About the Cover: Resembling an extraterrestrial landscape, an effervescent architecture exemplifies the evanescent yet transitory characteristics of an illusionary world. In the inset is the ever-changing universe whose living creatures judiciously lend themselves to diverse but distinct levels of evolution that lead each of them to a wide range of choices from ephemeral indulgence to eternal tranquility.

Journey to the East

(Hành Trình Về Phương Đông)

The Fourth Edition

The English re-establishment *Journey to the East* is first printed
in 2009 in the United States of America by CreateSpace at
7290 B Investment Drive
Charleston, SC 29418

Toll free: 1-866-308-6235

Journey to the East can be purchased at:
https://www.createspace.com/1000250244

For all comments and requests, please contact the copyright owners at:

povenleace@yahoo.com

ABOUT BAIRD T. SPALDING AND

HIS *JOURNEY TO THE EAST*

Baird T. Spalding (1857–1953) was internationally recognized for his six-volume set of books entitled *Life and Teaching of the Masters of the Far East*, the so-called "a breakthrough in Western spirituality." According to a recent New Age newspaper account, it was referred to as "a landmark work in spiritual literature." Shortly after its publication, it became a classic of the spirituality of the twentieth century.

Nowadays, this six-volume set has been translated and sold worldwide in many different languages and has remained a great attraction and interest to many people for the search engines. The account of his journey to the Far East in 1894 indeed offered the Western world a number of innovative resolutions that conceptually yet conventionally transcend spiritual and intellectual knowledge paradigm.

According to a Vietnamese translation entitled *Hành Trình Về Phương Đông* that literally means "journey to the east" by Nguyên Phong, published in 1987 via the Người Việt publisher, Mr. Spalding published *Journey to the East* in 1924. That was the same year as the first volume of his masterpiece *Life and Teaching of the Masters of the Far East* but from India instead of from the United States of America.

Unfortunately, this original English *Journey to the East* is no longer in print, and it is extremely rare, or even impossible, to find a copy of it. Owing to this scarcity, we hereby re-instate the English edition and sincerely hope that our direct re-translation from the Vietnamese version will effectively serve intellectual as well as spiritual communities.

During Mr. Spalding's early ages, he was known to be shy and highly reclusive but kind and generous. His simple life was fully occupied by extensive travels to engineer mining researches, to encounter great beings, and to grant people favors.

To honor his devotion to the Eastern philosophy and to respect his kindheartedness, we have been bestowed all royalties from selling this

English reestablishment to charitable consortia. By purchasing this book, you directly donate to people who are either poorer or much less fortunate than you are. We thank you very much in advance for your support and generosity.

—P. L.

ACKNOWLEDGEMENTS & OTHER BOOKS

Most of all, we are deeply grateful to Mr. Nguyên Phong for adapting *Journey to the East* by Baird T. Spalding into Vietnamese and to the Publisher Người Việt for publishing *Hành Trình Về Phương Đông* in 1987.

Without this Vietnamese translation, Spalding's masterpiece *Journey to the East* would have been lost forever. To the best of our knowledge, *Hành Trình Về Phương Đông* is the only trace from which Spalding's *Journey to the East* can be reinstated nowadays.

Over the last twenty-two years, *Hành Trình Về Phương Đông* has been a wonderful intellectual gift to only people who are able to read and understand Vietnamese. To extend this benefit to a larger group of audience, it is our great privilege to re-establish Spalding's stunning success back into English.

Special appreciations are expressed by the following persons who read the manuscript and provided editorial comments that help enhance this English reestablishment: Noel Hartlein, USA; Cảnh Quang Trương, Philippines; Hermanus Gundahar, Germany; and R. J. Putney, USA.

Illustrated comments are wide-ranging, from as short as a line that depicts the overall impression about the book as long as a paragraph that vividly describes rare experiences particularly in Chapter 9. These comments, along with short summaries of the corresponding readers, are registered in the Readers' Comments.

We are grateful to experienced remarks on technical layouts and thoughtful suggestions for practical methodologies of Mrs. Ngân Diệp Trương. Her forthright comments substantially improve the presentation of the book. A special thank you goes to Mrs. H. Triệu who provided thoughtful discussions and to Mr. Thiện Đại Võ who endowed technical and mechanical supports.

Finally yet importantly, we deeply appreciate our beloved spouses who have wholeheartedly supported and have enthusiastically played a significant part in this project. Without their wonderful understanding, steadfast encouragement, and relentless dedication, this adaptation might have to wait much longer before it can be released.

—P. L.

OTHER BOOKS

(1) *Journey to the East* (*Hành Trình Về Phương Đông*)
   by Nguyên Phong and Baird T. Spalding   **2009**

(2) *Lotus on the Snow* (*Hoa Sen Trên Tuyết*)
   by Nguyên Phong and Alen Havey   **2010**

(3) *Finding Your True Self* (*Bên Rặng Tuyết Sơn*)
   by Nguyên Phong and Swami A. Jyoti   **2011**

(4) The Resolve to Transform Cancer (Niệm Phật
   Chuyển Hóa Tế Bào Ung Thư) by the Buddhist
   Teacher Đạo Chứng and Thích Minh Quang   **2011**

(5) *The Four Noble Truths*—The Unabridged Version
   (*Tứ Diệu Đế*) by the Most Venable Thích Thiện Hoa   **2012**

(6) *Samsara* (*Luân Hồi*) by Chánh Trí Võ Văn Dật
   This book is only for donations, not for sale.   **2013**

(7) *Secrets of Self-Transcendence: Wisdom &*
   Common Sense by Bhagwan Shree Rajneesh
   and Ni Sư Thích Nữ Trí Hải   **2013**

(8) *Prevention Is Better Than Cure* (the Abridged Version
   of *Niệm Phật Chuyển Hóa Tế Bào Ung Thư*) by the
   Buddhist Teacher Đạo Chứng and Thích Minh Quang   **2014**

(9) *Siddhartha* by Herman Hesse   **2015**

(10) *Satyakam* by Nguyên Phong and Swami A. Jyoti   **2015**

(11) *Siddhartha and Its Insights* by Herman Hesse
   and Ni Sư Thích Nữ Trí Hải   **2015**

(12) *The Egyptian* (*Dấu Chân Trên Cát*) by
   Mika Waltari and Nguyên Phong   **2015**

TABLE OF CONTENTS

FOREWORD

. . . With a smile, Phương Vũ, a friend of mine, told me, "Do you know, Biện Giang, that book has changed my life." That was back in 1989 in Manila, the Philippines. In 2008, that same book was sent to Michaela Alisley, my associate in Nebraska, the United States. Barely a week later, Michaela emailed me, "With the help from a Vietnamese friend, I finished reading the book, which has indeed given me a completely different perception in life."

Hành Trình Về Phương Đông is the title of the aforementioned book.

Literally, *Hành Trình Về Phương Đông* [*HTVPD*] means *Journey to the East*. The Publishing House Người Việt first published *HTVPD* in 1987. It was released as a Vietnamese translation from a book entitled *Journey to the East* by Baird T. Spalding (1857-1953) printed by the Adyar Publishing House in India in 1924, and Nguyên Phong was the translator.

Since its first publication in 1987, *HTVPD* has been a blessing for numerous readers including Vietnamese and those who can read and understand Vietnamese. Being conscious of how *HTVPD* has affected us intellectually and spiritually, we wish that the original English version were still available so that the wisdoms from this book could be disseminated to a larger and more divergent group of audiences around the world.

Regardless of whatever the reason may be, either out of print or scarceness, it is extremely difficult, or even impossible, to find a copy of *Journey to the East* by Baird T. Spalding. Although *HTVPD* is widely disseminated from various bookstores and web sites, the number of its readers is considerably limited because it is written in Vietnamese. To overcome this limitation and the insufficient availability of *Journey to the East*, we hereby would like to reinstate the English version.

This English re-translation is dedicated to all fellows who appreciate a way to look at life that is full of peace and love, a path that leads to happiness, and an approach that helps themselves as well as others find tranquility. The translation is also an invaluable gift to all readers who realize that they were born into this world with empty hands, and likewise, they will leave it with bare hands.

First, *Journey to the East* will be offered as a gift book to a number of libraries and organizations that currently propagate *HTVPD*. After these gift books are exhausted, *Journey to the East* will be available to the public, and the profits will entirely be donated to charity. The primary objective of our English re-establishment is to help comfort and guide people to a path full of peace and tranquillity.

Since *HTVPD* has provided a large number of individuals with a happier and more peaceful path in life, we wholeheartedly believe that *Journey to the East* will reach out to many more people who wish to search for a different perception to look at life. Should you find *Journey to the East* beneficial to you in whichever way or under whatever circumstance, please open your heart to those who are less fortunate than you are.

"Thi ân bất cầu báo", a profound Vietnamese proverb, interprets as "Granting good deeds without expecting anything in return". If we all try to practice this principle, then this world is sure to be a better place to live. With distinct levels in the evolution of human beings, readers are encouraged to embrace ethical messages and moral lessons that are appropriate to your personal consciences.

Let us start our *journey to the East*

—P.L.

CHAPTER ONE

A STRANGE INDIAN

In the hustle and bustle of the present life, many people have lost their confidence. They believe that life is to enjoy and to satisfy material needs because death is the end. There is neither God nor the Supreme Being in the universe. Not long ago, a major newspaper in the United States released an article declaring that "God is dead!" The author of the article flat out challenged everyone to prove the fact that God is still alive. Of course, this article triggered a compelling argument.

An astrologist at the Palomar Research Center proclaimed, "I have used the best contemporary telescope to observe stars that are millions of light-years away from the earth, but I have not seen any paradise or God." Nowadays, the eccentricity of scientific experiments becomes so exaggerated that it challenges everything.

Nevertheless, while science was proud of its capability to prove and explain everything, an incident had happened. An ambassadorial delegation led by Indian King Ranjit Singh came to visit England. During the visit to Oxford University, King Ranjit ordered a monk to give a performance. The monk had upset scientific conceptions at the time. Not only could he drink different kinds of chemicals, including extremely strong reagents without being hurt, but he could also hold his breath for hours at the bottom of a pool. After Dr. Sir Claude Wade and his team examined him, he then entered into a coffin and was buried alive for forty-eight hours. Once exhumed, he was still full of energy. The monk also performed several more strange presentations that were also subjected to serious examination and severe verification by the scientists. These outlandish phenomena vigorously provoked public opinions.

The Royal Association had assembled a delegation of well-known scientists to investigate these observable facts. A delegation of many famous scientists led by Professor Spalding was instructed to go to India to observe, search, report, and explain mysterious events. The scientific delegation clearly conceived criteria to help scientists observe occurrences with an absolute scientific mentality. They would not accept anything that could not be explained clearly and logically.

To compile the final report, each scientist had to independently record what he/she saw and heard in his/her own notebook. Thereafter, all members had to compare detailed notes and carefully verify what they had witnessed. Observable facts would be recorded in the main minutes only if everyone agreed with one another's findings. This requirement was established to assure the best accuracy and the absolute impartiality. All happenings that could not be explained logically and scientifically would be eliminated.

When the scientists left England for the expedition, they were neither confident nor convinced. However, they were all changed after they returned. Professor Spalding revealed, "Easterners have important philosophical *Truths* that are worthy of examination and learning by Westerners. It is time for the Westerners to go back to the East for their spiritual homeland." It was regrettable that the homecoming of the delegation had faced vehement hostilities from a narrow-minded public society. The scientists were forced to resign and were not allowed to disclose what they had witnessed in India.

Shortly thereafter, the leader of the delegation, Professor Spalding, had published a book entitled *Journey to the East*, which had ebulliently attracted interest and attention of the public. Given its fascination and inquisitiveness, readers hastily searched for the scientists. Unfortunately, they had learned that all members of the delegation had left Europe for a monkhood in the Himalayan Mountain System. Nevertheless, the book's contents had created dynamic motivations in many people who went to India in an attempt to authenticate the published findings. The memoirs of Sir Walter Blake in the *London Science* as well as the investigation team of the reporters Paul Brunton and Max Muller uncovered the mysterious curtain of the East and confirmed the value of the study.

India is known as a country of many religions. Religion intimately bonds to daily life and becomes a powerful motivation that masters all activities in the country. Indians are often proud of their traditional culture that is considered as the religious civilization because they inherit a treasure of sacred wisdom that cannot be found elsewhere. This fact explicated why the British Royal Society financially sponsored a delegation of well-known scientists to go to India for the study of mysterious phenomena.

After the delegation had travelled for two years in India, from Bombay [currently known as Mumbai] to Calcutta [currently known as Kolkata], the scientists visited hundreds of temples and interacted with thousands of renowned monks and priests. They neither were satisfied nor learned anything new because the majority of the monks they met kept repeating the same conventional notions recorded in the classics.

In addition, these monks interwove superstitious beliefs and sanctified legends into their notions to glorify Indian culture. Most monks boasted about ranks and positions they possessed. Owing to the lack of typical standards to determine religious merits, everyone in India could easily self-proclaim with a title like a wise man [Rishi], master [guru], reverend [swami], or even an earthly saint [Bhagwan].

Hinduism does not have a particular program to train monks as Christianity does. Everyone can grant himself/herself with a religious title. Everybody can be a monk as long as he/she has his/her head shaved, dresses in a soutane, and gives him/her a title to attract disciples. Hinduism is not a uniform religion because it has thousands of different denominations. Each denomination is divided further into many independent groups.

Its splitting pattern is not in descending order like those of European religion. Monks have full freedom to interpret religious documents according to their understanding. Most of the time, they deliberately explain the documents in a way that serves them best. Besides, they also congregate either to promote each other or to strive against one another. Religious debates are very common because each group insists that its people or followers are official and faithfully follow the dogma of the Supreme Being.

This controversy explained why the religious study of the delegation did not lead to any fruitful results. Many times, the scientists felt lost and confused because they did not know what was right, and what was wrong. The British Royal Society instructed the study had to rely on the fundamentals of logical science. However, if the scientists applied this standard, they would encounter numerous predicaments because the culture of India was very different from that of Europe. The Indians accepted religious partitions by default, so no one would dare to interrogate monks' capabilities or to examine whether monks' assertions were plausible or not. Indians absolutely yet fervently believed in religious monks with an extreme patience.

Being disappointed with their religious findings, Professor Spalding wandered alone in Benares City. Among a jam-packed, noisy crowd was a bare-chested magician with puffed cheeks playing a flute to enchant a snake. A gigantic cobra in a basket straightened its neck and hissed. High intensity and low frequency sounds of the flute were rhythmically in tune with the dancing snake. The crowd whispered to each other with a great admiration. People did not realize that the snake's teeth were removed, and it was primarily fed with residual opium and carefully trained.

Everywhere in India, these kinds of bluffing games occurred unaccountably during the day. These games always ended when a few "accomplices" in the crowd applauded and threw a few coins into a basket to encourage people to do the same. While deeply in thoughts, Professor Spalding suddenly noticed a big, tall Indian man with an unusual manner gazed at him and smiled. The Indian politely greeted Professor Spalding with a bow in his perfect English. Professor Spalding responded likewise. As their conversation gradually became amicable, Professor Spalding asked the new friend for his opinion on the bluffing game.

The Indian replied, "Enlightened masters neither live in splendid temples nor have business cards with impressive positions and respectable titles printed. They do not need to advertise their powerful capability or religious merit and do not have to list their names in telephone directories, either. Besides, it is not necessary that an enlightened master must have many disciples. To meet enlightened masters, one must be able to distinguish him/her among other monks. All of those monks you have met are famous and have many followers because they know how to attract disciples with various manipulative forms of advertisements and how to make promises that disciples want to hear. The monks do not teach anything other than 'ordinary literatures' in praying books that an intelligent person can easily self-read and self-study. Are you disappointed because the monks you have met have never had any spiritual experience?"

Professor Spalding was surprised, "How do you know our disappointments so well?"

The Indian smiled, "You have discussed about these problems with each other and decided that if you cannot learn any new thing by the end of this month, you will return to Europe and conclude that Asia has nothing worth learning. Stories about wise men and sages are merely legends that are used to embellish Asian mysteries."

Professor Spalding panicked, "But how do you know about these discussions? We have just discussed about them among ourselves, and in fact, many of us are not even aware of them yet."

The Indian secretly smiled and gently emphasized, "My dear friend— thought has a supernatural power that can go beyond time and space. Your attitude is the reason that makes me come here and pass on a short message to you. It is no doubt that you are very knowledgeable about the Bible, 'Knock on the door, it will then open. Look for it, you will find it.' This is the message from a true master who has asked me to convey it to you."

Professor Spalding was thrilled by the fact that the Indian cited a quotation from the Holy Bible in the middle of the Benares market. He felt as if he woke up after being drunk, and his entire body seemed to shudder by a powerful electrical current.

Professor Spalding mumbled, "But . . . How do we know where to look for you? We have spent nearly two years and have gone to almost every town and village in India."

The Indian seriously replied, "Go to Rishikesh—a town that is enclosed by the Himalayan Mountains. You will meet monks who are completely different from those you have met. These monks live in simple huts and meditate in rocky caves. They eat very little and pray most of the time. To them, religion is as necessary as breath. They are true monks who devote their whole life to search for the *Truth*. A number of them have surmounted nature and have conquered invisible powers that are hidden in the universe. If you wish to learn about supernatural powers and mystical laws, you will not be disappointed."

The Indian was silent for a moment and looked at Professor Spalding intently, "If you want to go farther to find wise men [Rishi], you need a lot more time."

Professor Spalding queried, "You have just mentioned the word *wise men*. What is the difference between a wise man and a monk [yogi]?"

The Indian replied, "If you believe in the *Law of Progression* of Darwin, I offer to summarize. The progression of a soul goes in concert with the body. A wise man is the person who has made great progress in religious advancement while a monk is just starting."

Professor Spalding continued, "If that is the case, a wise man can perform miracles, can he not?"

The Indian gently shook his head and smiled, "He certainly can. However, mystical powers are not the ultimate purpose of his religious practice, but they are the natural results of concentration on thought and willpower. Rarely does a wise man perform his mystical power. The ultimate purpose of the religious practice is to liberate and to become perfect like the enlightened masters—Christ is one of them."

Professor Spalding argued, "Jesus, however, did perform miracles."

The Indian replied with a smile, "My dear friend, do you think that Jesus performed miracles to show off? Never, those miracles are the mechanisms to convert unsophisticated yet good-natured people and to give them faith."

Once again, the Indian talked about a religious leader who has been known by most Westerners.

Professor Spalding pondered and asked, "Why do wise men not become visible and teach people?"

The Indian earnestly said, "Do you think that those wise men will reveal to humanity who they are? If Buddha or Christ could come into sight and assert their commandments, would you believe in them? Do they have to perform miracles like walking on water or creating thousands of loaves of bread for people to convince you? Monks from low sects would do these kinds of miracles to attract disciples, but the enlightened ones would not perform anything for such purpose. My dear friend! Am I right?"

Professor Spalding asked, "But . . . But . . . When they live a secluded life, what good does it do for human beings?"

The Indian smiled, "Because humans do not know themselves well, they cannot judge themselves correctly. Who says that the enlightened ones are not helpful to human beings? If I assert that Christ frequently appears and continuously serves man, will you believe me? You would probably request evidence like a picture or something for verification, would you not? My dear friend, it is not easy for us to understand thoroughly the enlightened one's deepest thoughts. The simplest answer would probably be that they secretly and silently serve man by promoting love, charity, and kindness whose powers can penetrate through time and space. Although human eyes cannot identify, the effects are extremely powerful. Formerly, when humans were still primitive, the enlightened ones appeared to lay down a foundation and basis to guide them. Nowadays, humans are somewhat mature, so they have to be independent, make use of their abilities, and be responsible for what they do."

Professor Spalding pondered then asked, "You have previously mentioned that a true master has asked you to pass a message on to us. Is it possible for you to give me his address?"

The Indian solemnly replied, "My dear friend, everything depends on predestined affinity. When you have enough of predestined affinity, you will meet him."

After explaining, the Indian bowed to salute then disappeared from a jam-packed, noisy crowd in the middle of the marketplace in Benares City.

CHAPTER TWO

THE MONK OF THE BENARES CITY

Benares City was a site that had many historical vestiges and monks. Most Westerners who came to this city were always surprised because of the crowded population, closely adjoining houses, impressive temples, and magnificent monuments located throughout the city. Some temples looked ancient and solemn; however, what did people expect to see in there? A number of inexperienced followers simultaneously prayed and shook a little bell hoping that their prayers reached different deities. A large number of monks were in peculiar yoga postures. By posing in extremely difficult positions, they expected people to drop some money in a small bowl that was placed in front of them. We felt that they demonstrated circus performances to earn money for a living rather than to practice a true religious stance.

While other members of the delegation were busy with video-recording monks on nailed tables and large temples, Professor Spalding leisurely walked along a riverbank and saw a tall, muscular monk sauntering in close proximity. It seemed like an invisible force thrust Professor Spalding forward to look at the monk clearer, but he decided to turn on to a shorter path nearby a shrub to catch up with the monk instead. After a few steps, Professor Spalding was astounded because a big cobra blocked his way.

A cobra is an extremely venomous kind of snake that kills thousands of people every year. India has a countless number of cobras that appear everywhere. Moving forward or backward was like between the devil and the deep sea. Before Professor Spalding decided what to do, the snake sprang forward, straightened up its head, and snorted hissing sounds. All of a sudden, the Indian monk appeared, did not say anything, and walked right in between the snake and Professor Spalding. Spontaneously, the furious snake lay down quietly without making a move. When the Indian monk gently fondled the snake, it slowly crawled into the shrub and disappeared at Professor Spalding's astonishment.

The Indian monk smiled and leisurely declared, "Visibly destructible earthly selves are not able to perform such amazingly impressive attainment, but profound true selves can because the Supreme Being is within them as he is in all other species. In this case, his residing in me made the snake move away. When a person can eradicate his earthly self and allow his true self to reveal, nothing wrong can happen.   Once the Supreme Being's love and charity are developed, they penetrate through human beings and continue to disseminate to other creatures.   Hence, human beings can convert wild animals. When you saw the snake, you were frightened. I can sense your fear, and besides, it seems like you wanted to meet with me."

Professor Spalding stammered, "We are studying mysterious Asian phenomena. Honestly speaking, I feel confused and disappointed about what we have seen in the marketplace. However, since I have seen you, I have had an extraordinary afflatus.   It seems like an invisible force stimulated something to happen . . ."

The Indian monk gazed at Professor Spalding and signaled him to sit beside a very old tree.

The monk said, "During my meditation this morning, I received a message concerning you, so I left home for a walk outside.   You want to study the yoga method, do you not? I normally do not reveal this method, but the message I received has requested that I must help you. Hence, you are welcome to present your questions. I will endeavor to respond with the best of my knowledge."

Professor Spalding asked, "Please tell me about the yoga methods."

The monk remained quiet for a moment then continued, "No one knows exactly when the yoga methods actually began in human history.   Indian classics recorded that the god Shiva taught these methods to the philosopher Gheranda who in turn, educated his disciples.   Among these disciples, Marteyanda was the only person who apprehended all the essentials and disseminated the knowledge to intellectuals at the time. The Yoga methods belong to scientific fields that include many subjects like Astrology, Geography, Philosophy, and Mathematics. The method, I studied, is called Hatha yoga, which is only a small fraction of the entire yoga set. According to my master, yoga developed everywhere, so it attracted many philosophers and intellectuals during its prosperous period."

The monk continued, "As time went on, the golden period passed by, and man plunged into episodes of debauchery, dissipation, or materials and was eventually attracted to physical as well as material temptations. To prevent this spiritual obliteration, the philosophers discussed with each other to identify a possible solution. Finally, they concluded that the permission to teach people part of the yoga set was a way of resolving current problems. In the chosen part derived from the yuj [yoke] chapter are methods in which mind and body are under meticulous regulations. These methods concentrate in assimilating mind and body together with the universe. Thereafter, this particular part has been promulgated everywhere and is maintained until today. Since this part is taken from the Yuj chapter, it is called yoga."

The monk explained further, "It is important for everyone to realize that this so-called yoga is only a small part of the original yoga set. Even though it is a small part, very few people clearly and properly understand it. The majority of people who misunderstand it adopt the peculiar practice like injudicious, ascetic, and ludicrous postures. As you have seen, monks lie on nailed tables with arms held upward until they feel numb. These exercises are useless and bring no sensible results. These monks have damaged the reputation of science like yoga. For the majority of people, yoga has been relegated to an exercise for developing a healthy, vigorous body. Nevertheless, a proper practice can still bring good results to the body. On the other hand, the monks have a completely different perception because they are well aware that yoga will help them discover a mysterious energy as well as mystical power and to attain magic transformations."

The monk went on to elaborate, "To train their strength of mind, they concentrate their energy on activities like self-maltreatment and abusive challenges. For example, they lie under the sun, endure in the fog, sit on red-hot coals, stand on their hands, crisscross legs over their neck, self-starve, refrain from drinking, and pierce a sword through skin and muscles. To demonstrate their mental willpower, they publicly perform these ferocious manifestations to earn money and gain respect from inexperienced, naive people. The purpose of yoga is not to perform fascinating entertainments to gain people's respect."

Professor Spalding interrupted, "Should we criticize them? If the true monks conceal their indisputable trainings, misconception is unavoidable."

The monk smiled and leisurely explained, "Has a king ever displayed jades and jewelries for the public to enjoy? He carefully hides them, does he not? Likewise, the yoga methods are most precious, so the true monks never want to advertise them to the community. A person who truthfully craves for learning has to search for a proper monk, and this is the only avenue. A well-known monk does not need to advertise himself because he needs no eulogy from the disciples. On the contrary, he strictly chooses his disciples and only imparts esoteric knowledge to deserving disciples."

The monk carefully explained, "The yoga methods are confidential because these methods of training are considerably dangerous to persons who are inexperienced or short of ability. Opening secret points in a body is not a simple game. There are numerous kinds of yoga methods, but I concentrate on the Hatha yoga one that primarily concentrates on controlling the body prior to mind. At first, we must meticulously and thoroughly train the muscles and respiratory system then focus on the nervous system and brain. If the training is done properly, health will be improved, life will be prolonged, and spirit will be strengthened. This initial phase may demand from one to four years. A person can continue on to the next phase only if he has a healthy body and a strong spirit."

Professor Spalding repeatedly nodded, "What are the differences between these methods and the Westerners' methods? We also have techniques to develop healthy bodies."

The monk burst out laughing, "Westerners only know how to build up bones and muscles. This physical improvement cannot be compared to the Asian method that develops spiritual, mental, and physical growths. In the Asian method, the focus is primarily on four basic modes— *resting* to soothe the spirit and brain, *contemplating* to concentrate on determining, *regulating* the body to discard residues, and *exercising* to control respiration. For instance, relaxation is a simple yet discernible example. When a cat lies silently or waits patiently for a mouse beside a hole, the cat knows how to conserve its power and preserve its energy without waste any bit of them. It has carefully thought of every movement or posture before it makes a move to ensure its maximum comfort."

The monk analyzed, "Westerners believe that they know how to rest, but in reality, they do not. When they sit on a chair for a little while, they turn on this side and bend over the other side. They sometimes cross their legs and then stretch out their arms. It seems like they relax comfortably, but undoubtedly, their mind is constantly moving from one thought to another.

Realistically, they intellectually work in silence instead of pleasantly rest at ease. Creatures know how to preserve their power and strength because they are led by natural instinct that is the voice of nature. Human beings are guided by their brainpower; however, they cannot master it. Owing to the incapability to control, their mental power and physical welfare are adversely affected. Hence, never does a real rest seem to exist."

Professor Spalding sighed but acknowledged, "We have never thought of it. Would you be willing to explain more clearly on the Hatha yoga notion?"

The monk responded, "I certainly can share a few positions that help people improve their health. Everybody can practice a set of twenty-four positions [Asana] to enhance his/her vitality. These positions influence a number of secret points, so they exert a pressure on weak organs to help them perform more effectively. Western science has confirmed that besides main arteries, the human body has millions of tiny capillaries that carry oxygen to feed the entire body. If an organ or a muscle is less active or becomes weak, the number of tiny capillaries reduces. Conversely, exercising or swimming can increase activities of these tiny capillaries that help the weak organs become more active and consequently restore them. Similarly, practicing yoga positions makes the 'hot current'—Prana—circulate, which in turn stimulates internal organs not only to function properly but also to operate efficiently. Remember, practicing sports can induce organs to function, but yoga induces them to function according to their existing efficiency. Consequently, practicing yoga provides us with more miraculous results than exercising does. Human beings do not have to worry about sickness anymore. If illness exists, it will be cured completely."

Professor Spalding shook his head, "I do not believe Westerners will accept the fact that practicing yoga will treat illnesses."

The monk smiled, "How can a healthy body be sick? Sickness is caused by an imbalance of the body. Westerners know how to work but do not know how to rest. These are the reasons that trigger mental illnesses."

Professor Spalding requested, "That is all right. Would you please give more details about how to practice?"

The monk slowly explained, "The first step is to relax and sit comfortably. However, sitting on a chair, especially on a cushioned one with armrests and adjustable back, is very harmful to the backbone because it is the main passage of the Prana and is the causes of all backaches, paralysis, and rheumatoid arthritis. Sitting is quite simple, for instance, just sit on a floor with legs crossed, lean against nothing, tilt to neither side, keep the body balanced, maintain the backbone straight, and breathe steadily. Everyone can breathe soothingly for a few minutes, but shortly thereafter, his/her breathing becomes uncontrollable because his/her brain is used for activities and excitements. The man should keep his mind peaceful, calm, and undisturbed by trivial matters. At first, since a person cannot control his thoughts, he should think of beautiful flowers or a gorgeous spring. This is the first step of resting."

Professor Spalding interrupted, "It is not that difficult."

The monk laughed, "Resting has to be neither difficult nor complicated. When a person can keep his/her spinal column straight and regulate inhalation as well as exhalation, his/her current of internal energy freely travels everywhere in the body. Thus, it will fine-tune areas that are obstructed or stagnant. The second step is to lie down with head rested on the floor, legs stretched out, halluces faced away from each other, arms aligned down along the body, and eyes closed to assure that the body weight is distributed proportionally on the floor. A person has to lie down on the hard floor, not on a bed or on cushioned surface. Otherwise, the body weight will be distributed unevenly. During the resting process, the person must lie comfortably without any excessive endeavor. His mind has to be unoccupied and neither thinks nor longs for any indulgent desires. This lying position soothes the nervous system and helps it restore the equilibrium. You should keep in mind that the foundation of Hatha yoga relies on resting and preserving energy, not on punishing the body with eccentric twists and distorted turns."

Professor Spalding queried, "But yoga has these kinds of positions, does it not?"

The monk confirmed, "Adopting a particular posture for a certain period of time is not important, but focusing on how to execute the position properly is significant because the precise execution stimulates mysterious power in the body. This mysterious power is a secret of the nature because it only develops when a trainee follows an appropriate breathing [qigong].

Principally, proper position assists man to control his senses whereas breathing guides him to the spiritual world. Since the body and spirit always go hand in hand, a strong body cannot have a feeble mind and a perspicacious spirit will never reside in a sick body. In the advanced level of hatha yoga, a devout person has to contemplate and engross for a long time, so the proper sitting position is important because it facilitates the person to concentrate and strengthen determination."

Professor Spalding appeared to be confused, "I am still bothered by peculiar twists and distorted turns of the yoga such as standing on one's head and crossing legs over the neck . . ."

The monk gently reminded, "You should remember that the secret centers of the nervous system are scattered everywhere in the body. Every posture has its own mission and affects a specific secret point. Stimulating these secret points exerts a greater effect on different organs and mental activities. In general, peculiar and distorted gestures are merely to excite the secret points. You should bear in mind that these postures and breathing methods are simultaneously required. Strengthening and empowering muscles alone are not enough."

The monk elucidated, "Westerners exercise to build up the physical appearance, but realistically, they spend a large amount of vital energy to enlarge their muscles. Asians believe that the internal strength of intellectual power controls the muscles. You think a standing-on-head position is ridiculous, do you not? Gravitationally, this position allows blood to flow freely to the brain owing to gravity. Normally, the heart pumps blood to the brain. Compared to the pressurized transfer of blood via the aorta and arteries to the brain, the gravitational flow saves the heart a great deal of effort that, in turn, helps avoid heart diseases. Besides, this gravitational flow of blood to the brain benefits individuals who work a lot with their mind."

The monk explained, "When a person practices the standing-on-head position, he/she must be careful yet attentive and take it easy. He/she must ensure that he/she feels comfortable with each posture during his/her training process and avoids exerting excessive effort. He/she must keep in mind that the key to success is to rest gently and slowly, not to perform obstinately and tenaciously. The yoga method helps the body self-regulate in serenity and balance, so it is quite different from the Western method in which exercise involves aggressive and forceful movements. The Western method inevitably builds up muscles, but this assertive exertion disturbs the body and damages the mind."

Professor Spalding did not say a word because everything the monk said was logical, scientific, and rational unlike superstitious beliefs that other monks deified. Typical Europeans, who looked down on Easterners, viewed Asians as products of underdevelopment with food deficiency and from underprivileged regions with oppressively hot climate. They were undoubtedly surprised to learn that the Indians were well educated in exercises that were highly developed and scientifically sophisticated.

The monk continued, "Yoga is a science of the universe. Not only does it apply to Asia, but it also does to everywhere else. I cannot go deeply into details, but our blessed meeting this time is fruitful. I hereby offer you a secretly inherited key. The natural law discloses that man, on an average, breathes 21,600 times a day. A rapid respiration increases the number of breathings and thus shortens a lifetime. Conversely, the steadily slow respiration means to conserve vital energy and prolong life, therefore, lengthen a life span. This is the secrecy of qigong. Each breath we can save will accumulate and reserve for life extension. Food containing stimulants and cigarettes provokes speedy breathing and reduces the amount of air intake. These chemical excitements truncate the natural life even faster."

The monk looked at Professor Spalding with a smile as if he could read Professor Spalding's thoughts, "You are suspicious, are you not? The yoga method distinctively acknowledges the interrelationship between the respiratory and circulatory systems, and both of them intimately connect to the nervous system. The nervous system is the key on the door to the spirit; hence, breathing is the entrance to the mind. Breathing, however, is only the material aspect of a more subtle power. This power is invisible and latent in the body, but it is essential for all activities because it actually administers life. When this power leaves the body, breathing ceases and the body is dead. If we can control our breathing, we can partially master this invisible vital energy. When a man can dominate his body at an ultimate level, he can manage activities of various organs such as heart, livers, stomach, and lungs."

Professor Spalding shouted, "How could that be possible? When the heart stops beating, we are dead!"

The monk said, "If you do not believe me, please put your hand on my chest."

Professor Spalding rested his hand on the Indian monk's chest and felt the monk's pulse with the other hand. An outlandish pulsation occurred. The heart beating of the monk gradually slowed down and completely stopped. Was this a delusion? After Professor Spalding quickly looked at his watch and was silent for a minute, the monk's heart suddenly resumed beating.

The monk explained with a smile, "Do you believe me now? You surely think that this occurrence is contradictory science. I hereby offer an example so that you can verify for yourself. An elephant breathes slower than a monkey does; hence, it lives longer. If you observe respirations of other living creatures, you will find a snake breathes so slowly that it outlives a dog. If you thoroughly study, you will witness a mysterious relationship between breathing and longevity. A person with a peaceful life will live longer than the one with a pressing and aggressive life does. Several bat species sleep through the entire winter. They hang themselves from rocky walls, stop breathing many months, and wake up in the spring. Bears also sleep through the whole winter long. Why can humans not sleep as animals can? This habitual behavior is not against science or opposed to nature. Never do they accept anything else since scientists conclude that such a habit cannot occur. For Asians, everything can happen, and the nature is their best teacher."

Professor Spalding commented, "What is the advantage of living several more months or hours longer?"

The monk furtively smiled and answered, "You will understand what I say some day. For now, I cannot explain any further. Do you believe that if you practice this yoga method to the ultimate level, you can overcome the death devil? You agree that if we stop breathing, we will die. And if we can keep breathing, we can preserve our life, do we not?"

Professor Spalding immediately replied, "Of course, I do."

The monk explained further, "My dear friend, a monk can hold his breath not only for weeks, months, and years but also for centuries. Thus, he can prolong his life as long as he can wish, can he not? You have just agreed that wherever there is breath, life should be there, have you not?"

Professor Spalding asked, "How can a person hold his breath that long?"

The monk explained, "When you arrive in the Himalayan Mountains, you will meet these people, and the fact that they retain their breath is not as strange as you think. The genuine yoga can offer many mysterious and astonishing superpowers, but very few people would be willing to endure a meticulous training. In this dynamic, fast-moving world today, people are addicted to ephemeral fame, transient wealth, and impractical fantasy; hence, they do not have time to think about spiritual activities. This explains why people who truly want a spiritual state often conceal themselves in deserted places. They never look for disciples, but the disciples have to search for them."

Professor Spalding questioned, "Why do they live in the desolate places for a long time?"

The monk explicated, "Currently, you are still thinking as Westerners, meaning a one-way thought. To learn a new philosophy, you must discard existing prejudices. In the near future, you will understand what I want to say. Certainly, the true masters prolong their lives for a noble, legitimate reason. They do not long for life and are not afraid to die as ordinary people do. In the Himalayan Mountains, some masters have lived for hundreds of years, and others are even up to thousands of years. They all have specific missions, so they are able to keep their bodies intact. As a low-ranked monk like me, I do not have enough knowledge to raise my opinion. I predict that you will bring a fingernail of a four-hundred year old lama to England."

Professor Spalding asked, "Can you tell us how those true masters are able to extend their lives that long?"

The monk replied, "There are three methods to prolong life. The first method is to conscientiously, meticulously practice to perfection all asana positions and the secretly inherited qigong. An experienced master must supervise the practice of this method because 'A miss is as good as a mile.' The method also demands trainees to live serenely, peacefully, and honestly. Having an evil thought during a meditation can maliciously perturb the breathing that results in disturbance of the energy flow, madness, or sudden death. The second method is to use pharmaceutical products that are made especially from rare herbs. Very few people know how to prepare these medicinal herbs, and they only teach these formulas to selected disciples. Furthermore, the medicinal method will be used only in special circumstances because it has unpredictable results. The third method is to open mysterious points that relate to eight primary pulses involving life and death that is not easy to explain by science. I can only say that much, and it is up to you to believe in me or not."

The monk enlightened, "Deep inside the human brain is a tiny hole covered by a lid. At the end of the last vertebra is the refuge of the 'hot current', kundalini. Debauchery and excessive indulgence quickly consume the vital energy that makes people become old and senile. On the contrary, if we know how to control our body, we can save the vital energy. If we are able to master our body, we can conserve the kundalini. Only high-ranked masters of yoga have the audacity to train the kundalini. These masters are able to trigger the kundalini to flow upward against the vertebral column and open secret points as well as important centers located along the way. When they can open the tiny hole in the brain for the kundalini to enter and stay there, they can access powerful forces for rejuvenation and prolongation of life. Opening the lid in the brain is the most challenging task because a yogi may need help from the true master who must exert his internal power on eight primary pulses. This is a difficult job because a careless or reckless attempt may easily result in the yogi's regrettable fatality. Conversely, if kundalini can penetrate into the tiny hole, the yogi's lifetime can be lengthened, and his corpse does not deteriorate after death."

Professor Spalding remained silent because everything the monk revealed was strange and beyond scientific knowledge. Unquestionably, physiological science would never accept the conception of this invisible vital force because it could come from the imaginary and superstitious belief of this naive Indian monk. Should we believe in him, or should we not?

The monk smiled as if he could read Professor Spalding's mind, "I know you are in doubt because the conception of invisible vital force is contradictory to theoretical science. My dear friend, wisdom is the universal science that includes all scientific fields. Hence, this experimental science is only a fragment compared to the universal one. Some day in the future, science will advance adequately to address what I present here. By then, human knowledge should develop higher and can understand more precisely. You should understand that the universal laws confirm experimental sciences must go hand in hand with the progress of man. Several hundred years ago, science was rudimentary in comparison to that nowadays."

The monk elaborated, "If you traveled against history, you would recognize that the progresses of science and of humankind always complement each other. During the prehistoric period, a discussion about atomic energy was irrational, and people would not understand it anyway. In the Middle-Ages, if a person preached about space science, he would be convicted as a wizard. European history showed that super-intelligent people were ridiculed as lunatics and were burnt alive. Because of these absurd treatments, most true masters have never revealed their identities and kept their spirited performances not only extremely secret but also carefully hidden. Only scholars with a sincere devotion are educated by these true masters."

Professor Spalding asked, "Is there a mechanism for a European like me to receive this kind of education?"

The monk replied with a gentle smile, "There is, certainly. Would you be willing to leave a great comfort and extravagant life and live in an unpopulated area for religious learning?"

Professor Spalding answered, "That is fine, but I first have to settle my personal business."

The monk confirmed, "Are you ready to surrender all self-indulgent activities and mundane pleasures and devote your full attention to yoga training? This commitment is not for a few hours or a few days, but it will be your whole life."

Professor Spalding hesitated, "Do I have to spend the rest of my life training? If it is so, I will probably do it when I become old."

The monk burst out laughing, "My dear friend, the yoga method is not an entertainment when you have free time, or when your life approaches the twilight age. Why are Westerners so aggressive and dynamically greedy?"

Professor Spalding turned red and argued, "Why are we practicing yoga? What are the advantages to extend an austere life for several more years?"

The monk seriously said, "Who said the goal of yoga is to prolong life? Why should a person maintain a meaningless life? The majority of monks with a muscular body normally live longer than those without, but they do not comprehend the ultimate rationale. Do you think that the true masters only care to live a little bit longer? People often carry a one-way thought then directly jump to a conclusion. Being able to control the body is the prerequisite for mastering the spirit. It is easy to keep us from doing something wrong, but it is several orders of magnitude harder to imprison a brain to have bad thoughts because it requires a huge mental effort. Life is too short, and training to control the body requires many years. Thus, monks have to extend their life to train their spirit. As I have told you, Hatha yoga is primarily to control the body. After I have achieved it, I must focus on raja yoga to manage my spirit. In essence, Hatha yoga is the stepping stone for raja yoga."

Professor Spalding wondered, "Why can we not start the learning process with raja yoga?"

The monk just laughed, "Westerners are always in a rush. If you want to go far, you must go slowly. You must learn how to walk before you learn how to run. Taking a short cut to spiritual training guarantees a failure because if you cannot even control your body, you will never be able to manage your spirit."

Professor Spalding was anxious, "How can I learn raja yoga? Can you teach me?"

The monk calmly replied, "My dear friend, everyone has his/her own fate. If raja yoga is in your destiny, you will meet your teachers and friends. If you have a sincere desire for the *Truth*, your destiny will guide you."

Professor Spalding worried, "I do not know anyone, and those true masters are not listed in a telephone directory, how can I meet them?"

The monk secretly smiled, "Be confident, yearning for spiritual learning has a powerful thought, so it will be answered. 'Knock on the door, it will then open. Look for it, you will then find it.' You forget this command, do you not?"

Professor Spalding was startled because the Indian monk again cited another familiar quote from the Bible. He was too confused to say anything.

The monk smiled and continued, "Westerners are curious and want to know everything. Practicing is much more important than simply knowing it. The method of the body training is similar to that of the spiritual training. If a person exercises steadily and regularly, his/her muscles will firmly develop and so will his/her spirit. Many people with vicious characters such as selfishness, greediness, stinginess, and suspicion often exhibit bad behaviors toward others. The majority of people believe that these characters are natural and thus cannot be changed. Realistically, if we have a strong determination, we can reform these characters. If a proper exercise results in a brawny body, an appropriate control will create necessary virtue. The classic Rigveda has clearly indicated that people with a clear, precise vision of evolution are conscious of their privilege and happiness."

The monk elaborated, "If we want to be perfect people, we must have morality and courage. People who want to improve society must be self-disciplined first. They have to disregard their interests, concentrate on public responsibilities, and understand that all occasions to interact with people create opportunities to serve. Serving everyone means serving the Supreme Being. People who are enthusiastic about self-discipline must be aware of the unlimited power of thought because this power drives their actions. A man who searches for enlightenment in a religion must know how to keep his spirit under control and how to apply it logically and generously."

The monk went on to clarify, "Examining your thoughts is the primary objective of raja yoga. The worst obstacles for people who learn how to train their heart and sharpen their minds are being arrogant and being full of criticism. With a critical mindset, people readily attack everything, disgrace all virtues, and find faults in everybody. A raja yoga trainee must have the opposite attitude. He must find goodness in everyone and is conscious of reason in everything. With this mentality, he can assist himself and others. The second obstruction is irresponsibility. A man with this mindset often jumps from one project to the next regardless of whether the project is finished or properly done. As soon as he starts a new job, he already expects a result. If the result is not what he anticipates, he immediately abandons the job and undertakes something else. At last, he does not finish anything. His irresponsible, impatient mentality is unacceptable because perseverance and persistence are necessary for him to master his thought."

The monk interpreted, "It is obvious that no one can dispose of all faults and bad habits within a lifetime because life is short. Hence, self-improvement will last life after life. Once people have recognized the right path to follow, it is important that they concentrate all their efforts to go to the end. People will survive from one life to the next because whatever they have learned will never be lost. Until both the body and the mind are under the control of the will, humans will become sages. They are then conscious of the greatness of an endless life and leave their own self behind to join the universal evolution and to integrate with the everlasting true self."

Professor Spalding was optimistic, "Does this raja yoga training help us become a saint?"

The monk interrupted, "My dear friend, you should not quickly jump to this conclusion because there is not a unique way to become a saint. Many ways can take us to the *Truth*, and none of them is better than the rest. This is an extremely important notion that you should forever remember—the Hatha yoga method is not any better than the raja yoga method, and both of them are neither better than any other methods. Why do we have to think *this method is better*, or *that religion is more superior*? No way or no method is the unique one. The best way is to know oneself. Instead of searching for an absolute *Truth*, one should find the absolute within oneself because the *Truth* is for living, not for teaching."

Professor Spalding was utterly silent because the Indian monk's words seemed to send a powerful message to his heart. His previous prejudices suddenly disappeared, and he felt completely touched.

The monk smiled, "My dear friend, no saint would show off except for those egotistical people who have a passion for reputation and position. How can they be emancipated when they enslave themselves with ranks and status? The Supreme Being has bestowed us with intelligence to judge, so we must be able to distinguish among all things. Let us look at Benares City with hundreds of different temples, thousands of monks, and thousands of sects. Every monk brags that his/her sect is the closest one to the Almighty.

Why has the delegation not been satisfied with findings during the last two years even though you all have gone everywhere and visited many places? Is your differentiation at such a sophisticated level that it makes you reject superstition and blind-mindedness?"

The monk continued, "The Gita classic clearly stated, 'Like teacher, like pupil. A true master cannot have a bad disciple, and an intelligent disciple does not accept a dishonest master.' The natural law has substantiated experiences, 'Great minds think alike; and birds of a feather flock together.' A clear-sighted fellow cannot go along with an ignorant person. A knowledgeable monk must worry about how to control himself for liberation rather than how to recruit many disciples, construct marvelous temples and is proud of his results. Never will a monk liberate him if he shows off his ego and is presumptuously arrogant. You should use your rationale and intuition to distinguish these kinds of people from the true monks. If you sincerely yearn for the *Truth*, your wish will surely come true. Our meeting is quite sufficient, and it is time for me to go home."

Professor Spalding asked, "How can I see you again? And by the way, I do not know your name yet."

The monk gently replied, "Please call me Bramananda."

Professor Spalding silently looked at the monk disappearing behind a dense shrub. Twilight gradually came down on the Ganges.

CHAPTER THREE

EXPERIMENTAL SCIENCE AND MYSTERIOUS ASTROLOGY

Lawrence Keymakers, a rich English man, lived in Benares for many years. He owned many big companies and was very knowledgeable about this city. Lawrence welcomed the expedition to a magnificent mansion by the Ganges.

Professor Allen asked after a social conversation, "What do you think about things that the Indians called sacred wisdoms and superstitious events happening in the market?"

Lawrence shook his head, "India still has such peculiar performances, but besides what we consider supernatural or superstition, there are still concealed spiritual significances that are known by very few people. If you want to find out, you must investigate thoroughly rather than jump quickly to injudicious conclusions."

Professor Olivers burst out laughing, "Do you seriously believe that sitting on nailed tables and playing a flute to command snakes keep spiritual thoughts under wraps?"

Lawrence explained, "It completely depends upon your perception when you judge these performances. If you look at them through European lenses, they are comparatively marionettes. However, if you discard all prejudices, you may be able to learn many new things."

Professor Allen commented sarcastically, "You have lived in India for a long time, so you must have learned a lot of things, am I right?"

Lawrence smiled, "You are right. I have gained a lot of knowledge, and the first thing I have learned is modesty. Only having modesty can help us absorb new fascinating knowledge. If you look at a full glass of water in my hand, you will see the water overflows when I fill the glass with more water. Except when I pour some water away, I can add more water to the glass. Reminiscent of knowledge, only when we are modest and eradicate preexisting prejudices, can we accept more information. You wish to investigate and learn wisdoms from India, but you insist on keeping European preconceptions and looking down on everything in India. Your mental behavior is not different from a full glass of water, how can you fill the glass with anything else?"

Everybody was silent since Lawrence's forthright contention more or less invaded the delegation's pride. Regardless of the situation, they were still the most famous scientists of the British royal family who were always highly respected.

Professor Mortimer pointed at a strange piece of art on the wall and asked to break this icy atmosphere, "What kind of painting is it? It looks like a constellation, does it not?"

Lawrence responded, "You are right. It is my astrological forecast."

Everyone burst out laughing.

Professor Allen made a joke, "An astrological forecast? Our dear Lawrence, since when have you become an Indian?"

Lawrence seriously said, "This is an invaluable gift from Sudeih Babu, the best Indian astrologist."

Once again, the entire expedition broke out laughing because they were thinking of soothsayers squatting on sidewalks. Everywhere in India, soothsayers and physiognomists were ubiquitous because they made their living from superstitious people. Their professional instruments were a few threadbare books and several peculiar calendars. They were proud that they knew exactly the rich or poor destiny of people but nothing about theirs.

Lawrence shook his head, "Sudeih is the Master. He belongs to the noble, high-rank social class instead of a low-class soothsayer. He has studied Astrology since adolescence, so he is able to forecast many important events. If you want to study mystical phenomena, I strongly recommend that you meet him because he may be able to help you. Customarily, Sudeih has never received strange visitors, but I will introduce you to him since he is my dear friend."

Professor Allen shook his head, "We yearn to study the Indian civilization, not long for lucky-versus-risky or good-versus-bad destinies."

Lawrence secretly smiled, "Given what you desire, you have to meet this astrologist. You should keep in mind that I am not certain that Sudeih will agree to receive you. Not long ago, the King of Punjab personally waited for three days and three nights, but Sudeih relentlessly refused to meet the king."

The astrologist lived in a gorgeous mansion that had an attractive surrounding landscape. With a prearranged appointment, a housekeeper invited the delegation to an enormous living room that was luxuriously decorated like a king's chamber. Babu was a slender, small Indian with sparkling eyes as evidence of a rich innermost life.

Babu walked gently like a cat and courteously spoke English without an accent, "Keymakers has informed me that you are interested in Astrology."

Professor Olivers quickly replied, "We beg your sympathy, but we wish to search for mysterious occurrences and do not believe in Astrology."

Babu silently and indifferently looked at everybody, "If you wish, I can certainly provide you with an astrological forecast."

Professor Olivers looked suspicious, "Please do not be bothered with my future, luck or risk. Why do you not try to comment on my past?"

Babu nodded his head, asked Professor Olivers for his birthday, and drew eccentric symbols on a piece of paper.

Babu slowly disclosed, "You were born in a business family. During your early days, you craved for vocational travel, but your family severely forbade your longing. Your father wanted you to pursue business school at Oxford University to continue with his career. However, you were gifted in science, so you switched to physics after a short time. Your father was furious, determined not to support you, and entrusted his entire inheritance to your brothers. When you became a distinguished physicist of the British royal family, your father forced you to return home for a political enterprise. Under your family's pressure, you married a woman from an aristocratic family. Your marriage was not a happy one, so you spent most of your time in laboratories to find a distraction. With a liberated, outgoing individuality, your wife utterly obliterated all of your possessions and willfully committed infidelity. In sorrow and disappointment, your father passed away. Until your wife died, you had suffered for eighteen years. After arranging everything, you joined the expedition with the purpose of leaving London and fulfilling your travel dream."

Without saying a word, Professor Olivers sat still. His silence evidently indicated that everything Babu said was true. A disheartened, melancholy atmosphere seemed to dwell heavily in the living room.

Babu unsympathetically continued, "Would you like me to give more details or continue on to your future?"

Professor Olivers shook his head and hand-signaled Babu to stop. His pale face was indicative of the trauma that he just had experienced.

Professor Allen asked, "How can inaccessibly far stars influence each individual?"

Babu leisurely replied, "If the stars are too far away to exert any influence, how can experimental science explain the influence of the moon on low and high tides or on the menstrual flow in women?"

Professor Allen continued, "If I were involved in an accident, how would it relate to the stars?"

Babu shook his head and smiled, "You should think that stars are just symbolic entities. Stars do not have any effects on us. Realistically, our past indeed affects our present, and stars simply reflect this influence. People would not understand Astrology if they do not believe in reincarnation. A man dies and is reborn in many lives. His destiny follows and affects his life according to the *Law of Karma* or *Law of Cause and Effect*. If we do not believe that man dies and reincarnates to learn, to improve, and to become a better person, is everything just a coincidence? Can the fair and merciful Supreme Being tolerate such injustice?"

Babu continued, "When a person dies, his body becomes disintegrable and decomposed, but his characters, passions, and determinations remain unchanged. Once he reincarnates into the next life, these traits become his qualities. The stars are merely mirrors that record personalities and reflect them. Every single action creates a cause regardless of whether it is good or bad. For example, when we throw a balloon into the air, it will eventually fall back down because the gravitational force exerts on its weight. The time it reaches the earth depends upon how much it weighs and how strongly or gently we throw it. Astrological study examines the universal axes to predict when previous causes reappear."

Babu remained silent for a while and leisurely explained, "Before we proceed further, I would like you to understand the history of Astrology so that you will look at it properly. Since thousands of years ago, Astrology was always considered as an important science, and astrologists were in the second most important position after the monks. The objective of Astrology is the universe, but regrettably, it has been lost in the process. A small part that describes the relationship between human beings and the stars is handed down from one generation to another until today, but it is currently known as numerology. No one knows how long Astrology has existed, but the philosopher Bhrigu taught it to his disciples about six thousand [6,000] years ago."

Babu went on, "The essence of Astrology can be found in a set of books which is called *Brahma Chinta* and has been compiled by Bhrigu. Bhrigu had four disciples. The first one was excellent in science and went to Persia [currently Iran]. Thenceforth, Astrology spread to the west and subsequently influenced Greece and Roma. The second disciple was a brilliant philosopher. He travelled to the east to China and propagated philosophy in this country. The third disciple was fond of metaphysics, so he settled in the Himalayan Mountains and taught metaphysics to Tibetans. The fourth disciple stayed in India and became the king's advisor. The set of books *Brahma Chinta* compiled by Bhrigu turned out to be the national treasure; hence, it was kept in the imperial palace."

Babu revealed further, "Later, princes fought over the throne and tussled to possess *Brahma Chinta*. After several decades of war, the volume was subdivided, and each prince kept a part of it. Since then, Astrology was lost. The soothsayers have managed to collect some sections and manipulated them for a living. Although these soothsayers do not fully understand, grasping a few principles is sufficient for them to swing their practice. As you have seen, this forty-nine-roomed house is full of ancient books that I have collected. I have spent most of my fortune searching for these ancient books. I come from a royal family, but I am only fond of Astrology. I spent several decades studying Astrology and followed well-known astrologists until I collected *Brahma Chinta*. Of course, the original set of books had thousands of pages, but I only managed to accumulate several hundred pages and spend nearly twenty years studying them."

Babu smiled and looked at Professor Olivers, "My dear Olivers, the astrological forecast I sketch for you is unusual compared to those of other Europeans. It is up to you to believe in me or not because you are the only one who would know whether what I say is right or wrong. I, however, want to inform you that you have already paid off your retribution by karma, and your life is entering an important turn. This forecast reveals that you are on the verge of a religious revelation and will receive assistance from a sage."

Professor Olivers was so touched that he tightly held the astrologist's bony hands. The entire expedition was moved equally. Previously, everyone in the delegation was suspicious about numerology, but the anecdote about Professor Olivers' astrological forecast had changed everyone's mind. No one in the expedition had ever thought that Professor Olivers had such an unfortunate life.

Babu directed the expedition to large rooms that were stacked with bookshelves filled with thousands of antique books. Professor Mortimer, the archaeologist from Harvard University, was even amazed by invaluable treasures of literature. Several sets of books had scripts written on papyrus leaves from thousands of years ago. They were intermingled with other documents engraved on wood in the sixth century. The entire expedition felt that a large part of Indian wisdoms were concentrated here.

Professor Mortimer asked, "What are the subjects of these books?"

Babu answered, "These books are about religions, traditional wisdom, and Indian philosophy."

Professor Mortimer continued, "Then you are a philosopher, are you not?"

Babu smiled, "A person without philosophical knowledge is merely a simple astrologist or a low-class soothsayer."

Professor Mortimer wondered, "Do you recruit disciples?"

Babu smiled, "Many people have requested guidance from me, but I refused to accept them because I felt that they were either inadequately gifted or short of willpower to accomplish their ultimate goals. Furthermore, I feel like I am not qualified to be the master of anyone. I am just a man who has a passion for philosophy as you are scientists who are fascinated by scientific knowledge."

Professor Mortimer was curious, "You use Astrology to guide your life since you are able to recognize the past and foresee the future, do you not?"

Babu shook his head, "No, I do not. I have found the light of the *Truth*, so I do not need Astrology anymore. The astrological study is only useful to people who are still in the dark. I have completely devoted my life to the Supreme Being [Brahman], so I am no longer worried or anxious about my future. Whatever happens to me, I am willing to accept it as if it is his will."

Professor Mortimer disagreed, "If you were physically attacked by a ruffian or your life was threatened by a thug, would you consider it as his will? You would do something to protect yourself, would you not?"

Babu calmly replied, "I know that when I am in danger, all I need to do is to pray. Praying is necessary, and worrying is of no use. When I encounter difficulty, I am most conscious of his help. I tore my astrological forecast when I discovered the *Truth*. I am certain that the man can transform his spirit to harmonize with the Supreme Being. Everything that will happen due to the consequences from the past is unavoidable, why should we worry about it?"

The expedition always heard about perceptions of the Supreme Being. Asians have a very powerful religious spirit, so they fervently worship the Supreme Being. Asians do not understand that Europeans are actually suspicious and often substitute convoluted reasons for simple faiths. How can Westerners comprehend that the Supreme Being is only a conception or hypothesis that, like thousands of others, needs to be proven concretely?

Babu smiled as if he could read everybody's mind, "My dear friends, self-importance and arrogance are not useful to anyone. When people reach the most silent state of mind, they will realize the extremity of the mysterious universe and the insignificance of man. When they can detach themselves from a dull-witted state of reasoning, they will experience the utmost wonderful peace in concord with the Supreme Being."

Professor Allen shook his head, "Why do you not think of it as an illusion or imagination?"

Babu burst out laughing, "My dear friends, has a mother ever been doubtful that her child is not real? Reminiscent of the delivered moment, has she ever thought of that moment like the autosuggestion? When she observes her child growing up every day, how can she believe that the child does not exist? In life, the spiritual growth is an extremely important change that no one can ever forget because from that particular moment, the person completely changes and becomes a new one."

Babu glanced at the entire expedition whose members were famous professors and well-known scientists.

Babu smiled and announced, "We are only at the dawn of science. However, every novel discovery and new knowledge will bring us evidences saying that our universe is a tremendous effort of the Creator. To make things easy to understand, we should look at a mathematical problem. If we put ten small sticks labeled from one to ten into a pocket and gradually take out one stick at a time, after finishing, we then put all of them back into the pocket, mix thoroughly, and take each one out again, how can we take out from one to ten in order? Based on the statistical permutation, we must draw ten times to have a chance to take out the stick numbered 1, one hundred [or 10^2] times to pull out the sticks numbered 1 and 2 successively and one thousand [or 10^3] times to draw the sticks numbered 1, 2, and 3 consecutively. If you want to pull out the sticks from one to ten orderly, the chance you expect this special case to occur is 1 out of ten billion [10,000,000,000 or 10^{10}], am I right? If we apply this statistical mathematics to conditions that create life on the earth, the principle of fortuity does not satisfy the necessary requirements. Then, who creates life if accidental occurrences cannot be the case?"

Babu explained further, "The earth rotates around its axis at the equator with a speed of one thousand and six hundred kilometers [1,600 Km] per hour. If it rotates ten times slower, the daylight will be ten times longer and, naturally, the heat from the sun increases tenfold hotter. Consequently, all trees and living creatures will be burnt alive. On the contrary, whichever or whoever that can tolerate the heat will also die from the cold because the night time is longer in the same order of magnitude, and the earth is correspondingly ten times colder. Who makes the earth rotate around it in such a perfect speed? The sun is the life source of the earth, is it not? The sun's temperature is about five thousand and five hundred degrees centigrade [5,500 °C]. The earth is situated in an ideal location, neither too far nor too close, where it effectively receives the heat from the sun. If the heat from the sun slightly increases, we will be burnt. In contrast, if the heat from the sun decreases a little, we will be frozen to death. Why does the earth slope in such a flawless angle? The earth's axis slants at twenty-three degrees. If the earth stands straight up without tilting towards any direction, we would not have the four-seasoned weather."

Babu smiled and announced, "This inclination of the earth also prevents all water from evaporating toward two poles and becoming frozen. The moon is the earth's satellite whose attraction controls the ocean tides. If the moon is not three hundred and eighty thousand kilometers [380,000 Km] away from the earth, but eighty thousand kilometers [80,000 Km] closer, a deluge will occur. Owing to the moon's greater attractive force exerted on water at a three hundred thousand kilometers [300,000 Km] distance, the water will rise and flood all continents twice a day. In brief, all life forms on this earth will disappear if the conditions are aberrant a few. If we say that life exists merely by coincidence, the perfectly suitable condition that supports life on this earth may be one of quintillion [10^{18}] possibilities. In other words, given billions of billions of permutations for one ideal combination in which the positions and conditions of the sun, earth, and moon create a perfect situation, life existed on the earth is definitely not a coincidence."

Babu quietly looked at everybody. No one would imagine that an Indian astrologer could prove sonorously and eloquently the existence of the universe using scientific evidences in front of the audience including the most famous scientists in Europe.

Babu turned to Professor Allen—the biologist from Harvard University—and continued, "If mathematics seems to be too abstract to you, we should try to examine nature through the lens of biology. With the survival capability of all creatures, we must admit that the Creator's presence is perfect. Life has neither weight nor dimension, but it is truly powerful. Let us look at young, delicate rootlets; they seem weak, yet they can pierce through hard rocks. Life conquers air, land, and water. It dominates all elements; it forces the materials to disintegrate and then combine to form new structures. Life is a sculptor who molds new figures, an artist who paints landscapes to decorate nature, a musician who teaches birds to sing or insects to hum, and a chemist who creates fragrances and sweet fruits. Life from vegetation absorbs carbon dioxide and converts it to oxygen to feed all creatures. Drops of protoplasm are so transparent that they are almost invisible to our eyes, but they move because they absorb vital energy from the sun. These single cells contain germs of all plants, and animals are the origin of all life forms based on experimental sciences. By itself, protoplasm does not create life."

Professor Allen asked, "So from where is life coming?"

Babu explained, "My dear friends, salmons originally hatch in fresh water, travel to an ocean where they live until full grown, and then swim against streams to their birthplaces without any fluctuation and hesitation. If we move them to somewhere else, they will find their ways back to the origin. Who has taught them to distinguish these conventional practices so reliably? Sea eels have a similar living pattern. They leave their birthplaces—like ponds, canals, lakes, and rivers from everywhere in the world—and start a long voyage to the Bermuda Islands. To come here, European eels have to travel nearly four thousand kilometers [4,000 Km] whereas Asian eels must go farther, sometimes almost eight thousand kilometers [8000 Km]."

Babu elaborated, "Eels only reproduce and die at the Bermuda Islands. The baby eels born here do not know anything about their origins, but they return to their parents' far away native land regardless of whether at a canal in France or a lake in Indonesia. Each species returns to its homeland. French eels will not be lost to India, and Thailand eels will never go astray to Africa. Who gives these baby eels the ability to distinguish instinctively? Who guides these tiny eels on their adventurous journey of thousands of miles? Certainly, this long migration cannot be a coincidence. Do you agree?"

The entire expedition was utterly astonished by the exceptional knowledge of the small, skinny astrologist. No one would expect that an underdeveloped country like India could have such a brilliant scholar.

Babu elaborated, "You are probably wavering. To be more realistic, let us talk about the hereditary element in the small primary microorganism that is in all cells. Every creature has its own hereditary characteristics. This element indicates that life has been predetermined because a tree will produce a tree, not an animal. All creatures, including as small as ants to as big as whales are governed by this element. This genetic dependence is certainly not from people's thought or coincidently happens, is that right? Only the Creator has enough power to invent all of them. My dear friends, an absolute equality exists everywhere in the universe, so no species intrudes others. Let us look at insects, they reproduce very quickly, but why do they not take over the earth? Their overpopulation is impossible because they do not have lungs like mammals. They breathe through tracheas or windpipes that do not grow proportionally with their body size. Hence, even when they shed to grow, their body size is limited within a definite structure."

Babu smiled and continued, "Human beings are more superior compared to animals because of their faculty of reasoning. Animals' instincts are wonderful but limited by their mental simplicity. The human brain is marvelous because it can surpass beyond its limits. This far-reaching, exceeding intellect only exists in human beings. Hence, it allows man to recognize the Supreme Being's existence. We can call this recognition as imagination if we wish, but it allows man to perceive invisible and figureless phenomena. The imagination infinitely broadens our horizon; thus, we are conscious of a wonderful reality—the Supreme Being is everything. He is everywhere, but he appears most clearly in our souls."

The whole expedition remained silent but wholeheartedly admired the astrologist for his scientific yet simple illustrations. Several hours ago, everybody doubted the soothsayer's ability, but everyone now admitted that he was truly a knowledgeable scholar second to none.

Babu smiled, looked at everybody, and said, "As scientists, you should think about what I have just presented. If you examine the universe, eradicate preexisting prejudices, and eliminate the eccentricity of experimental science, you will then see that everything happens in a beautiful, harmonious order. You will also then realize how insignificant human beings really are relative to the gargantuan universe because science is built on the fundamental senses that are very limited and cannot perceive the universe. If we persist what we cannot hear and cannot see does not exist, we make a disastrous mistake. Uncountable occurrences have happened, and our restricted senses cannot feel them until we can open these senses someday."

Professor Mortimer surprised, "How do you know that?"

Babu calmly replied, "I have directly contemplated these questions during meditation. Besides, mysteriously inherited books also indicate that clearly."

Professor Mortimer hastily interfered, "Can we study or translate those books?"

Babu smiled, "Will you be willing to spend a few decades to translate? Books on spiritual mysticism are not common books for everyone to entertain. From my understanding, only a few people desire to study them because in their previous life, they have had spiritual inspiration, learned about the subject, and possessed enough knowledge to examine these books thoroughly. These people are on the spiritual door sill and are ready to enter the religious path. Only these people actually enjoy and focus their mind on barren-looking books in my house."

The entire delegation was silent. Although each member had his own thought, everyone agreed that the astrologist was right.

Professor Allen asked, "You have found the light of the *Truth*, but why do you still continue practicing Astrology and still tell people about their past and future?"

Babu proudly declared, "I live and serve people with this career, and it is not that I receive everyone. Whether you are a king or prime minister, I would not say a word if I sense that you do not have a kind heart, a good mind, and a sincere reform. Many people came to my door, but very few of them were invited to enter. Not long ago, a king brought a suitcase of gems here to exchange for an answer to his question, but I refused to reply. If I did not receive a spiritual message, it would be difficult for me to greet you. In addition, if I did not see Professor Olivers' astrological forecast, I would not reveal any secret to strangers, especially Westerners. For a long time, people have mostly misinterpreted and misrepresented Astrology. Since I have studied the original *Brahma Chinta*, I can share some astrological knowledge with you and hope overthrowing some prejudices of Westerners."

Babu started, "When we are born into life, each of us carries a different inherited asset that is retribution by karma. This asset can be good because of the causes that are in agreement with the Supreme Being's will or can be bad for the misconducts from previous lives. All of these causes are under a sub-conscience or Alaya-Vijnana and become the motive forces to control our life. These motive forces are distributed complicatedly by powers in the universe, and they become cosmic rays. These cosmic rays will not affect us immediately and drastically, but depending on the movement of the stars, they will reflect on the earth."

Babu went on, "This assessment is very logical because through innumerable life cycles, human beings have done numerous bad things that they cannot redeem in just a few lives. This is why humanity is constantly overwhelmed with misfortunes and revolves around reincarnation. From the movements and operations of the stars, astrologists can predict influences exerted on human beings in this lifetime. By studying Astrology, human beings understand clearly that no deity rewards, punishes, or controls their activities. Their destiny depends on the consequences that they create, so they must endure the results."

Professor Allen questioned, "But you did mention about the Supreme Being and his existence, did you not?"

Babu burst out laughing, "You still conceive the Supreme Being as an old man who sits high up there, controls life and death, and determines the destiny for everyone. How infantile your conception really is! The Supreme Being is much more superior. He creates everything and arranges them in a certain order in the universe. There is no such thing he determines destiny for each individual as you think. Everything proceeds according to the universal law that is '*We reap what we sow*'. Reminiscent of the law of reciprocal actions in physics by Newton that is '*To every action, there is always opposed an equal reaction*', there is nothing strange about that. None of us has a permanent predetermined destiny. Otherwise, we will be very negative and too passive to do things. At the worst, we completely entrust our fate to good luck and bad luck."

Babu explained, "My dear friend, Astrology is a practical, realistic, and advanced science instead of a superstitious discipline. Astrological forecast does not mean that people are slaves of their pasts, but it demonstrates the evolution of the universe in which people can change their destiny. Astrology studies human beings' reactions under the stars' influences. Stars are intermediate instruments that truthfully reveal equalizing actions of retribution by karma from the past. When a person is born at a certain hour on a certain day, the influence of stars will harmonize to his/her retribution at that particular moment. These stars reflect on his/her cosmic rays that make pulses move and cells change. Thus, these stars affect people's life."

Babu carried on, "Although man cannot change his past, he can escape and overcome the stars' influences with his liberal will. The case of your business friend, Mr. Keymakers, is a very good example. From his destiny, he had to die in the last war. Fortunately, a germ of charity sprung up in him when he witnessed the devastation and destruction from the war. His kind heart had felt for the victims, so he donated much of his fortune to help save many of them from poverty and suffering. Of course, he completely did not know anything about his destiny during the war, but his compassion and humanity had created a strong force that pushed the cosmic rays aside to save his life. His destiny has completely changed since then."

Babu elucidated, "You must understand that restructuring a destiny does not imply an obliteration of your past. It simply means that a major event that should happen in this lifetime does not occur. When our heart is set for good endeavors that are in agreement with the Supreme Being's will, a star's influence suddenly brightens up, and strong magnetic currents push against the cosmic rays in different directions. Hence, man is able to change his destiny if he performs good deeds and charity. Of course, appalling influences do not disappear, but they are latent and wait for another opportunity to reappear. Scientifically speaking, a human lifetime is like a mathematical equation, A times B equals C. A [multiplicand] and B [multiplier] are the causes, and C is the result. If we add another cause X [different from 1] to the equation, A times B times X are not equal to C anymore because of the second multiplier X."

Babu persisted, "This logical extension is the principle of destiny reforming that I have just presented. Human life is actually engraved on stars, but they are sometimes bright and occasionally blurry. However, the intensity is our decision. When we commit debauched sins, we generate malevolent motive forces that attract these sins and engrave them onto the stars. The stars rapidly reflect these new grooves, and of course, the consequences are immeasurable. On the contrary, if we are conscientious of the reflection and choose to treasure virtuous and useful deeds, then benevolent motive forces naturally dislodge bad influences aside. If man studies Astrology properly and scientifically, he will understand his destiny, believe in himself, and live comfortably. He will be neither pessimistic nor optimistic, but he will be happy and self-confident."

Professor Allen asked, "What will happen to a devout man with bad karma?"

Babu seriously answered, "A bad karma is like a suspended sentence. It is inactive, but no one can avoid it. To devout persons, they are well aware of the cause-and-effect principle, so they sincerely implore to redeem quickly. Although they do not create bad causes anymore, they have enough courage to endure their adverse karma. This is how they can shorten their time in life-and-death reincarnation cycles. The primary objective of true Astrology is to understand destiny and live comfortably."

Babu quietly thought. Finally, he walked to a large bookshelf and took out a beautiful box inlaid with gold. Inside the box was an ancient book written on papyrus leaves.

Babu interpreted, "This is a part of the *Brahma Chinta* set that I have collected. You should know that the mystical subject has two sections— exoteric and esoteric. The latter was taught to carefully selected disciples, who had spiritual enlightenment. The philosopher Bhrigu only propagated it to four chosen disciples. I regret that the small part of *Brahma Chinta* I have is incomplete and too complicated to understand. I spend twenty years studying it but understand very little. Since our meeting is a rare predestined affinity, I offer to translate several pages as a gift to you, 'All creatures in the universe, either invisible or visible, are organized and categorized based on the norm of number 7. All structural activities in the present galaxy belong to one of seven domains. Each domain has seven sections, and each section holds seven groups.' Our entire solar system represents the Supreme Being's manifestation, and each element in this system is a part of him."

Babu solemnly declared, "Besides, there are seven Logoi, and each of them is responsible for each domain. Practically, these seven Logoi are the centers of divine power and transportation system that the Supreme Being promulgates. Man has three main forms—body, soul, and spirit—which are corresponding to low, middle, and high worlds. This divided pattern also applies to the Supreme Being. All materials in the low world make up his body, those in the middle world constitute his soul, and those in the high world represent his spirit. In brief, everything is a part of the Supreme Being, from a grain of dust to the galaxies. All atomic materials that create a human body are also a part of the Supreme Being through seven domains. When the atomic materials pass through seven domains, they undergo some changes depending on each domain's influence. Astrology can distinguish who is affected by which domain. Astrology can also identify the person based upon the quantity of his/her constituent atoms that are emanated from the related domain."

Babu looked at the delegation and noticed that they were confused. Babu went on, "This subject is quite difficult to understand, so I will elaborate it further. In Christian terminology, these seven Logoi have appeared in Saint John's vision. The Apocalypse 4:5 clearly states, 'Seven candles lighted in front of Saint John are seven angels of God.' In the beginning, all of us were part of God, so it meant that we were of the same origin. Thereafter, we departed from each other and went through seven canals. From my understanding, seven canals represent seven characters of God via seven Logoi. The first angel is Michael [power representing the field commander of God's army] related to planet Mars. The second angel is Gabriel [knowledge regarding to the angel of death or one of God's messengers] related to Mercury. The third angel is Raphael [force referring to God has healed or God heals or God, please heal] related to the sun. The fourth angel is Uriel [light of God standing for a cherub and angel of repentance] related to the moon. The fifth angel is Zakiel or Raguel [angel associating with good intention] related to Jupiter."

Babu smiled and explained, "I do not know the related planets of the sixth [Jophiel or Sariel] and the seventh [Samuel or Jarahmeel] angels. Experimental scientists believe that planets are a random combination of materials. If this combination is accidental, why are they located at particular positions in the universe, and why do they travel around a fixed orbit? Everything seems to obey the natural law, but a controlling supernatural power is always behind this law. I am trying to use angels' names and Christian terminology to explain to you. This philosophy can be expressed differently depending on religious and cultural conceptions used, but there is still only one *Truth*. To understand Astrology, we must backtrack to our origin. Man comes from the same origin as water from the same source that flows along seven different springs to the ocean. Each spring has its own characteristics that affect its water more or less."

Babu continued, "Man can be distinguished from each other by seven characteristics depending upon through which canal he passes. Astrology studies man and influences of planets on his behaviors. Similarly, physiology differentiates people from one to another by their enthusiastic or apathetic character and calm or agitated temperament. Realistically, these studies are merely different methods used to illustrate man's characters. Of course, it is not easy to find the domain of each individual because he/she has been through many reincarnated cycles and has created convoluted retributions by karma. Consequently, reincarnations and retributions seriously dominate and significantly affect man's personality."

Babu elaborated, "If you can open your sense of *divine vision* or possess a profound experience in mystical subjects, you will know to which domain he/she belongs. When a person knows his/her domain and continues to improve his/her existing nature, he/she will rapidly make a big progress since the most effective instrument relates to his/her domain. For example, a person is talented in music but likes to study mathematics. It is not true that he/she will not make headway in math, but he/she will advance faster if he/she studies music since it suits his/her expertise. Knowing who we are and what potential capabilities we have will help us choose a proper direction to follow, and this is the real purpose of Astrology."

Babu explained further, "The majority of people who behave without thinking are influenced by the surrounding, so they are always disappointed and feel uncomfortable. They are self-acting or live with an unsuitable lifestyle. From the Bible, 'If you are not as innocent as a child, you are not able to enter the kingdom of God.' This maxim advises us to live honestly with ourselves. Astrology can help us figure out who we are and what appropriate actions we should take. Studying Astrology using these approaches is highly proper because Astrology is neither to reveal the past nor to predict the future or luck."

Professor Allen asked, "How can a person know for which domain he is suitable?"

Babu clarified, "An experienced astrologist can prepare an astrological forecast to find out which domain a particular person belongs to even though the preparation requires a lot of time. Another method is to look at people's actions. A person from the first domain will achieve his goal by power and determination. A person from the second domain carefully analyzes matters to select the most efficient method. A person from the third domain vigilantly examines time and the most propitious moment. In treating an illness, the person from the second domain tries to understand the causes and chooses the most effective methods while the person from the third domain studies about when is the best time to cure."

Babu elaborated, "Persons from the sixth domain will find a way to treat illnesses through faith, and persons from the seventh domain attempts to cure by rituals and ceremonies. However, the best method to determine the domain is to examine ourselves. We should eradicate those obsessions that we use to embellish our ego like reputations, positions, and desires. If we are truthful with ourselves, we can determine our domain. If we have a strong willpower and determine to work with a scientific spirit, we are probably from the first domain. If we are clever, like to debate, and work efficiently, we may belong to the second domain. If we are sensitive, like social work, and donate to charity, we are most likely from the fifth domain. If we have a strong faith and are prudent, we are most probably from the seventh domain."

Babu explained, "The subject of domain is very difficult to explain within a short time, so I can only provide a brief summary. The primitive matter starts to evolve through seven canals or seven important qualities. Only when a person completely develops these seven qualities, does he become perfect. Of course, we are all imperfect even though each of us has accomplished necessary underlying qualities. The Westerners are strong in deductive reasoning and science but seriously lack fervent belief and humanity. Their ability of reasoning is more predominant than sentiment, so they appear to be unsympathetic as well as insensitive and like to challenge instead of reconcile. In contrast, Asians are more intense in religious devotion and generosity but are deficient in logical thinking, so their sentiment often governs their behavior. As a result, they give an impression of endurance, concession, tolerance, and accommodation. Both groups of

41

people are at opposite ends of the characteristic spectrum without any absolute equilibrium, so there will be a fundamental change allowing the two ethnic groups of people to learn from each other and be more harmonized."

Babu contemplated for a while and said in a deep voice, "Throughout my whole life of studying mystically inherited books on various religions, I have never seen distinct discrepancies among their philosophies. In fact, they are essentially the same. Unfortunately, man likes to find differences to criticize or denounce others, and the resulting slanders eventually lead to complete ignorance."

Professor Allen disagreed, "Religions are different from each other, are they not?"

Babu gently reminded, "My dear friends, each nation has its own customs and traditions. Each era has different changes and values. Hence, the *Truth* can be taught by different methods. Although methods and languages are not the same, there is still only one *Truth*. It is just as the Supreme Being has seven different canals through seven distinct domains. Atomic elements in each domain have different vibrations, colors, and qualities, but they all originate from the Supreme Being. Similarly, you do not change your identity when you wear a different shirt. The shirt is not the same, but the person who wears the shirt is the same. If you travel back to the origin, you will understand the changes in each period through the influence of the stars."

Professor Allen wondered, "Would you please elaborate it further?"

Babu thought quietly for a while then replied, "Within the seven Logoi, changes happen periodically like circulation of breath in the respiratory system or blood movement from the heart. These changes occur under convoluted, multifarious formalisms. It is probably those humans' and Logoi' minds are created from the same atomic elements, so everyone on earth can more or less sense influences when the Logoi change. In other words, when a Logos who is in charge of a domain undergoes changes, people who pass through this domain will change accordingly because their atomic constitution has a high proportion of the domain. Historical evolution revealed that the human brain evolves with time, and so does his civilization. From my study, each cycle of evolution lasted approximately one hundred years, and dramatic events that occurred during the last twenty-five years often affected the next cycle."

Professor Allen was anxious, "Then the changes that will start from 1975 to 2000 will influence the twenty-first century, will they not?"

Babu nodded his head, "In reality, periods do not coincide exactly by year or month because the solar calendar is often not precise. Astrology utilizes the calendar derived from movements of the stars. Nevertheless, to simplify this issue, we can say that the last twenty-five years of each century is the transitional period during which many compelling incidences occur."

Professor Mortimer interrupted, "What are the evidences that indicate significant changes at the end of the twentieth century?"

Babu smiled and looked at everyone, "Since you are all Europeans, I will adduce with European history for your convenience. You can consider what has happened as coincidences if you wish. In 1275, Roger Bacon launched the cultural Renaissance movement that led to all changes in Europe one hundred years later. In 1375, Christian Rosenkreuz disseminated this culture to all social classes, so European people were liberated from the objectionable foundation of the Middle Ages. Were the years 1275 and 1375 the last quarters of the thirteenth and fourteenth centuries?"

Professor Mortimer, the archaeologist as well as historian, thought, "Indeed, the cultural universal movement via Renaissance has saved Europe from decadence. However, they are the only two examples. To be conclusive, I believe that we need more evidences."

Babu confidently smiled and further confirmed, "What do you think about the inventions of the printing machine and printing techniques in 1473? Were ideologies of philosophers and clergies universally popular and widespread because of them? Was the intellectual standard of people in Europe enhanced because of them? What do you think about Francis Bacon and his emulative movement in scientific research that used English instead of Latin to spread scientific knowledge in 1578? Did these evolutions bring science to society to improve the standard of living? Again, these events happened during the last twenty-five years of the fifteenth and sixteenth centuries. They must first restore culture to liberate Europeans from conservative prejudices, then restore and develop science so that people know how to deduce and henceforth change the society. Culture must pave the way for the reasoning that opens up a path for political and social transformations to follow."

Babu continued, "In 1675, secret organizations started establishing to call upon for help to abort social classes and to eradicate social injustices created by the Monarchy system. In 1789, the French Revolution finally broke out and completely changed European history. Once again, these two cataclysms occurred within the last twenty-five years of the seventeenth and eighteenth centuries. From that time on, you probably have seen, have you not?"

Professor Mortimer's forehead was sweating. European history was not strange to him, but Babu's explanations had awakened him. The entire expedition was stunned and unanimously admired Babu. Within the evening, the Indian astrologist had eloquently presented contentions on mathematics, biology, philosophy, religions, and even European history as if he was the most knowledgeable scholar. His intellectual sophistication had conquered everyone.

Professor Mortimer's voice trembled, "In your opinion, what will happen to the twentieth century?"

Babu silently thought for a moment then replied, "The year of 1875 marked an important breakthrough that was scientific development in mechanical civilization together with Darwin's evolution theory and the liberal Christianity movement. Since this time onward, the controversy between the spiritual and material world started. Two powerful forces that emanated from two opposite ends of the constellation created the spiritual and material movements. The twentieth century begins with the flourishing development of materialism. People who are dragged into material conditions will face with challenges in which stomach demands and corporal pleasures will intensely struggle with spiritual necessity. During the last twenty-five years, the spiritual movement will be strongly developed and disseminated widely to encourage spiritual progress. By the end of the twentieth century, the material movement will collapse, and the study of mysteriously inherited religion will begin."

Babu explained further, "My dear friends, you are all pioneers. Before a universal, secretly inherited teaching is implemented, we must help initiate the process like planting seeds in advance of germination. This is the reason you are encouraged to study mystical phenomena in the East. I cannot reveal anything else anymore, but through the astrological forecast of Oliver, I assure you that these predictions will come true. It is certain that many changes and efforts that assist humanity's advancement will happen during the last twenty-five years of this century that is the important period."

Babu elaborated, "This living world has two different kinds of people. The first kind of people has seen wonderful light of enlightenment at the end of the horizon and has oriented a direction to approach. Of course, they have to fight persistently against temptations and adverse environments, but to them, hope always shines. The second type neither appreciates honorable thoughts nor believes in noble deeds. They are strayed, pitifully because they will have to learn painful lessons until they understand and redirect them to the light of enlightenment. These situations have been happening."

Professor Mortimer wondered, "What will happen to the unaware people?"

Babu burst out laughing, "You think that the Supreme Being will punish them, do you not? No, he will not, but they will learn their lessons from mistakes and in pains. For example, a rural man wants to go to a city. He can take established highways and follow maps, but he can also insist to neither pursue accessible highways nor look at available maps. By ignoring common practices, he may end up passing through jungles, stepping on prickly paths, suffering pains, and going astray everywhere. Thereafter, he recognizes his ignorance. Life is a valuable lesson that everyone has to learn. Life is unpredictable because it can be easy in one moment but can also be difficult in the next. Never will life be quiet and smooth for anyone."

Babu stopped talking and looked toward the Ganges. On the other side of the river was a club with multicolored lights and lively music.

Babu sighed, "That place is the meeting home of commercial organizations. The club associates with merchants, hierarchies, intellectuals, and most wealthy persons in this city. They meet every week for luxurious entertainment. The majority of them are beyond sixty, but they still insist on maintaining their pleasures. Their bodies are asthenic, but their desire for material indulgence is still intense. They get together to talk about weather conditions and recreational life. None of them is conscious that every single one of them will leave this living world in the very near future. By listening to them, you would think that they could shed like snakes to live forever."

Babu looked at the starred firmament with a deep thought, "Everything in this universe is in the absolute equilibrium. This universe is not in excess or deficient from a tiny grain of dust in immense galaxies. Life is too short, but people are always drawn into hurly-burly. Very few people realize that today's extravagances will lead to tomorrow's sorrows. Everything is flickering like an illusion, but people consider it real. If they consciously observe what is happening, they can learn many good things. Regrettably, when people attain their ambition, they quickly forget their past. In contrast, people agree to learn only when they are in misery, humiliation, and embarrassment. Perhaps, these reasons indeed trigger extraordinary changes and urge people to learn."

Professor Mortimer interrogated, "You think that people are going to learn in sorrows, do you not?"

Babu sighed, "Unfortunately, that is true. We are often forgetful, so we have to learn sorrowful lessons repeatedly. When people are miserable and oppressed or their freedom is trampled on, they will return to their last hope that is faith. When people are happy, very few of them think of self-improvement to liberate. When they are sick, they realize that being healthy is the happiness. When they are in prison, they truly appreciate the value of freedom. Unfortunately, after recovering from a sickness, they are not conscientious of the cause. Hence, they continue with their old lifestyle that makes them ill all over again."

Professor Mortimer disagreed, "Man has learned a lot and has made great progress."

Babu interrupted, "What do you mean by progress? From the material perspective, people were in progress a little bit more compared to their progress during the last several centuries. From the spiritual perception, they are as poor as they have been since the past. They have not made any spiritual improvement as evidenced by their continually committing the same mistakes."

Professor Mortimer asked, "Are you referring to war?"

Babu kept quiet, continued looking at the starred firmament, and was deeply in thought. The entire delegation waited patiently in silence.

Professor Allen finally decided to break the ice, "In your opinion, can peace be established in the near future?"

Babu smiled and explained, "Given my limited knowledge, what makes you think that I know the answer? Since the presence of human beings on this planet, wars have been going on one after another. Have wars ever stopped? Realistically, wars are the manifestations of our inner feelings that are exaggerated to daily activities. As time goes on, wars become seriously worse owing to industrial activity and intellectual creativity. Never will the wars stop if the reasons that have triggered them still exist. If there is a huge old tree that we want to fell, we cannot climb up the tree and strip off its leaves because new leaves will grow to replace them. The only way to kill the tree is to excavate the root."

Babu continued answering, "Wars originate from ambition, anger, animosity, nationalism, tribalism, political organization, hatred, and jealousy. Eradication of these appalling factors is how to end wars. The unique method is to create a spiritual revolution. Only when people, who realize the real causes of wars, change their perception about life and obliterate hostility, will they have peace. It is unfortunate that everyone always finds faults in others—this mentality explains why we are in our current situations. Peace and goodwill must go hand in hand. People cannot achieve peace when their mind is full of animosity, hatred, and jealousy and want to exploit others for personal gain or for their party's benefits. All conferences and plans that intend to bring peace to humanity are unsuccessful because people are not at peace with themselves."

Babu smiled, looked at everybody for a while, and seriously said, "You all know of King Alexander the Great who conquered the world. To establish peace for Greece, he attacked and destroyed all neighboring countries that could potentially threaten Greece. After he won one battle, he had to prepare for the next one. Paradoxically, the war that was supposed to bring peace kept on going. Alexander was an intelligent person who followed the philosopher Aristotle. When Alexander was enthroned as the king, he confidently told Master Aristotle that, 'I will defeat Egypt and Turkey.'"

Aristotle asked, "And then?"

Alexander replied, "I will dispatch troops to attack Persia and to hoist the Greek flag. Shortly thereafter, I will conquer all of the Middle East countries."

Aristotle asked, "Then what else?"

Alexander replied, "I will then sweep through Afghanistan and India."

Aristotle continued asking, ". . . And then what is next?"

Alexander was thinking, "Thereafter, I can sleep peacefully."

[Note: during this period, Greek only knew India but not other countries in Asia.]

Aristotle smiled, "My dear son, why do you not sleep peacefully tonight? Would that be better?"

Babu went on, "I think people should ask themselves a similar question. We should honestly examine our mind to see what we actually want. Do we want peace or violence? It seems like we anxiously want something to happen. Every morning, we quickly grab a newspaper to find the most exciting news. If there is no news about war, natural calamity, devastating problems, or economic difficulties, we then throw the newspaper on the floor and complain that nothing is worth reading. Is it true? We want to live peacefully and do not like any disorders, but we like to hear about people's turmoil. We spend a lot of time to vigorously discuss about people, in particular, criticize men, and ridicule women. Is it true that we still do that? Have we ever asked ourselves why we do what we do?"

Babu concluded, "Our mind still wants money, reputation, position, and health, and we only pray for our peace. Thus, we are never satisfied. If someone ever asks about our mentality, we simply deny just as did King Alexander who only wished for a peaceful sleep. A tranquil sleep is neither difficult nor too far away, and it does not require any intensive labor or force, either. How can we plunge into ephemeral materials, establish reputations, indulge physical desires, and search for tranquility and peace at the same time? Longing for transient materials and personal satisfactions indeed destroys our serenity and affluent inner self. We create our own problems, not the environment or circumstance, is it right? Today, we have had quite a long conversation. You will continue with a long-lasting journey and meet many reputed teachers and erudite philosophers. I wish that you will find peace in your mind."

Babu smiled and waved his hands to say good-bye to the visitors. The moon was up high and cast its shadow on the glittering surface of the Ganges.

CHAPTER FOUR

ON THE ONE THOUSAND-MILE ROAD

The meeting with Brahmananda and Sudeih Babu had changed everything. Until now, the expedition admitted that behind superstitious beliefs, numerous transcendent *Truths* were worth learning and studying. The presence of a true monk who sent the mysterious thought message to Brahmananda and Sudeih Babu had greatly encouraged the expedition and made them believe that their research would exceed their expectations. The experience with Sudeih Babu had made everyone eliminate their prejudice, discrimination, conservative perception, and arrogance of Europeans and start learning to observe mysterious wisdoms of Asians.

The expedition started the journey toward Rishikesh. At the beginning, the roads were in good condition, so they traveled reasonably fast. Later, the roads were discontinuous, so the delegation had to ride on either donkeys or horses and sometimes walked on narrow paths between mountains. The fact that European scientists traveled by the ride or on foot through secluded areas had never happened, so the officers of the royal army tried to impede the delegation for security reasons. Although India was a British colony, many regions still did not cooperate with the authorities. Hence, the expedition required the escort of fully armed forces. In some regions, even local people rarely took a chance to commute because pirate clans were persistently active. To be cautious, the expedition was carefully armed, but no regrettable incident happened during the journey. Everyone felt that an invisible powerful force protected the delegation.

Along the way, the delegation passed by a temple of the Jainism, whose basis was developed from the principle of expanding compassion [Ahimsa]. Jains practiced Ahimsa so strictly that the rituals became meticulous and stringent. Sage Mahavira established Jainism over two thousand [2,000] years ago. He was a prince but left his imperial palace for the jungle hoping to find a religious *Truth*. With his perseverance and sincerity, he finally achieved enlightenment. As soon as people stepped into the temple, they immediately saw the statue of Mahavira in a meditation position with a large diamond on his forehead. Before entering the temple, all visitors had to take off their belt, shoes, or everything that was made of animal skins, horns, or tusks, etc. All items derived from killing had to be left outside the temple. Jains utterly obeyed these rituals since Ahimsa forbade all disciples to slaughter, eat flesh, and even store anything associated with killing in their houses.

Jains always dressed in white and veiled their face, except for the eyes to prevent flies and mosquitoes from entering their mouth and nose. If unlucky insects happened to fly in their mouth or nose and entrap in there, Jains would presume to commit murder because of their absolute belief in Ahimsa for all creatures. Moreover, Jain monks had to be on annual indoor retreat for the whole summer because insects reproduce during this period. They avoided being outside because they did not want to step on insects inadvertently. To Europeans, the practice of Ahimsa seemed to be excessively unreasonable and extremely ridiculous, but the majority of Jains stringently implemented the commandments. They believed that if they could not strictly follow the commandments, they would have no hope to advance further on the religious path.

Some Jains were even more extremists because after a learning period in the temple, they voluntarily went to the jungles and lived naked. They only drank spring water, ate fruits, and devoted all their time to meditation. They perceived that as long as they still ate rice and wore clothes, they were indebted to society. If they still enjoyed generous donation from devout fellows, they were in humanity's debt. When they took a religious vow, they had to divorce from life, leave everything behind, and detach from all kinds of temptations in the material world including wealth, materials, and even clothes.

Jainism believed that when people devoted their lives to a religion, they had to break off from the notion of possession because ownership in whatever form meant obligation and binding, which led to attachment and hindered religious learning as well as liberation. Jains even left beautiful temples for a natural life in the jungles. They took the ground as their bed, the sky as their roof, and animals as their friends. They devoted all their time to meditate on spreading love to all creatures. While many monks were meditating, wild animals gathered around them without any fear. European scholars called this religion as nudism because of its absolute rejection of everything. It was unfortunate that the term *nudism* was often assimilated with savage barbarousness and incivility.

When the British came to rule this country, many Jains were under arrest because they were accused of staining fine customs even though they lived in the jungles and had no contact with society. Once discrimination, prejudice, tradition, and custom were discarded, the delegation felt that the Jains' philosophy was practical. Jains believed that the power of love could annihilate all difficulties and obstacles. However, this love had to be extremely absolute. Its purpose was not limited to any particular class of people but intended to disperse equally to everyone regardless of social classes, races, or religions. This philosophical reform was extremely important because Indian customs were traditionally very biased and discriminative.

Jains believed that human beings, whether strong or weak, rich or poor, middle classes or lower classes, or commoner or royals, deserved love equally. Not only is love boundless but also intense like that of a mother for her children. For the sake of this love, she would not flinch from difficulties or dangers. Love must be sincere, profound, and sincerely originated so that it cannot be deceitful or biased under any circumstances. After disseminating love to all human beings, people had to propagate it to all animals from huge elephants to tiny insects. This was why they did not only avoid slaughtering but also stayed away from products involving butchery.

Jainism regarded the subjugation of their enemy by power as a bestiality that needed to be eliminated but considered the conquest of their opponent by love like a unique way to resolve everything. Jainism had many followers and strongly thrived in Northern India. Beyond this area, Jainism faced a challenging confrontation by Hinduism and Islam. Indian history revealed that Islam had obliterated Buddhism and Jainism barbarously. On the other hand, Jainism's ascetic rules had restrained people from joining it. Besides, monks with naked bodies and concealed faces were easily mistaken for unrespectable people. This was probably why Jainism only expanded in secluded regions and around mountains.

Ashmah was a small village that lay next to the foot of a mountain. The delegation stopped by at Ashmah for the donkeys and horses to rest. Another reason that the delegation visited Ashmah was the important historical monument—the so-called silent temple"—nearby. This temple was a white-rocked architecture built over four thousand [4,000] years ago. Inside the temple was an enormous solemn room without any statues. Stepping inside this quiet temple, people suddenly felt free from the commotion and sentiment with an indescribable peace. According to a legend, while King Rapoor led troops to conquer neighboring countries, he met a monk here. The monk advised him to give up the strategy of conquering people by belligerent power and take on the approach of winning people over by benevolence and righteousness. The king took the monk's advice, ordered the disarmament, and encouraged people to live with morals and virtues. Since then, the kingdom of Rapoor enjoyed peace and prosperity.

As time passed by, very few people knew of the era of King Rapoor, but the temple built in remembrance of his awakening still existed. When entering the temple, nobody could utter anything or make any noise. The reason that the temple did not have any statues was to emphasize the absolute *Truth* of invisibility and immateriality.

The monk who took care of the temple explained to the delegation, "The silent temple is a place of power because silence is synonymous with power. When people attain the spiritual silence, they reach the stage where everything is in unification with the mystical power. Human beings have the spiritual power, but owing to their unconsciousness, they inadvertently waste it. Dissipation of power is disturbance whereas the concentration of power is tranquility. When people concentrate their spiritual power to a unique center of vital energy, they are able to interact with the Supreme Being spiritually. When people are united with the Supreme Being, they are united with all powers, and that is the ultimate spiritual heritage. The only way for human beings to unite with the Supreme Being is to consciously interrelate with him and completely give up the external surroundings for innermost feelings because he lives invisibly in human beings' heart and mind."

The monk explained, "When people eradicate illusionary pride or ego, recognize ignorance or incapability, and are ready to learn or reform, they can improve themselves. People cannot teach anything to individuals who are haughty and arrogant because only modest people can see the *Truth* to learn. The Supreme Being does not listen to boisterous, repetitive prayers, but he pays attention to sincere prayers who come to him through their heart and worship him with their mind in tranquility. Whoever is in contact with him in silence would recognize his power because they realize what he does to their wishes."

The delegation asked, "If the disciples do not pray according to any books or sacred Bible, how can they understand the philosophical religion that they pursue?"

The monk explained, "Wisdom comes from silence. The Supreme Being does not need us to praise him vociferously or to use any particular language. When a disciple sincerely prays in silence, his thought will synchronize with sacred influence that is acknowledged only when his mind is calm. When our mind is completely peaceful, we can self-analyze, improve our dignity, and welcome inspirations from the Supreme Being. People can only be conscious of their ability and of the environment in tranquility. Potential power can only emerge and develop in silence. When the mind is at peace, external affairs will not disturb it, and personal desires will subside. When people can self-liberate from external commotions, they will receive wonderful harmony from the boundless world. People should realize that happiness is in their mind. Nowadays, the majority of people are looking for happiness from the external environment, but environmental factors can only provide them with a momentary entertainment rather than infinite happiness. All searching mechanisms of the environment are hopeless. People should focus on their innermost feelings because all corporal and ritual forms are only oppressions."

The delegation was bewildered, "How can you find anything when you sit quietly?"

The monk verified further, "People will gradually be conscious of themselves. Of course, this process requires time. They will find their happiness that is dependent neither on external factors nor on other persons. A liberated state of mind that no one can steal is the religious state. This state of mind is precipitated by the development and flourishing of deep secret thoughts from our innermost feelings. People will find their own answers once they realize their true self and sublime influences of the Supreme Being. By then, all external searches will end."

The delegation questioned, "What you said is fascinating. However, if people do not have any books to guide them, how can they attain that state?"

The monk argued, "The majority of Europeans are familiar with being active and relies on a method or religious philosophy to guide their life, so they are easily subjected to deviation and oversight. A proper approach is that they must think and find a way for themselves. The way to liberation demands personal courage and individual effort because none of the ways is alike. Human history reveals that numerous religions disseminate extremely wonderful *Truths*, but very few disciples thoroughly study them. Most of the disciples depend on the monks' guidance. Paradoxically, while monks cannot even liberate themselves, how can they guide others to liberation? This was the reason that King Rapoor built the silent temple with no statue, figure, or language to avoid entering the paths of different Hindu sects. The Supreme Being is omnipresent and absolute. Hence, no particular language or picture can represent him. Only in complete silence without any corporal or ritual forms, can people have freedom, live peacefully together, and understand the mutual relationship between them and their fellow men."

The monk elaborated further, "Human beings often contemplate relationships among themselves, but contemplations are more or less biased and always wrong if they examine emotional connections through a sense of self. People's thoughts are true only when they are liberated from prejudices and external conditions. Freedom of thought does not only mean that people can think in whichever way they wish, but it also means that they must unshackle themselves from being compelled to think in a particular manner. In short, this *Truth* can only be found in silence with the removal of all rites, corporal forms, languages, discriminations, prejudices, imposed thoughts, and fears originated from ignorance. Only when people are completely free, can they actually have peace and liberation."

The delegation said good-bye to the guardian. The visit was short, but it gave everyone a good impression. It seemed like an invisible magnetic current was floating around the temple because everybody felt overwhelmed by an indescribable peace. Practicing a religion in silence was no longer an abstract and useless matter as the delegation used to think. Indeed, India still has many things about which the Europeans should learn and think.

CHAPTER FIVE

THE SACRED CITY

Rishikesh! It was a name of the supernatural power and of the city of saints. For a long time, people had considered this city as a holy land where all people who actively searched for religious *Truth* came to blend themselves in this sacred ambiance. Rishikesh was at a special location and regarded as the entrance to the Himalayan Mountains. To the north is an impressive mountain range filled with numerous mysteries. To the south is the Ganges—the sacred river of Hinduism. Regardless of social classes, intellectual or non-intellectual, an Indian at least immerses himself once in the stream to receive the sanctifications brought by this river.

It was exactly as the secret Indian of the Benares City said. Monks and the disciples went for pilgrimages everywhere in the city. Some skinny monks walked and recited incantations while other ascetic monks leaned against their staffs and contemplated beside the Ganges. Hustling among clamorous followers were magicians in colorful garments performing strange entertainments. A big, strong built man who wore a tiger-skin waistband undulated in a yoga position. Next to the monk, a bony magician rolled on the ground and murmured prayers. Bonzes sonorously read prayers beside those monks who concomitantly played drums, danced, and sang the deities' names. There were monks who meditated in rocky caves deep inside a mountain and appeared to care nothing about worldly affairs. Adjacent to them were other monks with dishevelled hair and beards wrapped in ragged garments like mummies. There were also monks with imperceptible breath, lying quietly as if they were about to die. Alongside them were magicians who passionately called the Supreme Being's name noisily. Wallowing in the fragrance of incense, pilgrims with a sincere, reverent expression jostled and hustled one another in the midst of a crowd. The expedition felt as if they were lost in a strange, mysterious world filled with extraordinary, peculiar people.

Dr. Kavir, director of the Sanscrit Language Research Institute of the government, was a famous knowledgeable intellectual who lived in Rishikesh for many years. According to him, Rishikesh was not a city of true venerable monks like in the old days but rather a metropolis of hodgepodge-like individuals. The majority of people were monks and disciples who were physically and spiritually poor. They gathered some religious principles, several life-enhancement methods, and a few incantations to earn their living from superstitious people. Most of these monks were losers in life because they were lazy and refused to work. In an underdeveloped country like India, the easiest way to have food, clothing, and house was to become a monk and live off people's devoutness. Because no criteria were set forth, everyone could become a monk. As long as they wore soutane, memorized several prayers, and knew some ritual ceremonies, they could promote themselves to either monks or sages. These religious pretenders actually damaged honors of religions because they took advantage of faith to instigate wrongdoing for personal gain. Not only did these monks come together in a group, promoted each other, and praised one another, but they also criticized those who were not from the same group.

Being informed that a foreign delegation came to study ancient wisdoms, numerous monks and disciples found their ways to reveal secret teachings, of course with a price. When they were rejected, they immediately reduced the cost just like a business. A monk demanded to sell his mysteriously inherited book for fifty golden coins, but after numerous devaluations, he agreed to exchange his book for a meal. A group of monks who claimed to be well respected with high-ranking titles demanded to have philosophical discussions with the delegation. After these monks introduced their religious accomplishments, the delegation was extremely astounded because they were some sort of gods or saints, not human beings. Every single one of them was with religion for hundreds of years and possessed all different kinds of magical witchcrafts. However, when a police officer walked in, these gods and saints were flabbergasted and ran away all together.

Around the markets, many ascetic monks displayed their maimed, disabled figures as great exploits. The delegation did not understand what they could attain besides a few coins that pedestrians tossed at them. Some monks employed hocus-pocus publicly. With a particular tariff, they were ready to perform talismans, spells, or incantations, curse at your enemy, bring you a beautiful girl, or help you succeed in your business. Monks who advertized to sell amulets and charms or self-proclaimed to be these kinds of gods or those sorts of saints were everywhere.

A monk came to meet the delegation and introduced himself as the personification of the great Krishna and as the Buddha Siddhartha in two of his previous lives. Dr. Kavir became angry and gave the order to arrest this monk. When a police officer handcuffed him, he confessed that he was only a failing primary school student and could not find any job. He was lazy but liked to be a boss of others, so he always faced with difficulties regardless of what he did. At last, he shaved his head, dressed like a monk, and self-declared as the reincarnated great Krishna. Unfortunately, some country folks believed in him, so they raised some funds and built a temple for him. Since then, he comfortably lived on donations of devout people and did not practice any religion at all. Given such a situation, he demanded even more. He complained that the temple was too small to be comparable with his status. Being acquainted with arrogance and deceitfulness, when he learned that a foreign delegation came to visit, he plotted to play tricks and hoped gaining some money.

Indian history revealed that Rishikesh was the sacred, holy land where genuine monks came to practice religions. Subsequently, when pilgrims became popular, mendicants flocked to Rishikesh to practice their profession. When they realized that being a monk seemed to be an easier way to earn a living, many mendicants became monks or missionaries specialized in manipulating money from innocent, credulous devotees.

Of course, Rishikesh still had intellectual monks who dedicated their lives to search for the *Truth*. These committed monks remained practicing their religion in the vicinity and did not pay any attention to monks who took advantage of their presence to seek profits. This behavior was the specific characteristic of the Indian culture. A Westerner certainly would not accept such a situation. They either requested for law enforcement or gave dishonest monks warnings. However, Hinduism did not have a close organization as Christianity. Monks envisaged many different ways to practice religions, so they would bear the consequence of their choice. Impostors or manipulators would definitely endure corollaries in their next life.

Professor Kavir informed that when the culture degenerated with time, life became more difficult. Truly holy monks became rare while fake monks and magicians turned out to be popular. Thousands of illiterate, ignorant people wandered with high titles and positions like teachers [guru], scholars [yogi], or sages [Bhagwan]. They waited until festive days or holidays, appeared at temples or pagodas, and showed off how important they were to collect donations. Certainly, they were burdens of the society because they came in for their share and yet offered nothing in return. This was why Westerners looked down on the cultural heritage of India. Realistically, part of the problem was the blind belief in the religion of the people. They could not distinguish between a true monk and an impostor. A fervent belief in religion made them become naïve yet credulous and ready to obey monks absolutely.

Another part of the problem was the reliance on the supernatural power. The majority of devoted people were too busy to earn their living, so they did not have any time for their spiritual life. As a result, they entrusted a particular monk to pray on their behalf and assimilate their liberation as well as faithfulness. Most monks exhaustedly took advantage of these faithful people through promises to take care of their spiritual life by praying for them. These monks were proud that they attained enlightenment, were able to communicate directly with the Supreme Being, and acted as intermediaries for the Supreme Being and man. They did not only live in magnificent temples and enjoyed offerings but also demanded other things in the name of the Almighty.

Culturally, Asians did not like to be suspicious, so they accepted what the monks said as the Almighty's wills and scrupulously obeyed. As a result, religious Indian documents underwent considerable changes that made it difficult to distinguish between real and delusive matters. Monks were free to recite mysterious quotations and then to interpret these quotations in the ways that benefited them most. Discrimination among social classes was very clear in India.

Monks were always on the top, even higher than king and nobles. The monk class came along to share social services without doing anything while other classes were responsible to provide what these monks demanded. Because they were leisured, they opposed and criticized each other. Each monk established his own religious sect or school, claimed his sovereign boundary, and interpreted religious classics using his own philosophy from concrete to abstract matters including chronology, theory of orientation and space, monism, and pluralism, etc. Not only did these monks disagree with each other but also argued against each other. This controversy greatly confused the faithful who did not know what to believe in.

Because of the social poverty, religious turmoil and, deranged spirit caused by heretical doctrine, India has never become a strong, prosperous country like others over the years. However, with a great heritage and hidden wisdom, a number of virtuous monks still live discretely in India to keep the spiritual flame always bright. Even now, some people are eager for the *Truth* and willing to abandon everything to search for it. The fact that people voluntarily leave everything behind for the *Truth* is also a distinctive character of Asians because Westerners can hardly accept the notion of giving up material possessions to chase after something that is illusive, equivocal, and unrealistic. Westerners strongly believe that searching for the *Truth* is useless, and happiness is to enjoy everything that life offers because death is the end. Nevertheless, there are still Europeans who ask themselves whether there is anything after death or not.

Professor Evans-Wentz asked, "If life is so, what is its purpose? Why are we born to die?"

Professor Kavir offered, "The Western culture cannot provide a straightforward answer to this question, and this subject becomes a big headache for many renowned philosophers because most of them can only provide a roundabout response which leads to no definite conclusion. All they can say is that it may be this or perhaps that. When Westerners are actually in touch with Asians, they are suddenly and completely astonished because everything they are wondering has been answered by Asians since thousands of years ago."

History has recorded that some Europeans who came to visit Asia were so fascinated about Asian cultural wisdom that they did not even remember the main purpose of their trip. The classic example was King Alexander the Great of Greece, the so-called all-victorious, invincible king. He conquered the world by crushing Egypt, destroying Persia, and expanding his empire as far as the Indian Ocean. When he came to India, he was the authoritative conqueror with famous power and reputation. However, when he returned to Greece, he became a modest and courteous philosopher. King Alexander the Great was a disciple of the famous philosopher Aristotle but was convinced by Indian sages. After he overpowered all Indian armies, he ordered all Indian commanders to come for interrogations.

The arrogant king raised his voice, "Being defeated as such, are you submitting to me?"

If it were from other countries, kings or commanders would be on their knees to beg for forgiveness and surrender because of the power of Greece.

The Indian commander loudly replied, "You are just a cruel and ruthless fellow, why should I submit to you? You can militarily win, but how can you govern our people?"

King Alexander became very angry, "I have ruled the whole world. Which country would not admire my talent? Wherever people betray me, I will kill that entire country. Do you not see great nations like Egypt and Persia asking for submission, much less the weak country like India?"

The Indian commander burst out laughing, "Subjugating by military conquest is easy, but winning over people's hearts is hundreds of thousands times more difficult. A wicked person like you cannot preside over India."

Professor Kavir explained, "This unexpected statement indeed startled King Alexander. It should be remembered that Alexander the Great was the king who was a perfect fighter as well as a scholar rather than a person who only relied on power. Since childhood, the Greek philosophers educated him. At the age of fourteen, he dispatched troops to mount punitive expeditions all over the Mediterranean region and achieved many brilliant feats of arms. He followed the famous philosopher Aristotle to study while tens of other scholars always surrounded to consult him. The reasoning of the Indian commander made King Alexander think hard. Instead of ordering to kill the Indian commander to set an example for others, King Alexander was not even mad but brought up the subject of conquering people's hearts to discuss with him. Throughout European history, King Alexander the Great was the only emperor who reasonably debated until he gained respect and admiration from his enemies. The detailed discussions between King Alexander the Great and the Indian commander was not reported in history, but shortly thereafter, King Alexander the Great invited Indian philosophers to come and discuss with Greek scholars who always accompanied the expeditionary force."

Professor Kavir grieved over the king's death, "Within a short period, King Alexander the Great recognized that Greek philosophers were not intellectually comparable with Indian scholars, so the king changed his attitude and treated Indian scholars with respect and courtesy. Instead of governing by power as he still did to other countries, he took advice from scholars and respected the rights of Indians. The expeditionary force ceased to advance further into India, so the king could have more time to learn and discuss with Indian sages and philosophers. The discussions sometimes lasted for weeks or even prolonged for months. After that, the king ordered to bring all troops back to Greece because he gave up his dream of becoming the universal king. King Alexander planned to revolutionize his policy on how to govern the world using the Indian philosophy as the model. Unfortunately, King Alexander passed away when he was not even thirty years old. "If King Alexander the Great could live a few years longer, Western history would have been completely different."

Among the renowned philosophers, Ramakrishna was considered as the saint of Hinduism. His reputation spread as far as Europe. The delegation found their way to meet with his disciple, Sage Mahayasa, who practiced his religion in a temple nearby. Across from a small terrace was a long-standing room built with an ancient architecture. The delegation was welcome to sit on a carpet. After a few minutes, it sounded as if someone slowly walked in. It was an old, healthy man with a long white beard, serious countenance, and shiny eyes that seemed to sparkle holy-like. Everyone felt strangely moved, and Professor Evans-Wentz started to present the aims of the delegation.

Mahayasa smiled, "The Supernatural has led you here, so you will have opportunities to meet with many great philosophers in this country. The Supernatural has a clear objective, and you will see."

Professor Evans-Wentz asked, "Even though we have heard a lot about Saint Ramakrishna, can you tell us more about him?"

Mahayasa was gracious, "I am very pleased to talk about him. He died half of a century ago, but I still vividly keep his memory in my heart. I was twenty-seven years old when I met him and always stayed beside him until the last days of his life. Thanks to him, I have become a new person, and my perception about life has changed drastically. His influence on people is so profound that whoever has come to interact with him are all converted, including suspicious and cynical persons."

Professor Evans-Wentz wondered, "But if people do not believe in him, how can they be converted?"

Mahayasa smiled, "Given peaceful influences emanated from the holy Ramakrishna, even though people feel distrustful, they still sense the tranquility and comfort."

Professor Allen hesitated, "We know that he did not have much education."

Mahayasa gently replied, "You are right. He was very simple, knew very little, and did not learn a lot, but all well-educated, talented Indians admired him. They bowed to his spiritual halo. He always taught that money, titles, and positions are ephemerals. They appeared to be transient compared to spiritual worth."

Professor Allen continued, "But Westerners cannot understand why royal people and sophisticated scholars bowed to a man who did not even finish a secondary school."

Mahayasa gently justified, "They cannot understand because they assume that the monks must possess academic degrees, graduate from renowned universities, and communicate eloquently. Indian conception about monks is quite different because it is not necessary for a monk to graduate from a specialized school and write highly sophisticated books but rather to inspire and awaken consciences. When you were close to him, you would understand how peaceful it really was. How wonderful it was to be with him! He used to wallow in spiritual deep meditations that made us feel as if we were with a saint rather than with a worldly man."

Mahayasa relayed his own experience with Ramakrishna in the details, "I will tell you about my experience. I was educated according to a European system, so I was proud that I read a lot and had a much broader knowledge than those around me. At the time, I was the English teacher at the Calcutta secondary school. Venerable Ramakrishna was practicing a religion at the Dakshineswar institution that was not too far away from where I was. One day, I followed my friends to the Dakshineswar institution in Venerable Ramakrishna's preaching. In fact, I intended to debate with Venerable Ramakrishna whom people highly regarded as a saint instead of listening to him, but a strange feeling came over me as soon as I heard his words. I was invigorated with an indescribably strange, peaceful feeling. He neither talked with a common language nor used ostentatious terminologies that I thought he would but communicated with the audience with the voice of his heart. I was passionate by his simple, sincere teachings like a long-standing drought waiting to receive water. Thereafter, I came to his teaching every week. A short time later, he accepted me as his disciple and personally advised me, 'Looking at your physiognomy, I know you will become a monk [yogi], so you should try to fulfill your daily life responsibility, but your mind must always think of the Supreme Being.'"

Professor Allen said, "We have heard about Ramakrishna since we were in Europe, but European public opinion probably does not know anything about him except that he was an uneducated man."

Mahayasa explained, "From my knowledge, he did not want to go to school because his innate nature leaned completely toward spiritual intellect. A person like him certainly does not pay attention to literature, diploma, rank, wealth, or fame. When he became a teenager, he experienced a strange occurrence. At the ages of sixteen and seventeen, most adolescents go through crises or undergo personal character changes particularly in emotional romance. To high-minded persons, adolescence is the beginning of a real life with the development of magnificent, spiritual skills. This beginning also starts with a panic when one faces death. The majority of people think of death more or less but only for a while, very few of them give it a deep thought. Great philosophers, however, are different. They try their best to understand 'What is death?'"

Mahayasa smiled and nodded his head, "It was similar for Ramakrishna. He contemplated 'What is death. My body is dead, but how about me? Do I die? If I were this body, would I be this body when I die? If I were not this body, I would not die, but how would I find out? The only and unique way is to experience death.' Thereafter, he determined to meditate and contemplate about this subject. He imagined that his body was dead meaning that it neither breathed nor felt. With a vehement willpower, he withdrew all vital energy from his body, and he was eventually successful. One day, his body became stiff and immobile like a dead person, but immediately at that very moment, an indescribable power sprung up sincerely and overwhelmed his innermost feelings. He did not say anything about what happened thereafter, but we could guess through his teachings. We could think of that power like grace."

Mahayasa explained, "Once Ramakrishna attained that revelation, he advanced deeply into a source of life to harmonize with the supernatural—he then unified with his true self. Since then, he experienced that the true self resided deeply in his innermost feelings, but he had not yet experienced another *Truth*, 'The true self was the unique *Truth* because there was nothing else besides it.' When advancing deeply into the innermost feelings, he actually experienced the genuine peace. He, however, was not satisfied when he became conscious because the provisional peace he felt was just for saints. With all his heart and mind, he contemplated on this sensation of deficiency; hence, his body at that moment was often under intense heat that lasted for many months. Unfortunately but expectedly, people around him did not understand and assumed that he was ill. He remained sunk in this selfless state for a long time and took no heed of everything around him. His uncle was also unaware of this kind of experience, so he often scolded Ramakrishna for being lazy and refusing to study."

Mahayasa continued, "One day, Ramakrishna heard about the Dakshiniwar temple, the name with a mysterious fascination, and decided to go to that temple. Upon arrival at the temple, he immediately stepped right to the front of the Shiva statue and said, 'Father, you have called me, and now I come.' At this particular moment, the feelings of intense heat and deficiency disappeared altogether. He confirmed a new *Truth*, 'My father and I are one.' Since then, he did not have to meditate to attain the joyous, peaceful feeling, but he was always in it. He underwent various challenges—for example, being picked on by children, criticized by other monks, and provoked by all different kinds of people—but his mind always remained unruffled and quiet without any disruption."

Mahayasa explained, "The Gita classic has taught that once a person achieves the selfless state, his/her mind will no longer be in commotion caused by external factors no matter how painful or miserable those factors might be. Mahayasa's peaceful, joyful nature attracted many neighboring fellows who loved, admired, and respected him. As time went on, the number of fellows, he had, rapidly increased. It was noted that he neither went to any school nor read any documentation about selflessness, but he attained it during his adolescence. Besides, no one ever guided him through this transcendent state, either. Nevertheless, whenever disciples asked him to explain a certain religious paragraph or section, he just skimmed through and understood it easily. These kinds of religious scripts were highly sophisticated, but he only glanced at them and grasped the contents quickly because he actually authenticated them by personal experiences."

Mahayasa elaborated in further details, "He taught religion using a silent interaction rather than a verbal communication. Many people came to interrogate him, but once they met him, their queries naturally disappeared as if he already answered them. If a question was raised, he gently provided a brief yet easily understood answer. He did not write any religious books like other monks, but he taught religion by using his calm demeanor or a few simple phrases. His disciples came from everywhere in the country, so they had different sources and degrees of comprehension. Although their impressions of him were different, they all recognized that he was the most venerated teacher, and all respected him highly. Because Ramakrishna attained the selfless state, he did not distinguish between him and others, between the rich and the poor, and between man and woman. To him, all people were absolute and equal including all animals."

Professor Allen commented, "Since Ramakrishna did not leave any books or teaching manuscripts behind, Europeans do not understand why he was so famous. Would you fill us in with some of his teaching philosophies?"

Mahayasa smiled, "After he passed away, many disciples have left home to disseminate his teachings, but I still remain practicing at home. I go to work every day and live in this world but do not depend on it. Even now, I still remember he once taught, 'We rush into life with the idea that we can find happiness. Even when we are close to the end of our journey, many of us still do not bother to ask whether our idea is correct or not.' In reality, never do we want to stop and contemplate. We always think that we are on the brink of attaining what we long for. We only halt when life neglects or torments us. Ramakrishna anticipated this mind-set to be natural and explained it like a dream. In a dream, if we only experience enjoyable events, we continue with the fantasy and startle to wake up when we stumble upon a painful or sad situation. A beautiful, peaceful life is usually not conducive to contemplate important matters. However, if life is just a dream, it will certainly be over at some point. During many consecutive years, we try to search for happiness. Many times, we think we have attained and enjoyed it permanently, but we are disappointed every time. Shortly after, we continue to go after the illusion as we previously did."

Mahayasa went on, "If we stop and think about it, we will recognize that we pursue happiness but know neither its real nature nor mechanism to attain it. We should try to understand what happiness is. Everyone knows the characteristic of happiness is perpetual that means it will forever be with us, and we will always be cheerful for the rest of our life. Unfortunately, all that life brings to us is ephemeral. They are merely temporary pleasant feelings, not everlasting ones. Since these feelings are overwhelmed and come like a flow, we believe they are happier and conclude that as long as they continue to come, we are enjoying happiness."

Mahayasa analyzed, "If we carefully think about these pleasurable feelings, they are just our emotional responses to external occurrences that attract our attention. These external events sometimes create joy but sporadically present us with sorrows. Moreover, the same incident can give rise to joy or trigger misery depending upon when it happens. Hence, we must realize that happiness is not from external factors; otherwise, we must always be happy when we have more factors, must we not? Realistically, the rich people with countless materials are not necessarily happier than poorer ones. In other words, the poor people with much less possessions are not necessarily sadder than the rich ones. In summary, we clearly see that we chase after happiness, but we neither know what it is nor exploit which way to attain it."

Mahayasa further elaborated, "People who sincerely search for happiness will ultimately find that it is in their innermost feelings. Pleasures do not have any characteristic of ownership but are merely small sparks of a genuine happiness that belongs to the natural character of human and are hidden by ignorance. Reminiscent of a dog that gnaws away a piece of bone injuring its mouth, it is bleeding, but it thinks that the blood is from the bone instead. Similarly, we think that we will have happiness when we run after external materials. You probably have a hard time to accept this perception, but at least, you believe that joy or sadness depends on us more than on external elements. Even if we adopt this perception, it is not adequate to bring us happiness owing to two threats—desire and fear. The more we long for, the more we scare. The more we scare, the worse we suffer. As opposed to eliminating these threats, we beseech them. When personal desire impulsively urges 'Grasp that thing, and you will be happy', we believe in it and search for all means to grab it. If we cannot attain it, we feel miserable. In contrast, if we prevail, our thirst for something else drives us further. Strangely enough, we do not realize that we are deceived at all. Indisputably, hankering is like a roasting hot flame. It fiercely roars through the air as more fuel is added. As long as we are slaves of desires, we will never be happy. Once we obtain what we want, we are then afraid to lose them. The more we own, the worse we feel. Is it true? In brief, to achieve a genuine happiness, we have to rise above trepidation and yearning."

Mahayasa was quiet as if he was sinking into the past then continued, "From here on, I need another teacher to guide me further. This teacher has to unambiguously understand where happiness is and unmistakably know which path to follow. He also has to overcome all threats like dread and longing and actually attains the boundless happiness. Only with such achievements does he then have enough experience to guide us. Like a patient searching for a renowned physician, a religious disciple desperately needs a master. Ramakrishna was my teacher. Ancient books and classic masterpieces confirm that wisdom can help people escape from misery, but we can neither find wisdom from books nor by reasoning. In the past, teachers like Buddha and Christ found their own happiness and led others. After they left, their disciples recorded their teaching philosophies in Bibles, but these religious documents are far from perfect. Regardless of which languages are used, words are neither adequate nor effective to describe everything compared with the direct preaching of the masters who are still living beside us. Ramakrishna taught that all causes of miseries are from our inner thoughts, not from external influences. Some people asked Ramakrishna, 'Are there any bad things in our living world?' He answered, 'It is very beautiful.' What is considered bad is the human mind because it misunderstands the world. Our current mission is to travel against the historical time, search for the original mistakes and eradicate them, and everything will then become beautiful."

Mahayasa dissected the subject, "Discovering and obliterating fundamental blunders are like major medicines while all other means are provisional. At the most, these temporary methods help us identify the aforementioned medicines. Searching for the right medicines represents the values of religions and rites. Unfortunately, dogmatic partitions among religions often weaken the spirit and hinder the advancement of disciples.

Once people questioned Ramakrishna that how come human was always miserable and afraid, the reason he replied was the poor judgment that stemmed from the lack of self-understanding.   Some people understand themselves very well but believe that this self-understanding is unnecessary because the daily life is so full of complications and exigencies that they need to exploit—for example—creating benefits and earning a lot of money.   To take advantage of the situation, people grant education with an excessive value like forcing everyone to go to school.   Since the ancient time, man has received much of his knowledge including history, geography, astronomy, physics, philosophy, and metaphysics.   If the knowledge of these areas is a proper comprehension, it should bring happiness to humanity.   The reality is completely in reverse.   We learn how to control natural power and go against natural laws that make the society more and more miserable and disappointing.   This dominance, known as the science's offspring, only brings benefits to a minority.   Therefore, a number of people are rich and comfortable but not happy because the majority of people are sorrowful.   In brief, science creates more obstructions for man than solves fundamental conditions in life."

Mahayasa looked at everyone in the expedition and continued, "A university professor once asked Ramakrishna about the wall of ignorance that science could not overcome.   Scientists knew small entities like atoms and electrons, but they simply guessed instead of derived from direct evidences. They also knew gigantic entities like galaxies, but they could not make any further advancement.   Ramakrishna replied that external factors only led humans to ignorance.   According to him, if humans strived to search for things other than their nature, what they found would not be real knowledge. This statement seems to devalue science, but he has delivered a good sense if we carefully think about it.   Current scientific understanding still has many uncertainties.   While scientists still disagree with each other on a certain subject, people raise their voice to support the majority.   Hence, the minorities of scholars who do not agree have to obligatorily subside even though they may be right."

Mahayasa explained, "Within the scope of science as well as philosophy and religion, ideas are often divergent more or less depending upon the scholar's heart and mind.   To search for the *Truth*, scholars have to possess noble characters because their heart and mind must exert a great effect not only on the search but also on the comprehension. These searches and intellectual capacities are considered genuine only when researchers have adequate qualifications. This is the reason science is stumbling over many mistakes that are difficult to rectify. The failure of science originates from a fundamental mistake—for example—the scholars think they know the problem without the necessity of knowing themselves. In both situations, they begin their searching journey with incorrect prejudices about their nature. Hence, although what they discover are valuable, their premises are fundamentally erroneous. As a result, today science leads humans to a deep abyss instead of to bright horizon."

"One day, some disciples came to ask Ramakrishna about idolatries that they did not like. They wanted him to accept their opinion that was not to worship the Supreme Being under any form of statues. For example,

One disciple specifically asked him, 'Does the Supreme Being have a stature?'

Ramakrishna replied, 'Who says that the Supreme Being has stature?'

The disciple continued, 'If the Supreme Being does not have any stature, why do we have to worship the so-called his statue?'

Ramakrishna explained, 'Let us forget about the Supreme Being for a moment. Would you tell me whether you have a figure?'

The disciple quickly said, 'Of course, I do. Look at my body.'

Ramakrishna firmly asked, 'Are you this grayish black body with disheveled hair and shaggy beard?'

The disciple was surprised, 'Certainly, I am this body and no one else.'

Ramakrishna continued to interrogate, 'When you are sound asleep without any dream, are you this body?'

The disciple was confident, 'Yes, I am. Because when I wake up, I see that I do not change at all.'

Ramakrishna went on, 'And what happens when you die?'

The disciple confirmed, 'Then I am still this body.'

Ramakrishna interrogated further, 'When people are about to cremate the dead body, why does the body not say that it does not want to go and wants to come home?'

This disciple now realized that he was wrong and answered, 'I am not this body but rather its life.'

Ramakrishna reminded the disciple, 'You should carefully think about your recent reply. A moment ago, you said that you were this body, but now you say that you are not it. It is a fundamental mistake to affirm that you are this body. As long as this erroneous perception exists, it does not matter whether you say the Supreme Being has a figure or not. Once this fallacious perception is abolished, everything will be clear.'"

Mahayasa elaborated, "In summary, according to Ramakrishna, the cause of fears, infatuations, and desires are the initial misconceptions, which assume that we are this body, because fears or desires start from this body. Of course, many people agree with Ramakrishna and believe that humans are not their body but rather their perpetual life. Books also recount a lot about this everlasting life, but in reality, people do not do anything differently. At the beginning, they think that with the knowledge they have attained and the transcendent *Truths* they have understood, they will be different from ordinary people, but they still act as if they are the body. Why is it so? For example, if their body is petite, they assume that they are small. If their body is huge and beautiful, they consider themselves big and good-looking. If their body is unhealthy, they claim that they are sick. If their thought is imaginative, they presume that they are intelligent. In brief, fears and desires remain the same. Perhaps, these feelings are even more intense because they are proud of their presently superior knowledge. In other words, they behave as such because they have not experienced their true self. The original erroneous belief about their body still exerts a strong effect on them. Their knowledge has not created a real evolution in them yet."

Mahayasa commented, "Ramakrishna taught that a spiritual knowledge attained from books was often more insidious than an illiterate, ignorant person. People who are knowledgeable yet sociable and own diplomas as well as reputations are often selfish and arrogant because they believe that they know abundantly, understand profusely, and refuse to search or practice more deeply into anything else. They do not realize that their comprehension from books is merely superficial knowledge rather than a spiritual experience. Books are only compasses for guidance, not genuine wisdoms. Hence, acquiring knowledge via this manner creates a perplexed situation in philosophy and theology. Philosophers and theologians ceaselessly discuss about difficult problems including initial causes, final *Truths*, the nature of time, human destiny, freedom, and liberation, but they do not reach any conclusions. Great philosophers do not participate in these discussions because they have their own way to solve the problems, and they are contrary to intellectual solutions. Instead of discussing, they try to discover the *Truth* by themselves. Once they identify the *Truth*, the abovementioned problems are naturally solved."

At this very moment, Mahayasa was silent and seemed to sink deeply in a fond atmosphere.

Professor Evans-Wentz queried, "But human beings cannot only live by faith because they must be satisfied with their faculty of reasoning. What do you think about people who have an intellectual inclination?"

Mahayasa smiled, "If my teacher, Ramakrishna, was still alive, he would advise you to pray."

Professor Evans-Wentz questioned, "Why should I pray?"

Mahayasa explained, "Praying is the last alternative of human beings. When arguments seem to be irresolvable, praying will be complementary, supportive, and redemptive."

Professor Evans-Wentz continued, "What should I do if I cannot pray?"

Mahayasa affectionately looked at professor Wentz with glistening eyes, "You should be in touch with true monks because they will guide your spirit to sacred places and kindle your best holy ability. Perhaps, you need a teacher."

CHAPTER SIX

THE MYSTERIOUS EVENTS

- I -

Dr. Kavir informed the expedition that if they wanted to investigate mysterious events and extraordinary magic, they had to meet the magician Vishudha. This magician never used to receive visitors even the most faithful, respectable followers. He lived in a small house with a few trusted disciples and rarely went outside. The disciples informed the delegation that their master never performed witchcraft even in secret places and refused to welcome the expedition. Dr. Kavir fully exploited his talents of diplomatic persuasion as well as authoritative intimidation, but these disciples still refused to budge. The presence of a European group quickly attracted the attention of people in town and pilgrims, so within a short while, a big crowd surrounded the delegation. Perhaps, the disturbing noise drew Vishudha's attention; hence, he commanded his disciples to invite Dr. Kavir to come in for a talk.

Dr. Kavir walked out with great joy on his face after a while, "Vishudha does not receive strange visitors, but he specially makes an exception for us."

Vishudha was a big old man with white hair like silky gut. He sat on a grass woven mat, exhibited a cold-looking face, and consciously stared into the air as if he did not even pay attention to the expedition.

One of Vishudha's disciples asked, "For what purpose do you come here?"

Professor Allen replied, "We have learned that Vishudha has an extraordinary power. The purpose of our journey is to investigate mysterious events and scientifically record things that we actually hear and witness."

The disciple confirmed, "So you want to see some magic?"

Professor Allen continued, "We hope that you do not mind."

After listening to the interpretations, Vishudha smiled and requested

Professor Olivers to lend him a handkerchief and a magnifying glass.

Vishudha raised the magnifying glass and faced it against the sun so that the sunlight shone on the handkerchief then said, "I will collect fragrances in the air . . . Now, what scent would you like?"

Professor Olivers said, "I like jasmine."

Vishudha smiled and handed the handkerchief to Professor Olivers. The perfume permeated the entire room, and everyone knew that it was the aroma of jasmine. Everyone carefully examined the handkerchief that was neither wet by any liquid nor indicative of any sign that someone dropped a little bit of aromatic scent on it. It seemed like Vishudha read everybody's mind, so he asked Professor Mortimer for another handkerchief.

Professor Kavir interpreted, "Now please choose a distinctive smell from your country's flora that has never grown in India."

Professor Mortimer replied, "All right, I like the tulip fragrance."

Vishudha smiled and lifted the magnifying glass to the sun so that the sunlight reflected onto the handkerchief, and this time, the tulip scent strongly suffused the entire room. The expedition hurried to ask for other peculiar smells, and he pleased them every time. Even with chemical odors and acidic stenches in the laboratory, he could also create it. Everybody carefully examined Vishudha to see if he concealed something under his coat. Vishudha smiled and rolled up his sleeves to prove that he did not play any tricks or hide any special fragrant materials.

Professor Mortimer inquired, "Would you please explain what has happened?"

Everybody was astounded because according to the Indian customs, interrogating a monk was a sign of lack of respect.

Vishudha spoke a few words to Professor Kavir who then translated, "That is the science of the sun, the so-called solarology. Sunlight contains a very powerful capacity. If you know how to select and segregate its components, we can create everything we wish."

Professor Mortimer was stunned, "Solarology—is it the science of the

Atlantean people?"

Vishudha explained, "Indeed, it is a field of science that was once popular in the Atlantis, but it does not particularly belong to the Atlantean people."

Professor Mortimer was overwhelmed, "Then the continent of Atlantis was real. It went under the sea a long time ago, and Plato was the only one who recorded its existence in his books. How true was this story?"

Vishudha pondered, "It is up to you to believe it or not. Europeans always demand proof in one way or the other. If you want to call it a legend, it is perfectly fine. Science always originates from somewhere. Once it advances to an incomparable level, time and space do not matter anymore. The solarology actually emanated from Tibet in a very distant era when India was still an island, and the Himalayan Mountains were merely a shoreline. Nevertheless, these facts are not useful to your study, are they?"

Professor Mortimer asked, "What can you do with this solarology?"

Vishudha wondered, "What else do you want? Are you not satisfied yet?"

Vishudha stood up and walked to a vase of flowers nearby. Although the vase was full of blossoms, some of them already withered. Vishudha raised the magnifying glass to converge sunlight on the faded ones. Upon everybody's astonishment, the dried, shriveled flowers suddenly became fresh and fragrant. Everyone was too stunned to utter a word. Vishudha now directed the sunlight through the magnifying glass onto his palm. A bunch of fresh, delicious grapes appeared all of a sudden. One should bear in mind that India is a tropical country where grapes cannot grow, and furthermore at the time, Europe is in the winter when grapes are off the season. Having a bunch of fresh, picked grapes are unbelievable but extraordinary.

Vishudha handed the bunch of grapes to Professor Allen and calmly explained, "This is the Pajouti grape which only grows in the southern region of Italy, and this kind of grape has never been exported. It smells nice but has a slightly acrid taste."

Everyone gathered to look at the grapes, and some of them even put several grapes in their mouth, ostensibly afraid that it could be an illusion.

Vishudha gently reminded everyone, "This must not be the first time you have seen a peculiar event appearing. Have you ever heard of the 'bread story'? Do you not remember the story in which Jesus Christ asked Saint Phillip at Galileo, 'Where shall we buy bread?' even though He certainly knew that the bread people needed was not bought from a market? Christ just borrowed the opportunity to show the disciples that people could create bread from the power of the spirit. Normally, people only think that they have so much bread or money, and both of which are limited within a framework. What Christ actually wanted to convey was that once we lived with the spirit of the true self, we were neither deficient in anything nor bounded by any limitation. Christ looked at the Supreme Being as the Creator of all creatures and was grateful to the Supreme Being for granting human beings the power and necessary materials to satisfy all their needs. Lord Jesus cracked the bread and asked the apostles to distribute it to everyone. After all of the people were full, there were still ten baskets of bread in excess."

Vishudha solemnly said after waiting for everyone to finish eating, "In a similar case, Elisée provided more than enough oil to a widow in the Jerusalem city for an infinite length of time. Elisée did not ask the people who had plenty of oil in their house because it would mean that the quantity of oil was limited. What do the stories in the Bible teach us? Is it true that contemporary sciences cannot explain these phenomena? Is it true that some people consider these stories as legendary parables? Perhaps, you assume that these anecdotes, which were recorded a long time ago, were partially erroneous, do you not?"

Everyone in the expedition was startled because of this unexpected question. To them, the Bible was not a strange book. The majority of people know the Bible by heart, but very few of them meticulously contemplate about accounts that actually happened in it.

Vishudha smiled, looked at the delegation one by one, and continued, "Jesus has taught that nature has all the materials to make everything, and people can find their food from these resources. They only need to extract the components of the natural materials to create all necessary things, but owing to being cowardly and lack of faith as well as confidence, human beings do not believe that they can procure their necessities. Are demands also the intentions to create? Instead of striving to achieve yearnings and to create materials, people constrain themselves and think that they cannot engender those desires. Hence, human beings are further and further away from God as time goes on. Nowadays, human beings believe that they are entities that are completely separate from God. They have utterly deviated from the perfect path and missed the beautiful, noble purpose. They do not let God reveal himself through them as he wishes. Jesus, himself, has said, 'Whatever I can do, so can you. In fact, you can even do many more important things.' What did he want to imply? Is it true that human beings, in genuine position, are the children of God? Jesus' mission in this world was to prove that in certain positions, human beings are perfectly able to create as God is. When he commanded the blind man to go to the Pool of Siloam and wash his eyes, has he proved to them that God has sent him to the earth to create as God has?"

When Vishudha stopped talking and raised his hand, a big loaf of bread unnoticeably appeared in his hand. Everybody was silent, held their breath, and did not utter a word. The fact that an Indian monk did not talk about any tradition or religion of India but about the Bible as a pastor did had surprised everyone. Suddenly, the loaf of bread disappeared as if it was destroyed.

Vishudha gently continued, "As you have seen, I have just abused the mysterious laws to satisfy my aspiration. I burned the object that I created. By doing so, I have improperly used the immutable law of nature. If I continued to do like that, it is not only the objects are obliterated, but their creator also endures the same consequence. You have smelled the fragrances, observed the resuscitation of the withering flowers, and witnessed the appearance of a bunch of Pajouti grapes. In essence, I can use this mysterious power to perform things that are useful or benevolent to humanity because these acts accord with the universal laws and God's will. On the contrary, with a bad intention like showing off, I will deviate from the right path and be responsible for my action, meaning that I will encounter treacherous effects of my behavior. For example, when I burn an object, I can be burned into a piece of coal immediately. If man would serve God, behave properly according to His will, and act suitably with natural laws, he could have entered God's kingdom. Otherwise, he could be entering the door of hell."

Vishudha looked straight at everyone, "Gentlemen, the great scholars, have I satisfied your wish and curiosity? If you still have a passion for studying and recording the strange phenomena that science cannot explain yet, hundreds of monks and magicians everywhere in this city can perform to please you. It is very regrettable that few of them understand the consequence they will have to bear later. For what purpose do you want to record these wonder workings and witchcrafts? Are you going to disseminate them widely to Westerners? What good is it? How many people would believe what you say are not imaginations? Perhaps, they will even condemn you. Have you ever thought that you are doing things uselessly? You probably will write reports on these strange phenomena, but where will they lead you? Life is not to observe, record, and then make statistics, is it? My dear scholars, have you ever discovered the purpose of life? If you have not wondered about the purpose of your life yet, what good is it to record and investigate anything? When you have not yet found the answer for yourself, records and statistical data are useless, are they not?"

A silence seems to cover the room. Vishudha leisurely sat on the grass woven mat without saying anything further. Doctor Kavir signaled for the delegation to leave. After leaving the stone house, everybody was too emotional to utter a word. The events that just happened upset all normal perceptions about physics and chemistry. Exactly as Vishudha said, 'How can you prove a miracle? How can you inform Westerners who are busy with making their living in New York or London that the East has endless secrets and superior philosophies that Westerners cannot understand?' Eastern philosophies exceedingly surpass, very far in advance compared to the best philosophies in the West. Perhaps, Eastern philosophers smile at the eccentric and the chaos of the so-called advanced science. The question of Vishudha made everyone mull over assiduously. At the beginning, everyone yearned to record strange happenings to study, but owing to phenomena that science could not explain, the entire delegation became bewildered and did not know what to do.

Professor Spalding recalled the Indian's words at the Benares City, "If you only want to study the wonder-working phenomena and mystical power, you will not be disappointed when you come to Rishikesh. If you want to go further to meet true teachers, you need more time."

Meeting with the true teachers and holy scholars was extraordinarily attractive to the delegation, but they did not understand why they had to wait for an additional time. It seemed like there had to be a profound reason that the delegation could not explain. Everyone had an afflatus as if a mysterious pre-arrangement had been made for this study mission to the East.

Harishchandra was a monk of the Swami religious order. He often traveled everywhere and rarely stayed in any particular place. This time, he stopped by to visit Dr. Kavir for several days; hence, the expedition had the opportunity to meet him. Harishchandra was about sixty with a large stature and very bright eyes. After several introductory salutations, he revealed to the delegation that his real age was beyond one hundred and believed that he could live at least several more decades.

The delegation asked, "Why do you think you can live that long?"

Harishchandra replied, "Because my creating ability is very strong at the present, I believe that my brain is still as active as that of a young man. Given this is the case, I am sure that I can live fairly much longer."

Dr. Kavir smiled and continued on behalf of Harishchandra, "Not only is he a knowledgeable monk in yoga but is also an artist. He can play all musical instruments including classical and modern. He also paints pictures, sculptures, figures, and writes poems, in short, there is not any type of art that he does not know."

Dr. Mortimer was curious, "Where did you study? And how can you know so many types of art?"

Harishchandra laughed out loudly, "Dr. Kavir is too generous to me. I only know a little bit about a few types of art. Never have I had a chance to go to school, but yoga has helped me."

Dr. Mortimer rushed in, "Which ones do you mean, the qigong method or various positions?"

Harishchandra burst out laughing, "It is neither of them. I became conscious of my creativity during a meditation session, and since then, I can perform various types of art. The majority of people view art as a means of entertainment because they manipulate art like a mechanism that helps them escape personal burdens. Listening to a song or a tune makes them forget their present sorrows. That is not the enjoyment of the truth, the good, and the beauty of art. When art is segregated from life, it is only a technique displaying shallow effects and superficial aspirations. The source of inspiration cannot be an invitation, but it is rather a natural feeling. All efforts that try to capture the inspirations through all means are only illusions. Talent and genius only help us recognize our ego, satisfy our despicable aspiration, and disable our creativity. A true artist is the person who actually overcomes all illusions of his/her self-worth and glory and is conscious of the beauty of the art like the reality."

Harishchandra smiled and explained when he saw everyone seemed to be confused, "The innermost feeling of human beings is a permanent battlefield where conflicts among conceptions, formalities, theories, and practices are always happening, and these controversies often cause mistakes. When people listen to a song or enjoy a painting, they fill themselves with enthusiasm and feeling. This emotional feeling is different from one person to another because it depends upon personal opinion and pre-existent prejudice. If I like Mozart's music, it is difficult for all other musicians to compete with him. Of course, people who love Beethoven will disagree with me. In brief, my feelings are bias for Mozart, so I lose my sensitivity for other creations. An artist will become a machine if he/she only knows how to serve his/her own ego, to work to show off individuality, or to satisfy personal desire instead of to create beautiful arts. He/she only knows 'I write', 'I compose music', 'I paint', and 'I create', etc. From this moment, he/she loses his/her wonderful, creative capacity and is only a body without soul. The successes and compliments will inflate his/her ego and cast a shadow over his/her feelings for the true beauty."

Harishchandra continued to elaborate, "The mentality of greed for honors and eager for fame and/or wealth is not the mindset that loves the beauty but is a state of mind that originates from the thirst for desires. Desires require a guarantee for security, so an artist becomes afraid. Subsequently, he/she builds an imaginary wall to segregate him/her from everything else. He/she does not take pleasure in the beauty anymore. Of course, the beauty still remains, but his/her heart becomes insensitive because of the prejudices and secluded tendency. Instead of looking at everything as it is in reality, he/she views it through the lens of collection and possession and eventually transforms it into an object. The true artist only knows how to create, and we only know how to enjoy. We read a book, listen to music, and contemplate artistic work, but we never have the deep feeling of the creator. Wanting to sing, we need a song, but because we do not have a wonderful song, we tend to turn our emotional attention to the singer. We feel lost because of the lack of connection between a song and singer. Given a beauty, we tend to compare it to a painting. Granted a natural reverberation, we are inclined to imagine a particular song. We only feel the vibration through the feelings of others, and this is not a creation."

Professor Mortimer shook his head, "Wanting to create, we need a talent or have to be gifted. It is neither that anybody can create nor is talented."

Harishchandra disagreed, "It is not right. Everyone can create without the necessity of a special talent because creation is a wonderful state of the art that is not influenced by the sense of self. Creation does not mean composing music, writing a poem, or painting a picture, but it is a state that the *Truth* can be revealed. The *Truth* can only come into sight when a thought is deeply converged. The convergence of thought only precipitates in the absence of self. Once the mind is completely at rest and not compelled by desires, a creative capability will disclose itself. When the self does not exist anymore, everything is a sacred union, and the beauty can be described in a poem, a song, a smile, or a silence. For the most part, human beings do not have an inclination to be quiet. We do not have time to observe drifting clouds in the sky, a sunset, a magnificent mountain, or a half-opened flower because our mind is always in the hustle and bustle."

Harishchandra explained, "Our eyes are with the sceneries, but our heart does not move because we still have a passion for illusions. Occasionally, we feel a throb of emotion while enjoying a beautiful song. However, if we repeatedly listen to this same song and hope retrieving our initial feeling, we inadvertently annihilate our own creation. A true artist is the one who has a big heart to welcome natural inspirations and to see the truth, the good, and the beauty everywhere rather than to acknowledge art through a capability of recollection or utilization of stimulant. A true artist creates because he loves the beauty, not because his work brings him the fame, money, or position; otherwise, he integrates himself with the objects. Whoever experiences a deep vibration because of the beauty, is an artist and a creator for his/her true, wonderful sensation is an 'awakening' and union. This sensation cannot be self-created or found anywhere; it naturally comes and goes."

Professor Mortimer asked, "You have experienced it, have you not?"

Harishchandra explained, "In a meditation session, I have recognized this sensation, and since then I see beauty everywhere. I live in this conscious revelation and can vigorously create through multifarious aspects or forms like music, painting, and poems."

Professor Mortimer requested, "Would you let us listen to a piece of your music?"

Harishchandra smiled, pulled a long bamboo flute from his coat, and raised it to his mouth. However, no sound was perceived by anyone for quite a while.

"We have not heard anything. Are you playing?" Professor Mortimer was impatient.

Harishchandra deliberately replied, "You do not yet know how to enjoy the music because your mind is still full of prejudices. Please keep silent because the sound of my music is very peaceful."

Professor Mortimer was about to argue, but Harishchandra raised a finger to his mouth to signal Professor Mortimer to keep quiet. Suddenly, Professor Mortimer shuddered because of a peculiar sound resonated from somewhere. A peaceful feeling slowly, gently penetrated through his body, and he felt overwhelmed in an indescribable pleasure and in an extraordinary world of reverberation. The sound of music was very slow, quite calm, and soft like the wind whispering on the top of the trees or the water bubbling through spring crevices. Time seemed to stand still. When Professor Mortimer started to gain back his consciousness, the sound had ended a while ago. Harishchandra remained sitting with a discreet smile and laid the bamboo flute in front of him. The entire expedition was dumbfounded and looked at each other without uttering a word.

Professor Mortimer shook his head and was perplexed, "What is that strange sound? Would you please explain?"

Harishchandra smiled, "As you are aware, our body is surrounded by many states, for example, the vital, soul, and spirit states. These states are composed of very light, high pitch, and nearly invisible atoms. Music itself has vibrations that are in tune with those of these states, so it exerts a great effect on human beings. The sound you just heard is based on 'a quarter tone' that affects your spiritual state. Sound derived from 'a third tone' influences the soul state whereas the one with 'a semitone' acts upon the body. These relationships are quite easy to understand because the quartertone has higher timbre, so it has a bearing on the lighter state. People only know the musical impacts on the material world but do not understand its influence in the upper world. The music leaves a mark on the body and directly influences his/her characters and actions. This phenomenon is comparable to that of a stone being thrown into a pond. The stone sinks, but the waves still ripple on the water surface and sinuously move wider away. A leaf floating on the water certainly endures a great deal of effect in many ways. The consequence of music is even more dramatic than that of the stone. Hence, selecting a type of music to listen to is very important. The religious classics of Veda stated that, 'The universe is created by the synchronization of multifarious sounds.' The Bible also recited that, 'Mysterious sound appears first of all and remains with the Supreme Being. This mysterious sound is the Supreme Being.'"

The delegation looked at each other, and once again, the Indian monk explained a new subject citing the Bible that was not alien to Europeans.

Harishchandra explained, "Thanks to the sound that makes all creatures sympathize with each other. This communicative mechanism is very simple among animals but gradually becomes convoluted amongst human beings. The progression of language in rudimentary sound is only a few steps apart, but these steps eventually create music. Music is a subtle, secretive formula to communicate, but it has an extremely powerful impact that can shape a nation, society, and tradition. It is even more influential than religious teaching and philosophical lessons because it influences the invisible states. Human beings only understand that when they listen to sad music for a long time, they become morose. In contrast, once they listen to upbeat music, they feel excited. Realistically, their mind only unconsciously reflects changes among different states. Since a long time ago, music has held an important position and considerably influences people, from kings to ordinary citizens."

Harishchandra gave more details, "Have you ever noticed eras during which the more changes and alterations music undergoes, the more fine customs as well as good traditions disintegrate, and the worse the societies

become? In contrast, when music is restricted, society becomes conservative.
You assume that music is the cultural product that represents each period.
This assumption is not quite correct because history has revealed that
whenever music changes, politics, and cultures alter accordingly. Music is
constructive as much as destructive. Only sophisticated sounds that are truly
created by selfless spirits can lead us to our spiritual homeland. To create
this kind of music, man must let his true self brightly shine and improve his
peaceful mind to harmonize with the universe. The sounds of music of the
universe are always far-reaching for people who are conscious of them, know
how to enjoy them, appreciate the love of beauty, and are aware of
mysterious sounds of boundless silence. Let us remain silent, and you will
learn many new subjects. Let us endeavor to look at everything realistically,
and you will be creative. When you live with an artistic mind, you are the
artists who know to love the beauty and to have compassion for the truth, the
good, and the beauty."

- II -

Doctor Bandyo, the former director of Calcutta Hospital, was a famous
university professor in surgery. This Indian scholar was once the prospective
candidate for the Nobel Prize in medicine. After a major catastrophe, he
resigned and secluded himself at a small village near Rishikesh to take care
of villagers' health. He was the man of whom the merchant Keymakers
deeply admired and spoke so highly that the delegation searched for him.

Professor Mortimer inquired after several social conversations,

"We have learned that you resigned in a very special circumstance. The
merchant Keymakers told us to ask you about your anecdote. Would you
please fill us in with the details?"

Dr. Bandyo remained silent for a short while then replied, "This is a
personal account of an incident that I should never share with anyone.
However, I am willing to disclose it because the merchant Keymakers
introduced you to me. As you know, I am a well-known medical doctor and
vow to devote my life to science. I neither know anything about yoga nor
trust any invisible, mysterious events. I only believe in whatever science can
clearly prove. As a medical doctor specialized in tropical diseases, I used to
be fascinated with researches about strange illnesses that are difficult to cure.

I was successful in more than a hundred peculiar cases that other physicians gave up. I carefully recorded symptoms, pathological progress, as well as methods of treatment and wrote detailed medical documents to teach at different international medical universities. I travelled many times to give lectures on tropical diseases and was a prospective candidate for the Nobel Prize award. Of course, this proposed nomination was a great honor for me, personally, and for India."

Dr. Bandyo explained, "One day, people sent a little girl of thirteen or fourteen years old to the hospital. She carried a strange illness that had never been known. I was very interested in it and devoted all of my time to investigate this sickness. A medical committee composed of the most famous physicians was established to tackle the predicament for several consecutive months. Unfortunately, we tried our best to treat her, but unfortunately, she did not have any improvement. Finally, the medical committee capitulated. I felt so hopeless when I sat beside her and waited for her to take her last breath. Never had I felt once in my life that I was completely powerless to face an ephemeral life and death as such."

Dr. Bandyo continued, "Unexpectedly at that particular moment, I suddenly realized a strange phenomenon that was the presence of a fresh, calm, yet indescribable atmosphere. Everywhere in the room was abruptly lighted up with a magnificent bright and colorful radiance, and I saw a woman appearing right beside the girl's bed. Her body was a luminously bright halo as the water stream was glistening under the sunlight. At that moment, I consciously recognized that she was the Mother of the world. She is known by different names like Mother Maria of Christianity, Bodhisattva of Buddhism, and Avalokiteshvara of Hinduism. She is ranked second after the Supreme Being but symbolizes mercy as well as charity and always responds to the implications of all human beings. Within that second, my mind utterly changed. I was completely on my knees even though I had never prayed all my life. With all my heart, I earnestly and respectfully begged her to save the patient. I voluntarily promised for the rest of my life to honor her activities and forever to follow her."

Professor Mortimer was impatient, "And then . . . What happened to the girl?"

Dr. Bandyo was quiet as he recalled the past, "My dear friends, what else could happen? When the Mother takes actions, all sicknesses can be cured. The next day, the entire hospital was in commotion because I had cured the girl. All of my friends criticized and accused me of keeping the treatment secret. They assumed that I waited until everyone capitulated and then showed off my talent. The medical school requested that I disclosed the healing procedure and offered to name the illness after me. With this discovery, they were certain that the Nobel Prize would be awarded to me. Pharmaceutical companies eagerly demanded that I reveal the mystery medicines. It was not only Indian companies but also international companies, which insisted on licensing exclusively the patents."

Dr. Bandyo continued, "Of course, I could not answer, and even if I did, nobody would believe me anyway. The medical council was extremely furious because they believed that I was adamant to conceal the information. My dear friends determined to interrogate me for the medical treatments and vehemently censured my uncooperative behavior. The secretary of the health department contacted and informed me that ten medical doctors in the world were potential candidates for the Nobel Prize, but only one of them would be the winner. He said if I divulged the medical discovery, I would surely be the winner. I honestly told him that the Mother of the world appeared and cured the girl. Everybody agreed that I was crazy."

Dr. Bandyo continued, "At last, a doctor from another country received the Nobel Prize of that year. The Indian medical council was so enraged and threatened to expel me. My colleagues shunned me. Besides, newspapers, magazines, and press contemptibly criticized and denounced me as a 'sorcerer'. Can you imagine that the most famous medical doctor in the country suddenly became a low-ranked quack doctor? At that particular moment, I genuinely understood what ephemerals really meant. I did not know what to do other than praying to the Mother helping me have enough courage to bear this unfortunate event. Everybody cursed at me and ridiculed me except for the merchant Keymakers, the only person who believed in me. He took advantage of his influential authority to defend me and to pressure the medical council to restore the honor of a well-known physician who was a victim of a glaring injustice. He spent a lot of money to bribe media, so the public opinions gradually subsided. Finally, people did not pay attention to me anymore. During the crisis period, I believed that this event happened for a reason, so I wholeheartedly prayed to the Mother."

Dr. Bandyo was so moved to recognize the *Truth*, "In one praying session, the answer came to me through a sacred manifestation. In my long-standing past life, I was a talented physician, but I refused to believe in supernatural powers and criticized people who had faith and often prayed to the Mother. Because of this disrespect, I had to pay for the consequence today. Since the day I saw the Mother, my mind has changed drastically. Throughout my childhood, I had never known of any religion. I have been absorbing the Western education, so I have absolutely believed in science. Witnessing the miracle from the Mother has changed everything. It is as the blind regaining eyesight. My spirit is completely different from the past. I feel so peaceful, tranquil, and full of courage that I endure people's denunciation. I devote all of my time to pray, vow to follow Mother's footsteps forever and help save human beings. One day, when I was praying, the Mother suddenly appeared with a smile. Since then, I feel like I have plunged into a new, strange world. I am conscious of the facts that I have never thought of them. I also clearly perceived other worlds and witnessed perpetual activities as well as progresses of all creatures. In simpler words, my Divine Vision suddenly starts to operate, and since then, I have observed and learned the supernatural worlds."

Using ordinary languages to describe invisible worlds without exaggeration or understatement is very challenging because words can only describe something that is visible. Explaining events that were indescribable obviously appeared awkward, but this was not the case for Dr. Bandyo because he could deliver descriptions about the invisible worlds as fluently and lively as he did about obvious scientific phenomena.

Dr. Bandyo looked at everybody and calmly continued, "You probably do not trust me much, but it is not important. I only want to share my spiritual experience with you, and it is up to you to decide whether you should believe in me or not. Because of my active Divine Vision, I know that a large invisible world, that has other living creatures, exists around us. I label it as the "invisibility" because our naked eyes cannot see it. However, science will prove that the invisible world exists some day. We often call creatures in this world ghosts, devils, and mischievous spirits. Owing to our lack of knowledge about these creatures, we pass off something wrong onto them. Realistically, some of these creatures are good while others are bad, and so are human beings. Among these creatures, one closely cooperates with the Mother to do her activities. The most appropriate name for that creature is probably an angel [Deva]. There are many different kinds of angels, and each kind handles a particular job. Owing to professional duty, I have often contacted angels who take care of health. Here I offer to relate about the invisible world to you."

Dr. Bandyo went into detail, "Health angels frequently keep close contact with people like medical doctors and nurses who have the responsibilities to treat and take care of patients. A guardian angel always protects a physician who has professional conscience and works to help other people. This angel often follows, encircles the physicians with a bright halo, and exercises a supernatural power on the physicians' intuition when they treat patients. The angel also keeps the physicians calm and ceaselessly emits soft, silky, and sparkling halos that transmit the vital forces to patients. The angel's task seems to harmonize and blend invisible vital forces in the supernatural world together and then spiritually transform them into silky lights that flow into the patient. A devoted physician has vibrations that resonate with invisible influences. Naturally, he absorbs sophisticated magnetic forces into his body and then releases them through ten fingertips to heal wounds easily and mysteriously. People cannot explain why one physician is better than the other one even though they have received the same education. An excellent physician bears a resemblance to a 'cool hand' doctor, but in reality, it is due to his noble-minded thoughts that vibrate with mysterious powers of the universe and become a center transferring vital forces to the patients."

Dr. Bandyo elaborated, "Although medicine is proud of its capability to cure many diseases, in reality, it capitulates in numerous challenges involving metaphysics. A physician is like an instrument of the Supreme Being that helps save man. Hence, if he is not conscious of his sacred responsibility and exhibits inhumane behavior, he will bear very serious consequences. Obviously, abundant goodness cannot come to him; hence, bad influences will not only strike on his life but also on his profession and ability. With my divine vision, I witness that physicians who specialize in abortion are constantly surrounded by the souls of martyrs. Careless physicians who have abused the sanctified powers of the Supreme Being to injure patients will certainly face extreme misfortunes. Since long ago, people have been well aware of the rules of ethical practice, so Hippocrates established the Hippocratic Oath. Unfortunately, very few people pay attention to this vow nowadays. Physicians practice their profession as other typical professions do, without any consciousness of their sacred functions. As a physician specializing in surgery, I can speak from my own experience, 'During an operation, the patient's life is entirely in the hand of the physician and guardian angels.' A careless or inattentive moment can also cause regrettable consequences. Hence, practicing medicine is a duty and a sacred function that requires a conscience, charity, and immeasurable sacrifice. It should definitely not be regarded like a normal profession, merely for living."

Professor Mortimer further requested, "Would you please elaborate more on the world of angels? What have you seen?"

Dr. Bandyo smiled and continued, "Because of the medical profession, I often observe angels' activities in hospitals, for instance, in the maternity room where women are waiting for their accouchement. In this room, the angels create a peaceful, fresh atmosphere to welcome new souls to join the earth. To the invisible world, this moment is very solemn as it is a ceremony. The healing angels cover the physicians and nurses with a halo and continuously transmit vital energy to the mother to help her tolerate painful moments. Every single ritual step occurs precisely in a proper manner until the child is born. When a new soul is reborn, he/she just seems to regain consciousness from a coma. Hence, his/her soul feels suffocated, gloomy, and heavy. He/she needs to be reassured. As soon as he/she first cries, a light and flowing influence resounded from the invisible world vibrates into the child's spirit to soothe him/her. The angel who is in charge of the entire ceremony has a dignified looking face and spirit. This angel always connects closely to the heart of the Mother. The angel's face bestows the affection on the woman to praise her for the lofty function. At that moment, the spirit of the woman is elevated and blended together with the Mother's grace in glory."

Doctor Bandyo paused for a little while and leisurely continued, "You are all men, so you cannot understand the emotional state of a mother during parturition. Regardless of how difficult and painful the circumstance may be; all mothers are extremely happy when they hear their child cry because at that particular moment, their spirit is harmonized with the Mother's grace. In their heart reflects the lively presence of the Mother and dazzles her compassion as well as indescribable love. During this time, the in-charge angel also receives a stream of radiance in which everyone sees something glorious yet beautiful and feels a wonderful source of well-being that pours onto the mother and her child. Thereafter, the guardian angel starts assisting the child to regulate his/her disturbed life. The guardian angel also emits a magneto-electric field to surround the child like a soapy bubble and to protect him/her from outer noise. Owing to these protections, the child dozes for a short time while the guardian angel concentrates on harmonizing the child's spirit so that he/she can adapt to the new environment."

Doctor Bandyo remained silent as if he was wallowing in a deep thought and finally continued, "To a newly born child, science only cares for his/her sufficiency in food and nutrition. It does not realize that he/she actually needs an extremely important element that is love. In whichever way the physical state is cared for, other states must also be supported to the same extent. The foremost nourishment of all states is love. Without love, it is very difficult for a child to survive because the sentimental need is sometimes far more important than other necessities. Love is the nutritional factor that is vital for his/her psychological and spiritual developments. Because parents do not adequately provide their children with love, they grow slowly and are underdeveloped. Mental and psychological illnesses are often caused by love deficiency. The cause is quite simple to understand because a child imagines the universe according to the way the parents treat him/her. Depending on whether a child is loved or hated, life will appear to be lovely or hateful to him/her correspondingly."

Doctor Bandyo confirmed, "Since infanthood, children receive the love potential energy from the Mother. If they continue to receive love from their parents and others, this love potential will strongly develop and become a center to disseminate love. On the contrary, if the children are neglected, they will become aggressive because the embryo of love is destroyed. The parents' obligation is extremely sacred, and their responsibility is exceptionally important because giving love to their children is far more crucial than providing sufficient food and clothes to them. Love is a powerful creative potential that renders people who love and are loved to be prosperous. In this world, love is the only commodity that everyone can give everlastingly and generously without any fear of being wasteful. A true love has a value of harmonization and is irreplaceable. Love never causes any damage, but on the contrary, it creates good influences. Love is the vital energy that can cure all illnesses, and science needs to focus more attention on it."

Doctor Bandyo cited, "The *Journal of Medicine* mentioned about a research conducted by Dr. René Spitz from New York University. Experimentally, two groups of newly born babies were raised in different environments. The first group was taken care of by their parents while nurses brought up the second group. All babies received exactly the same nurture and nourishment except for love. Only within a few months, the babies from the first group strongly developed, gained weight, and were very healthy while those from the second group ate less, grew slowly, and suffered from multifarious sicknesses. Doctor Spitz concluded that young children desperately needed love to have a normal development. Experimental science has clearly proven the facts, but not many parents reserve a lot of time for their children nowadays. Once the parents provide enough food and clothes for their children, they feel like they sufficiently fulfill their responsibility. Because of this mentality, although Western societies are materially comfortable and educationally advanced, there are all sorts of crimes, mental illnesses, and illegal offenses that are so abnormal compared to situations in the third world countries. Why do intellectual scholars not wonder if parents spend adequate time with their children to enable them to develop normally?"

The entire delegation was quiet because they felt that Dr. Bandyo made perfect sense on this subject.

Professor Mortimer spoke, "Let us go back to the topic of angels. What other effects do they have on people's lives?"

Doctor Bandyo explained, "Rarely do Angels interfere with a man's life. In fact, they are very busy with their specific activities. Their world is composed of fine, light atoms that have rapid vibrations; hence, they do not like to be associated with the visible world that has a sluggish vibration. This setting can be visualized as if you are living in a cool, clean location, so it is unlikely that you would want to plunge into an ill-smelling, humid area."

Doctor Allen was curious, "Can you apply your divine vision to other businesses like the other side of the living world, the so-called dead world?"

Doctor Bandyo smiled, "My dear friend, I first want to confirm that death is not the end. It is only a transition period from one lifetime to the next.

The man simply leaves his corpse. Death does not have anything that needs to be afraid of as people often think of it."

Doctor Allen continued, "Then do dead people see us?"

Doctor Bandyo explained, "They only see us through our souls; hence, they know our affection or thoughts and emotion even though they cannot hear words or sounds from the visible world."

Doctor Allen was more interested, "Then the dead people still live around the living ones, do they not?"

Doctor Bandyo elucidated, "Immediately after death, they are still deeply attached, so they stay at the house to be close to the family and relatives. As time goes on, when they are conscious of the invisible world, they then detach themselves, meaning that they join the invisible world and will not be around the living world anymore. The attachment is very insidious to the dead people, especially those who died prematurely or unexpectedly. They still have a lot of desires and passions, so they hang around the living world and refuse to go elsewhere."

Doctor Allen went on, "What happens to the children when they die?"

Doctor Bandyo explicated, "They have very little passion and desire, so they are more leisured and relaxed. At the beginning, they still play around their parents without being aware of their death. Their reincarnation occurs very quickly, and they often come back to the same family owing to predestined affinities. For example, in a case of a mother who has a miscarriage by the physician's negligence, the child still continues to be around his/her mother and will reincarnate when a chance arises. It is different from abortion, the child does not understand why his/her mother hates and hurts him/her. Pitifully, he/she stays around and tries to ask the mother, and of course, he/she cannot find the answer."

Doctor Allen wondered, "Asians often believe that their relatives' souls are able to help their living relatives and have special powers. Hence, Asians have the custom of veneration for their ancestors. What is your take on this tradition?"

Doctor Bandyo burst out laughing, "From my knowledge, how humans are in the living world; they will remain to be the same after death. Nothing will change. They neither become more intelligent nor gain more knowledge. Moreover, the invisible and visible worlds are so far apart that the dead people can hardly help the living ones. Naturally, the dead people want to be in touch with their living relatives who are often not conscious of their presence at all. This is another reason that makes the dead people feel miserable. Furthermore, the dead people can read their living relatives' thoughts through the spiritual state, so they sometimes suffer even more owing to knowing the *Truth*. Let us try to imagine that when the parents read the thought of their child who is so happy because he/she can inherit the fortune. A husband is happy because his wife dies that gives him full freedom to do whatever he likes. A dead husband witnesses his wife to be happy because she had gotten rid of her burden. Based upon these examples, you should realize that people who suffer the most with miseries are largely the dead people, not the living ones. Hence, the dead people need to be consoled and counseled."

Doctor Allen queried, "But how can we console them? Did you not just say that the two worlds are too far apart?"

Doctor Bandyo smiled, "There are many ways to help the dead people, including passive and active means. To the relatives of the dead, they can actively contribute by helping the dead feel relieved and comfortable, so the dead can be liberated quickly. The first avoidable actions are to weep and to moan which prevent the dead from being emotional, regrettable, as well as attachable and from having difficulty with leaving the living world. The second preventable acts are not to organize memorial anniversaries and not to slaughter animals because these activities inadvertently invite bad souls and hungry spirits to the house that cause dreadful influences on the dead. It is good to pray continuously for 49 days because the dead people are in the important state during this period. The prayers render the dead people's spirit to be perspicacious and comprehensible, which make it easy for them to liberate. In addition, it is better to cremate the body rather than to bury it because the dead people will be miserable to witness their body being rotten or bored by maggots. Once the dead people emotionally detach from their body, they will easily liberate themselves."

Doctor Bandyo smiled, "In India, all dead people are cremated, which is a very good custom because no souls hang around graveyards. Monks are usually in charge of active assistances. Their spiritual state enters the invisible world of comfort and counsels the souls. The monks who are accountable for this responsibility must be devoted to serve completely and must undergo a training period to keep their mind lucid because many horrible scenes and strange creatures in the dead world will make the inexperienced and unknowledgeable people terrified. Only when monks are able to completely control themselves and be undisturbed by external influences, their spirit will be always peaceful and not be worried or afraid. In addition, they must have an unconditional love that is widely spread to all creatures, so their assistances can be secretive, impartial, and effective. You should keep in mind that all creatures in the invisible world are able to read each other's mind, so dishonest words can lead to immeasurable consequences."

Doctor Allen asked, "How do you know that so well?"

Doctor Bandyo smiled, "Because I am under training for this responsibility, my divine vision helps me absorb knowledge about the invisible world and to recognize the duties that the Mother entrusts me. I vow to devote the rest of my life to perform her will. This is why I left the hustle and bustle of the city and came here. During the day, I am a physician taking care of patients. For the rest of the time, I serve the Mother by fulfilling what She assigns me. My dear friends, throughout my life, I have never lived a life as fully as I have now."

CHAPTER SEVEN

THE MONK WHO CAN HEAL
ALL KINDS OF ILLNESSES

Ram Gobal Mukundar was a famous monk who could heal all kinds of illnesses. He established the Ashram monastery in the suburb of Rishikesh city and had a large number of disciples. With the introduction of Dr. Kavir, Ram Gobal agreed to receive the delegation. Ram Gobal had a robust body like an athlete. The way he walked was steady, lithe like that of a tiger. His voice was forceful like that of a gong. Since he reserved a certain period of time every day to speak with his patients, he asked the delegation to sit and watch while he treated them. His patients comprised all different social classes from high rank nobles who sat on palanquins to low status commoners, including the poor and hungry who dragged on foot. They carried multifarious sicknesses from incurable diseases such as cancer and leprosy to heartaches, rheumatism or rheumatoid arthritis, and diabetes, etc.

A patient with a very pale face in luxurious and elegant dress disclosed that he was a rich man in Madras [currently Chennai]. He suffered from a serious heartache that was at the dangerous stage. Dr. Mukundar said that if he had another heart attack, he would certainly not be able to survive.

Ram Gobal quietly listened to the patient spinning a long yarn about the symptoms and then told the patient, "Your breath was interrupted many times, so I think your heart attack will recur in the near future."

With a pale face, the rich man knelt down and begged me to save his life.

Ram Gobal leisurely informed him, "You can live many more years longer if you are patient with the treatment. Certainly, you know my method of treatment."

Ram Gobal explained to the delegation, "Sickness is the consequence of a process that is contradictory to the nature. Living in agreement with nature cannot result in sickness. Man is innately healthy. People become ill because of their destructible habits and unnatural way of living. As time goes on, these daily practices invade and consequently weaken their body. When the illness first begins, people rely on medicines and scientific discoveries.

Unfortunately, these methods of treatment can only temporarily prevent diseases from further development rather than cure them from the root. Western medicine only impedes the diseases from threatening life for a certain time, but it then surrenders thereafter. The unique way that can completely fight against a disease is to obliterate it from the root. The only person who can cure it is 'the patient himself/herself' and no one else. Once the patient is conscious of this fact and determines to follow the treatment, every single illness can be cured."

Professor Mortimer said, "Would you please elaborate it further?"

Ram Gobal smiled, "The treatment is quite simple. The first thing a patient must do is to decide whether he/she can pursue this method. If he/she is determined to follow, he/she must immediately abandon all of his/her patrimony—career, family, and including external situations—and join the monastery until he/she is completely cured."

Professor Mortimer surprised, "Do you mean that he/she has to become a monk?"

Ram Gobal laughed out loudly, "No, I do not mean that. This residence is not a religious monastery. I have never forced anyone to learn religion, to believe in any commandment or ritual, or to worship any invisible deity. The primary objective of this Ashram monastery is to treat illnesses. What I want to attain is to segregate the patients from their old lifestyle whose environment is the cause of their sickness. Worries, heartbrokenness, and malnutrition are primary reasons of almost every illness. It is necessary for the patients to shake off then eradicate all problems so that their mind can be completely unoccupied and comfortable before the illness can be treated. This mindset is the most important requirement for my method."

Professor Mortimer wondered, "Why is it necessary for a patient to give up everything? Would it not be effective enough that the treatment is far away from home?"

Ram Gobal burst out laughing, "Without surrendering everything, the sickness cannot be cured from the root. Although the environment may be different, their mind is still unrelenting, thinking about the problems and worrying about materials.   How can they completely annihilate their miseries? Only an absolute abandonment of everything can create a mind that does not possess any concerns. This new, fresh way of thinking is the only chance that the patients can be healed."

Professor Mortimer commented, "Forfeit all wealth, property, and family is not easy. How many people can do that? It is really simple to say it, but it is a real major problem to actually do it . . ."

Ram Gobal firmly said, "My dear friend, if you die, will you bring those things with you? Will you adamantly hold of those fake materials to suffer from the miseries and let death haunt you? Eventually, you will lose them all. Would it be better to leave them now? This way of treatment assumes that we are dead, lost everything, and are looking for a life in the death. The origin of illness is that man wallows in fame and wealth, worries about everything, thinks about trivial materials, and hoards physical commodities but forgets about his/her ephemeral nature or worthlessness in this world. People only see the small benefit and are oblivious about the significant danger. They are worried about material enrichment and forget about improving their spirit as well as nurturing their mind; hence, their body deteriorates, their mind becomes crazy and their spirit is inconsistent. In addition to overindulgences in wine, women, and debauchery, they unpredictably exhibit happy versus angry personalities and neglect nutrient, and thus sicknesses gradually evolve. When the illness is still insignificant, we do not pay much attention to treating it. Until it becomes life threatening, we panic and rely on scientific discoveries for treatment."

Ram Gobal carried on, "Medicines can temporarily prevent a disease from rapid growth, so people can prolong their life and continue to submerge deeper into indulgence as well as troubles for some more time. When medicines become ineffective and the disease aggressively develops, science gives up, and human beings have to accept the unavoidable consequence as their destiny. Very few people pay attention to this corollary that is indeed a major mistake. The fundamental cause of illness is the demand of daily occupation. The more comfortable life becomes, the more intellect and energy people consume to make life even more at ease."

Ram Gobal firmly said, "Besides, the greed to conquer and the competition to satisfy evanescent desires have made their body deviate from equilibrium and have seriously impaired their nervous system. Since the central nerve is the origin of all ailments, these illnesses gradually penetrate into internal organs that make people become unstable, contradictorily live against nature, and lose the existing well-being as time goes on. In other words, they lose themselves. Emancipation followed by eradication of everything is the first step for people to restore their original mindset and is the necessary condition to terminate their long-standing disease for good. Perhaps, when the spiritual system regains its equilibrium and the sorrows disappear, illnesses become treatable."

Professor Mortimer disagreed, "Given many potential causes for an illness, what do you think about illnesses caused by microorganisms?"

Ram Gobal shook his head, "In a healthy body, how can microbes invade? People who live according to the natural rules cannot be sick. Bacteria are everywhere, but people do not catch the same kind of sickness. If the microorganism is the main cause, why are some people sick, and others are not? Even during periods of epidemic, hundreds and thousands of people die, but some survive. In short, a healthy body can fight against all kinds of sickness."

At this moment, the patient looked up to Ram Gobal and spoke a few words to him.

Ram Gobal shook his head and turned to the delegation to relay, "This patient wants to go home for several months to a year to organize his business and then come back to continue with the treatment. This time of the year is the weaving season, and he is the owner of many factories. I have informed him that if he refuses to be treated, it may be difficult for him to be alive another month."

Professor Mortimer raised his voice, "But if you ask him to immediately abandon everything, how can he arrange everything on time?"

Ram Gobal explained, "Going for a treatment is not like going for a vacation. I have examined his spiritual appearance very carefully and found that his chance of survival is very slim. If he is too dull-witted to recognize his worse condition and wants to go home to take care of his business, his deviated mind will further deteriorate due to worries that trigger a heart attack and terminate his life. As you see, the most important criterion in treatment is to cure from the root, and this is the moment deciding his life and death. He is the only one who can cure him. People must understand when is the right time to break off from the past because there is no such method called a halfway treatment that can prolong the time. In fact, science has been trying to extend a life span, but this approach subsequently surrenders. This is not how I treat patients."

After the patient pondered on the pros and cons for a while, he hesitated to utter a few words then stood up, hurriedly walked out the door and did not dare to look at anyone. The decisive moment had passed. Ram Gobal sighed and called the next patient. After the treating session, only a few people accepted this strange way of treatment, and they were guided to the monastery by Ram Gobal's disciples. Ram Gobal also told the delegation that each patient was only allowed to have one set of clothes and absolutely could not receive visitors during the treatment period. Of course, once the treatment was over, the patient could leave this place at his/her own will. Even after becoming a member of the monastery, if the patients realized that they could not abandon the worldly life, they were free to leave the monastery. The number of people who changed their mind was not small.

Professor Allen wondered, "After they enter the monastery, what do they do, and how do you cure them?"

Ram Gobal gave details, "As you are aware, the first criterion is the determination to be treated until the illness is completely gone. This criterion demands the permanent abandon and eradication of everything. The second criterion is to self-treat because no one can cure any illness for anyone else. This second criterion requires the patient to control his own sentiments. At the monastery, patients eat very little. At the beginning, they only drink mineral water and eat plain rice. The purpose of this method is to flush all poisonous substances from the body because one of the most important causes of all illnesses is the habit of eating and drinking without moderation. To help the digestive system discard poisons that have been long-standing absorbed, the patients only eat plain food, meaning without any spices, sugar, or salt.   [Note: Indians eat many spices and salty foods]. Every day, the patients eat once before noon and drink water several times."

Ram Gobal continued, "Drinking less water will help the heart beat slowly because the quantity of liquid passing through it diminishes. When the heart and kidney can rest, the body will quickly regain its equilibrium because these two organs play an important role in health recovery. Eating plain food forces the liver and stomach to discharge poisonous materials that have long deposited. With this routine, most of poisons are flushed out within two weeks. If you wish to try to eat plain food for several weeks, you will feel the difference in your body right away. Besides maintaining appropriate nutrition, the patients have to devote the rest of their time for practicing yoga to reestablish equilibriums for the brain and nervous system. The first position in practice is to sit properly with the back straight so that the hot current can circulate without any hindrance. Two arms rest freely on the knees and breathe naturally with no excessive efforts. While practicing this position, the patients must keep their mind undisturbed as well as free from worries and must be in the stage of 'no wish and no prayer'. In addition, the patients are not allowed to exploit any incantations or ask deities for anything. As long as they behave naturally, their illness will gradually improve with time."

Professor Mortimer was surprised, "Is that all? It is so simple, not difficult at all."

Ram Gobal calmly said, "Of course, they must, however, conscientiously and continuously practice throughout their entire stay, or until the recovery is complete attainable."

Everybody looked at each other. They all thought that this monk had to have an extraordinary method or use mysterious medicine to treat his patients because the method he explained was too simple and appeared to be too fabulous to believe.

Ram Gobal seemed to understand their concern, "When human beings return to themselves and to their original status, they become harmonious with the nature. Under this condition, health and sickness are merely relative, so they do not fight against each other. Our true self has always been present, so it should not be restricted or difficult to find it. When we give up everything, we remove the burden from our mind. When we eat and drink properly, we eliminate the factors that cause sickness. When we practice yoga correctly, we restore our original equilibrium and come back to our true self. Thus, we cure ourselves and do not rely on any other forces or external factors."

Professor Mortimer still wondered, "Besides those methods, do the patients have to take any medicine?"

Ram Gobal shook his head, "This method does not utilize any medicine. It is very natural yet scientific. Of course, if you bring me a patient who is about to die or has a broken leg or arm, I cannot treat the patient using this method. In other words, if a person catches an epidemic or other common disease, he would rather go to see a medical doctor than come here to see me. Most patients who come to these deserted jungles and high mountains are hopeless or suffer from diseases that are difficult to cure or incurable by medical doctors. You should know that the human body has a miraculous capacity to heal itself. The body becomes weak and sick because the patient does not live naturally—it is as simple as that."

Ram Gobal elaborated further, "Not only does living naturally help the patients keep the body healthy but also assists them to reach the ultimate goal that is to eradicate their earthly self and return to their true self. When they can eliminate their low self, they will be liberated, leisured, relaxed, and unified with the universe as well as nature. Hence, they do not have to worry about anything else. Theoretically, it sounds easy, but practically it is a challenge. Humans are accustomed to living carelessly and becoming a slave of desires for so long that they are sick. Thus, it is not easy to get rid of all of them. After becoming accustomed to delicious food and beautiful clothes, it is very difficult for these patients to accustom with plain rice and spring water right away. Unfortunately, to eradicate the sickness from its root, the patients have to take bitter medicine which is the natural way to live through life."

Professor Mortimer was suspicious, "Do you have any evidence about this method? How do we know that the patients are healed, and their lives are prolonged by this method?"

Ram Gobal did not seem to be angry at this disrespectful statement, "I have more than three thousand [3,000] disciples in this monastery, and they are all patients with incurable diseases. A majority of them were refused by the hospitals because of their incurability. They are still alive for many years. Every day, hundreds of people request an admission to join the monastery, and only a few determined people are accepted. Even so, many people cannot overcome the initial challenging period and have left the monastery. All those who have remained are cured completely. You should remember that I do not accept any compensation or request any favor in return and do not self-proclaim any title or position. Life in this monastery is completely and independently self-support. Healthy people must cultivate, sow, plant, and harvest crops."

Ram Gobal emphasized, "According to the rules, the monastery does not accept gifts in any forms under any circumstances. Many patients have expressed their intention to offer properties and fortunes upon arrival and hope for special treatment. I have told them that once they decide to eradicate everything, they should donate their belongings to charity or pass on to their descendants and relatives. All they need is a set of clothes that they wear. Whether the patients are kings or mendicants, they are all the same to me. Their purpose is to come here for treatment, and they are the only people who can cure themselves. The monastery is established only for practicing treatment. It is neither a detention place nor a religious site. To join the monastery, all patients must obey these rules. When they want to leave, they are free to go without any obligation or hindrance."

Professor Mortimer asked, "But you teach the yoga method, do you not?"

Ram Gobal replied, "Yes, I do, but yoga is a science, not a religion as many people have misunderstood it. Besides, I also advocate a method of self-improvement for those who wish to follow a religious path, but this bespoke method itself is not a religion, either . . ."

Professor Mortimer requested, "Would you please explain more on your self-improvement method?"

Ram Gobal smiled, "As you have seen, the nutritious approach and yoga practice can help people overcome most sicknesses. Likewise, the self-improvement method will help people defeat obstacles to enter the religious path. There are many different ways to practice a religion depending on the individual's conception, social environment, and religion, etc. Nevertheless, the common goal is to liberate ourselves. I do not favor any particular method, so I let each patient choose his/her own. I only advise them to examine the method wisely and coherently to avoid common mistakes. As you know, when a large ship glides on big waves in an ocean, the captain has to look at the map, check the compass, and measure the orientation every half hour or so to determine the position of the ship. Knowing where we are and which destination we will go to are two important questions for us who are on a religious path. It is the same with religious practice. Religious followers must constantly self-interrogate so that they can correct ordinary mistakes in time because 'A miss is as good as a mile'. When a ship leaves a wharf, a minor glitch from the point of departure can make the ship go astray by several nautical miles. Similar to a religious path, an erroneous thought may lead them to the heterodoxy of that they are not even aware."

Ram Gobal explained, "The method from this monastery does not focus on formality, but it rather aspires to a frequent examination of the patients' perception about themselves and others around them. They have to examine themselves and control their thoughts every day or even every hour and then contemplate on themselves versus their true self. The Veda classic teachings have taught, 'We are not these material bodies, but we are rather noble yet everlasting souls and sacred lights of the Supreme Being.' In other words, humans are eternal souls, and their bodies are only temporary, rudimentary instruments. People who understand religion thoughtfully and mindfully care for their soul rather than their temporary body. This philosophical *Truth* helps religious followers avoid crimes and despondencies. Because the majority of people hold a misconception that they are the bodies, they try to take care and please their bodies in everything. Given this delusion, people do not hesitate to kill, hurt, and cheat each other to make their bodies happy. Altogether, everything they do to each other is bad, ugly, and disturbing. If people were conscious of this philosophical *Truth*, they would not want to hoard material wealth because these physical assets are not useful to their souls at all."

Ram Gobal went into detail, "People, who truly comprehend a religious path, realize that their souls are, indeed, they, the owners, whereas their bodies are merely the horses for riding on the road. People, who do not yet understand, admit that they are the horses and satisfy their needs with their best endeavors. They do not recognize that they are the valiant, everlasting horse-riders, so they willingly accept the fate of pusillanimous animals that take the absolute order from time and space. The first fundamental of religious followers is self-realization and self-examination of their paths to find a suitable means for self-improvement. The Veda classic teachings also instructed, 'Although you and I are different in appearance, but in fact we are internally related because all of us come from the same origin.' This receptive *Truth* reveals that we are leaves, flowers, and fruits from the same tree of the same root. Although we look different, we are all children of the Supreme Being. If we are conscious of this *Truth*, we will not be angry at, hostile to, and hate each other anymore. Have you ever seen the right hand with a knife to cut the left one and witnessed siblings with the feeling of resentment and hatred to harm each other?"

Ram Gobal smiled, "The discrepancies among men are distinguishable by multifarious levels of evolution through numerous generations. Have we ever hated a person who is inferior compared to us? By reasoning that 'All creatures are equal', we are ready to forgive others because they do not understand and are not cognizant of their actions. Furthermore, they are not different from us. Once we understand that 'One base but thousands of forms', we will look at all creatures as if we look at ourselves, from human beings to animals to plants to metals and to rocks. Moreover, once we are conscious that everything is a living thing and the Supreme Being resides in each of them, we will eradicate prejudice and extend our love to all living creatures. A religious follower is the person who lives peacefully with him/her as well as with all other people and is willing to exist happily with all creatures in the universe and resides harmoniously with the nature. From my knowledge, this way of living is the most serious path to a religious practice."

Ram Gobal looked at everyone and smiled, "If we follow the religious path for a period of time and find that we feel unhappy and apathetic, carry a tense facial character, have inflexible gestures, experience harsh behavior, speak forcefully, and possess a hateful mind, we certainly do not live according to religious wisdoms. We probably follow unorthodoxy and do not even realize it. If our mind is confused, our spirit is untrustworthy, we are greedy as well as antagonistic, and we feel bitter about others when we follow a religion, there is no question that these are the symptoms of contravening the religious teachings. Once we recognize our ill behaviors, we must immediately review the religious method for reform and determine to restart our religious path. If we do not rectify ourselves, the situation is incurable. It is like a sickness that attacks the patient's mind, and he/she still has the passion for materials. Without the determination to eradicate physical attachments, the illness is not curable."

Ram Gobal went on to elaborate, "My dear friends, all religious teachings instruct us to love, to forgive, and to help our fellow creatures, but why does the social activity not reflect them? Why do comprehension and practice contradict each other? Is it true that people cannot resist temptations for materials? Although they are aware of good logic and true reason, they just ignore them and continue to commit nefarious deeds. Sick people behave similarly. When illness just starts, they do not really care for a treatment. When their life is threatened, they panic, take whatever medicines available, and do whatever the doctors say to prolong their life. Why do these circumstances share many similarities? Science confirms that balance in food intake can help prevent various illnesses. Even though people are aware of the facts, how many of them follow? It seems like people still crave for good food and exotic cuisine albeit they know that these gastronomic dishes are toxic. If we accept that all of us are children of the Supreme Being, why do we still kill and harm each other? If we acknowledge that animals are our delicate brothers, should we refrain from killing them? Why do we continue killing our "little brothers" for delicious meals? Is it true that scrumptious tastes from sophisticated meals have made us forget everything?"

Ram Gobal expanded the logic, "Wealth is also a predicament because we know certainly that it is transient and we cannot take it with us when we die, but in reality, conflicts occur wherever there is wealth. Let us look at a flock of chickens in the yard; they are happy and enjoy playing together. Once a person throws in a handful of rice, they are all in a scuffle. Likewise, let us now look at a litter of puppies from the same parents; they caress and lick each other. However, when their owner throws a piece of bone at them, they immediately wrestle with each other for it. Human beings are more intelligent than animals, but wealth, reputation, and materials make them disagree with each other. Are they different from animals? For thousands of years, human beings are always guided by noble *Truths*, and every religion teaches them the best of everything. Why do they not make any progress? Is it true that we only speak of the *Truth* on the tip of our tongue and do not really mean it? We come to the most spectacular yet solemn chancels in the most elegant dress with the most beautiful offerings and the best reverential commandment that is known by heart, but we still do the most despicable things. Have you ever thought of these terrible actions?"

Everybody was silent and looked at each other without uttering a word.

Ram Gobal smiled, "Let us open the Bible and see what Jesus has taught us, 'You should not worry too much about clothes and food. Is life not more precious than food, and is body not precious more than clothes? Let us look at the birds in the sky; they neither sow nor reap. They do not keep food in storage, but the Father in heaven still takes great care of them. Are you not more valuable than those birds and beasts?' Jesus' teachings are clear and simple, and you certainly have heard of these teachings many times. Perhaps, very few people absolutely believe in him; hence, the world is full of killings because of food and clothes."

Once again, the delegation was astonished because the Indian monk who lived in a secluded desert at the Himalayan Mountains foot clearly quoted the Bible to the Western audiences.

Ram Gobal remained silent as if he was thinking about something and finally said, "Because I know that wealth and materials are the roots of all sins and temptations, everyone in the monastery can only keep one set of clothes on his/her body and must completely eradicate the material world. Worrying about protection of property implies being afraid of losing them. How can they liberate themselves if they still attach to the materials? Keeping money, wealth, or reputation is like a person who wears a yoke and jumps into a river. He/she will certainly sink because how can he/she swim with that heavy object? Is that true my friends?"

Professor Mortimer said, "What you said is very logical, but it is not always true that every religion avoids being associated with wealth and materials because they do need physical commodities to buy food and construct chancels. Money has its own function."

Ram Gobal nodded his head, "Using money correctly is one issue, but letting it seduce you is another. Jesus himself has taught, 'The rich following a religion is like a camel going through the eye of a needle. A man cannot worship two masters. Whom do you venerate, the Lord or money?' A true religious follower cannot be a slave for money in any form under any circumstance. You are probably wondering why I am so adamant about the absolute eradication of all sorts of possession, are you not? Since our meeting today is a predestined affinity, I offer to tell a story so that you can understand why the religious method assumes that money and materials are major obstacles for the religious followers. The story is as follows."

Ram Gobal started, "A disciple who was determined to follow a religion asked a monk to accept him. After a period of diligently working together, the monk had to go afar, so he instructed his disciple to stay home and devote the time to study. The disciple seriously took the monk's instruction and meditated without any negligence. Because of the simple, poor religious lifestyle, the disciple only had one set of loincloth to cover him, but rats often nibbled it. As a result, he periodically had to go and beg for another piece of loincloth. Given the situation, villagers offered him a cat to eliminate those rats. Since the disciple brought the cat home, the rats did not dare to do what they liked. However, the disciple now had to take care of another meal for the cat. Besides vegetable food for him, the disciple had to beg for milk to feed the cat. Knowing the situation, a follower volunteered to offer a cow to the disciple to provide milk for the cat. The disciple was happy to receive the cow; however, he now had milk for the cat but did not have straw for the cow. Therefore, besides begging for food for him, the disciple had to beseech straw for the cow. Seeing that, the villagers bestowed him a piece of land and agricultural equipments to grow crops for the cow."

Ram Gobal continued, "With the disciple's great effort and working hard, the harvested vegetables were much more than enough for the cow to eat; thus, he had to bring the remainder to a market for sale. Since this piece of land brought him so much benefit, he was completely overwhelmed and requested villagers for help. Amazingly, the land continued producing a variety of good crops with high yields, and within a short time, the disciple had a fertile and prosperous plantation. Provided with a large amount of profits, the disciple built a big, beautiful temple, hired workers to make sculptures, and cast a colossal bell. Unfortunately, the time he now had for religious practice was not much at all because he had to take care of the plantation, maintain bookkeeping on transactions, manage agricultural workers, invest money, buy more land, and continue to cultivate."

Ram Gobal shook his head, "One day, the monk came back and did not see the old simple hut but a majestic temple that was crowded with pilgrims. Inside the noisy temple, followers simultaneously worshipped and traded commodities. Seeing the monk, the disciple was so happy and ran to greet him. The monk gently asked for the reason of such a dramatic change. The disciple replied, 'Dear Sir, I wholeheartedly wanted to practice religion, but the rats kept nibbling away my loincloth. To protect my loin cloth, I raised a cat. To feed the cat with milk, I reared a cow. To feed the cow with crops, I had to cultivate. Because of many consecutive good harvests, I could not manage the work alone and had to hire people to help."

Ram Gobal continued, "Since the business became so successful and brought in more money, I was obliged to oversee everything directly. Thereafter, I had a large temple built, a big Buddha figure sculptured, and a colossal bell cast. I also had to hire people to carefully look after worship and incensement.' The monk sighed, 'Building a large temple is rather to chain you than to liberate you. Gathering too many followers is to generate more noise, to convolute your situation, and to obstruct your religious practice. It is just because of a torn loincloth, and you have gone astray too far, far away from the path that I have taught you for liberation. Although you have just made a minor mistake, you are completely off track without even realizing it. By being bound to those things, how can you liberate yourself?'"

Ram Gobal was silent as if he sank deeply into the past.

Ram Gobal spoke very softly shortly after, "You see the story was really ridiculous, do you not? However, it was a true story because I was that young disciple. After I listened to the monk, I realized what I did and understood what the true path to liberation was. I immediately left everything behind and followed him to the Himalayan Mountains for studying religion. Throughout several decades of earnest practice, he finally instructed me to come here to establish a monastery that is primarily for treating illnesses and teaching disciples how to self-improve. Because of my own experience, I have determined to lay down a policy that all religious followers must absolutely abandon everything and constantly self-examine every hour or even every minute because 'A miss is as good as a mile.'"

Everybody sat quietly and imagined a scenario in which a young disciple wallowed in temptation of material successes.

Professor Mortimer asked, "Given your experience, what other difficulties do religious disciples encounter besides materials? Will eradication of materials lead to liberation?"

Ram Gobal elaborated, "Regardless of what kind of eradication, every single kind will lighten the burden that prevents the disciples from attaining liberation. The materials are good servants, but they are callous masters. Many religious followers inadvertently pay so much attention to money and forget that it has two faces. A number of people assume that consuming material is to propagate a religion and to help disciples practice. Of course, the intention is very good; however, if they focus too much on formalism, they will neglect the spiritual aspects. Disciples must be conscious that they are still on a religious journey and are trying to search for the *Truth* to liberation. He must also realize that he has not finished the entire religious voyage, so he should not demand to handle important missions. He should work with enthusiasm but should not be a slave for a job. On the other hand, a major obstacle along a religious path is the lack of enthusiasm. The majority of the disciples have the habit of complacency, hesitation, and lack of determination, so they have to go through bitter, painful experiences to learn precious lessons. All of us still agree that life is illusionary, ephemeral, temporary, and artificial, so only religious paths can lead to a real liberation. Why are we still going after materials and refuse to improve our heart and mind?"

Professor Mortimer protested, "Religious disciples and laity are very different. We have to earn our living to feed ourselves . . ."

Ram Gobal smiled, "Each day has twenty-four hours. Is it logical that you devote the entire twenty-four hours to worry about your means of living? At this monastery, everyone spends only one hour per day to grow crops, and it is still sufficient. When we have more than enough food to eat, we want to eat delicious food. When we have an adequate condition of living, we yearn for a luxurious life. When we are rich, we long for being richer. Realistically, we just counterfeit that we have to work for a living; is it true? Westerners work ceaselessly and consider their job as a pleasurable activity, so illnesses and sorrows emerge. Hence, their nervous system deteriorates and worsens owing to dissatisfaction of spiritual demands. Why do we not work hard to nurture our spiritual needs?"

Professor Mortimer argued, "Westerners cannot accept to work for something that is equivocal and for an illusion that is unrealistic like spiritual perspective."

Ram Gobal shook his head, "When the material life becomes extremely convoluted and heartbreaking, then human beings will be conscious of their spirit. Many kings and millionaires have eliminated all of their fortunes and come here to practice religion when illnesses threaten their lives. At least, they know that they cannot embrace their wealth and die with it. Once they give up everything, their mind is relaxed and at ease. They recognize that the spiritual improvement is truly valuable, so they volunteer to practice religion and enjoy their clean, deliberate, and happy life. If it were merely for food, an hour of working per day would be adequate. Since people are never satisfied, they bind tightly with materials without any escape mechanisms. You believe that practicing religion is just to dress up nicely, go to the temples, bestow gifts, donate money, and read a few religious teachings, do you not? They are all external formalities and have no meaning. Reminiscent of religious disciples, they do not want to self-improve or to enhance their spirit; thus, their effort is actually useless because their sorrows and miseries remain in them."

Professor Mortimer asked, "What is then a true religious practice?"

Ram Gobal commented, "Entering a religious path is to self-improve. When you recognize something cruel, you should not do it. When you realize something good, you have to pursue it. You must always be voluntary self-conscious, self-disciplined, as well as self-examined and constantly study. If you were in business and made profits, would you make a great effort to expand your commerce? Of course, you do. A counter argument should also hold for religion. Why do we not nurture our spiritual needs as we support our material ones? Why do we keep promising that we will change our characters tomorrow as a debtor requests to delay his payment? Following a religion is not playing a game, so we cannot carry it out carelessly. It is, in fact, an important decision. You should not think that a frock will make you become a monk, and a deity will help you through every problem that you have because these kinds of thought are detrimental misconceptions. It is sad that the majority of disciples are expecting assistance from the deities they worship. They assume that once they memorize a few verses of religious teachings, carry out several ritual ceremonies, and donate offerings, they fulfill their duties and deserve salvations."

Ram Gobal elaborated, "If the aforementioned belief were true, kings and queens would have all gone to paradise because they make more contributions than everyone else does. Practicing a religion requires a wholehearted endeavor and conscientious effort to self-improve so that we deserve to be the children of the Supreme Being. Relying on a few external appearances does not reflect sincerity, and it will never do. A majority of disciples view practicing a religion like catching a bus. Wherever they want to go, they just buy a ticket, jump on the bus, enjoy the sceneries during the ride, and deliberately wait for the driver to do everything. At the destination, they leisurely get off the bus without feeling tired at all. A genuine practice of religion is a self-fulfilling performance. Paradise is not a place where we can go with a ticket. We cannot expect that deity will protect us because we make donations."

Ram Gobal elaborated, "Liberation only comes to individuals who have spiritual advancement. Once we understand this fundamental, we should initiate our practice without any delay. We should take faith as a companion, exploit available opportunities to self-improve, and eventually liberate ourselves. There are hundreds of ways to practice a religion. Although none of them is the same, they all lead to the same destination. Choosing a particular path depends on each individual, but he/she must carefully mull over it to avoid going off track. A true religious practice relies on the principle of 'knowing oneself' because on the religious path, there is no question of glory or humiliation but only progression. Hence, all followers have to repudiate pride, arrogance, as well as self-pity and do not feel humiliated or disappointed in order to proceed. If they fall down, they have to stand up and continue. At all times, they must identify their orientation to prevent themselves from getting lost. It is very pitiful for those who are too vainglorious to improve themselves because, like the sick people, they are about to die but refuse to take medication and decline to abandon everything to be cured."

Ram Gobal stopped talking because the dusk had long gone and left only a few sunrays that lingered on the healthy body of the Indian monk. The delegation kept silent but sincerely admired the simple explanations on the *Truth* of the modest man whom people called "the monk who can heal all kinds of illnesses."

CHAPTER EIGHT

THE SUPERHUMAN LIFE

Meeting with the monks who represented the traditional wisdom of India greatly encouraged the expedition, but how about the true monks [Rishi] or saints, who were they? Why had the true monk secretly sent a message to ask other monks to help the expedition? This important question puzzled everybody.

Professor Mortimer asked Professor Kavir, "Would it be possible for us to meet the true monks? Where are they?"

Professor Kavir informed that he knew a monk, Akila Bakthir, who often came and went to the Himalayan Mountains many times and had an extensive knowledge about great philosophers or true monks sheltering in this area. The delegation then went and searched for Akila Bakthir who was an old, crane-like thin man with a smiling face.

Professor Mortimer was impatient, "People say that you have met the true monks in the Himalayan Mountains, have you not?"

Bakthir confirmed, "Yes, I have. I have come across those saints."

Professor Mortimer questioned, "Do you believe that they are saints?"

Bakthir authenticated, "Of course, I do. They are not only saints but are also great scholars."

Professor Mortimer further interrogated, "What are the criteria that make you feel so assertive? Do they demonstrate any mysterious powers or perform something that makes them different from human beings? Should it be possible for such superhuman beings to even exist?"

Bakthir nodded his head, "The presence of these saints in the world is perfectly logical if we believe in reincarnation, retribution, evolution, and cause-and-effect. If we carefully observe, we will find that people are at all different levels. Some people are inferior compared to us while others are obviously more superior than we are. If human beings orderly undergo revolutions through many generations for a long time, there must be people who have made progress far in advance. From my knowledge, a few people have proceeded much further ahead compared to human beings today because they have opened a handful of superior senses and transcendental powers. Thus, we call them saints. In fact, these potential powers are latent in each one of us and wait for an opportunity to develop. Once these transcendental powers are opened, we will clearly see all evolutionary levels of human beings and recognize that people are in every single level."

Bakthir explained, "History of many nations reflects significant achievements of great men in all domains of activity. In their specialty, they are far better than the general population and are more knowledgeable than their contemporaries including great scholars and thinkers are. The evolution is simply the manifestation of the sacred life, and human beings become kinder and gentler because infinite life needs to be revealed through these sensations. The existence of the perfections is naturally logical because it is the flawless crystallization at the ultimate degree of a long, continuous pathway of evolution. All religious classics have demonstrated the presence of superhuman beings. When a religion is established, saints always appear. Indians are renowned for deities such as Brahma, Vishnu, and Shiva or for prominent sage like Krishna and Sancharacharya. Buddhists have Siddhartha and Bodhisattva while Christians have Jesus, prophets, and saints. Unsophisticated tribes also have their own deities."

Professor Mortimer requested, "Would you please elaborate more on this evolutionary advance?"

Bakthir elucidated, "The laws of universal evolution stipulate that everything changes with time in order to move forward on the predestined paths. Naturally, the progress is either fast or slow depending upon each individual and his/her surrounding environments. Vegetation comes from rocks and stones. Animals are the evolution of vegetation while human beings are the products of animals and birds. Likewise, human has a definite objective and limitation. Once they overcome these restrictions, they will enter a new stage. In other words, the advanced life form of human beings is the supernatural life. Each person has three main parts—body, soul and spirit. The spirit is sacred enlightenment hidden in the body, and we often refer to it by different names like Buddhist spirit, true self, or deist spirit . . ."

Professor Mortimer asked, "From what evidence do you propose this hypothesis?"

Bakthir explained, "This is not a hypothesis. I am conscious of it while practicing religion. Major religions also confirm it. The Buddha stated, 'All creatures have the Buddhist spirit.' Saint Paul defined man as three parts including body, soul, and spirit. Evolution is the return to the Supreme Being, going back to our true self and development of our perfect Buddhist spirit to come to reason. Although terminologies are different, the subject matter is the same. I will try to explain this concept by using connotations that Europeans can understand. The unification with the Supreme Being means coming back to him because we are part of him."

Bakthir substantiated, "According to my knowledge about the evolution, the body of human beings has developed to near perfection, but the majority of them cannot control their body. A person with advanced development is able to control his/her body and place it under the management of the spirit and soul. An unsophisticated person is the one who still has many bestial instincts. They only think about corporal desires like eating, drinking, sleeping, and passion. Because of these undignified characters, they will experience multifarious miseries to learn how to control their body."

Bakthir justified, "This world is a school that contains an element of misery. Once the body is under control, the soul must be under regulation thereafter. It is very difficult to control and conquer the soul or thoughts. Although we have seen that many people have power over their body's activities, their thoughts meander around like an undomesticated horse that has no definite direction. The intellectual determination that forces our thoughts to follow a certain way of thinking will lead us to the control of our soul. The last step is the conquest of the spirit that means utilizing intelligence to think, distinguish, and destroy evil thoughts as well as facades of ignorance. Thinking intellectually is one aspect, but thinking genuinely and virtuously is a completely different perspective. Until when the body, soul, and spirit are completely under control, we will harmonize with the true self. Thereafter, earthly being and true being are unified into one, and man will advance to a new stage and become a true immortal. At this stage, man enters an eternal life of the spirit, Christ's life. This life is so splendid and beautiful that it is beyond our knowledge, and words cannot describe it."

Professor Mortimer surprised, "Do you really believe that we will all reach for that kind of life?"

Bakthir confirmed, "Of course, evolution is the law of the universe, and everybody will have to go through the entire process. We can have evil actions, be selfish, and go against the stream of evolution, but by doing so we only delay our own evolution rather than staunch the evolution of human beings. The main issue is the length of time that human beings take to reach their destination, either the shortest or the longest. For instance, we can choose to swim downstream, propel upstream, or float at one position, but the stream of water continues to flow. Regardless of whether we like it or not, we will ultimately slither down the stream to the ocean. Living according to God's will is to swim downstream, and living against his will is to swim upstream. The majority of people often float in an indecisive mindset. They are sometimes sinking, floating, swimming upstream or sliding downstream because they are not wise enough to decide which road to take."

Professor Mortimer queried, "But how do they know which path to follow?"

Bakthir elaborated, "Because people are desolate and go astray, saints are always willing to advise and guide them. The presence of great sages like Buddha, Jesus, Krishna, and other religion founders is to guide human beings. Regrettably, people only like those who speak the same language with them and have the same desires like theirs. In the same token, they do not like to hear the *Truth* and do not want to be awakened."

Professor Mortimer queried, "How can they realize where is the truly true path?"

Bakthir replied, "For what purpose do human beings have the intelligence and the brain to distinguish among all things? Why do they not exploit them to choose a good road to follow?"

Professor Mortimer queried, "Are you referring to a religious road? How can we enter a religious life?

Bakthir fondled his beard and smiled, "There are four predestined affinities leading us to a religious life. The first predestined affinity is to be close to, to be in contact with, and to be faithful to the kind yet knowledgeable sages who are on their religious roads. For example, in a previous life, we had the opportunity to meet a monk, priest, or the Mother Superior with whom we had a profound spiritual experience. We highly admire and wholeheartedly hope that we will spiritually experience the same. Such sincere aspiration will definitely guide us to come across a religion in the next life. The second is to study books or manuscripts and listen to religious teachings. The more we are passionate to the religious study, the more we want to understand the religion and the deeper we want to be involved in it. Certainly, when we comprehend, we will change our life to make it more meaningful, and this is how to enter a religion."

Bakthir went on, "The third is to develop intelligence. For an unknown reason, we are conscious of what happens then waver and question why it has happened like such. From this suspicion, we think, observe, and learn from the strength of our thoughts from which we can discover a sacred key for religious principles. You have heard of this meditation mechanism. The fourth is to enhance character, improve oneself, practice charity, exercise generosity, and help people with an altruistic mindset. When we are able to achieve these steps, a spiritual light will gradually illuminate our soul."

Professor Mortimer requested, "Would you please give us more information about the superhuman beings that you have met?"

Bakhir smiled and gently stroked his white beard, "I have met many monks with supernatural forces. Some of them have lived several centuries and attained extremely high power. A special characteristic about them is that they evaluate everything with a perception that is completely different from ours because in their mind, they are not at all selfish like the majority of us. They have eliminated their low self and lived for everybody else instead of himself or herself. Besides this characteristic, they have also completely developed other aspects as well. The majority of us are imperfect, and very few of us can reach the highest level in all facets. Even the gifted scholars and intellectuals, they only reach the top level of their own expertise but not in many others."

Bakhir continued, "We all have the seeds of every characteristic, but only a few of these characteristics develop and yet they germinate unevenly. The superhuman beings are those who have completely developed all characteristics in every aspect that are beyond our comprehension. The majority of these superhuman beings have beautiful appearance. Their bodies are so perfect that it seems like they are not aged with time. Some of them have lived for several centuries, but they look healthy as if they were fifty years old. I have met a monk who is over two thousand [2,000] years old, and he currently manages an archaeological museum in the heart of the mountain."

Bakhir elaborated, "This museum contains many valuable and informative documents. It seems like they have recorded all vestiges of the entire historical evolution of human beings. These documents contain statures of many races that had lived on the earth, from the Lemurians to the giant people in the ancient time. There are miniature models that illustrate the evolutions of the earth's crust after natural catastrophes as well as movements of different races among continents. The museum also has very old manuscripts from monks and religious leaders, for example, the handwritten manuscript of Buddha when he was still the Prince Siddharta. There are drawers made from strong ironwood that hold mysterious teaching documents among which are writings in strange characters from civilizations that had long disappeared. Along with these teaching documents are maps, models of old cities from an ancient time as well as vestiges of very old animals."

Professor Mortimer interrupted, "Do you remember where the museum is? How can we go to that place?"

Bakhir seriously said, "The Himalayan Mountains are not the place where people can come and go at will easily because it has many mysterious secrets that are guarded by spirits. People must have a predestined grace in order to come to this holy land."

Professor Mortimer wondered, "Why do these superhuman beings keep eluding people? Why do they not appear to help human beings and disclose miraculous documents to the public? What good is it to hide them like that?"

Bakhir justified, "They always help human beings by distributing currents of miraculous power to the earth so that all creatures can benefit from them just as vegetations do from the sunlight. Their assistance is so immense that it is beyond what human beings can imagine or acknowledge. Divulgence or concealment of these documents has its own reason, and I cannot discuss it."

Professor Mortimer was curious, "According to the evolutionary theory you have just presented, if there is a superhuman life above the human life, there must be still a higher superhuman life as well."

Bakhir laughed for a little while then answered, "You still conceive hierarchy, comparison between superior versus inferior, and positions. Once the superhuman beings liberate themselves from reincarnation as well as life versus death and become the holy ones [asekha], the saintly religion is divided into seven paths for them to choose. Of course, my knowledge is still limited and insufficient; hence, I can only explain cursorily. These superhuman beings can enter divine places that are beyond our knowledge, and these divine places bear different names including nirvana, heaven-above immaterial world."

Bakhir explained further, "After entering these divine places, they will reincarnate on the earth some day as a religious founder in the future. This is the path of Dharmakaya. They can enter a spiritual state with a mysterious meaning that I do not clearly understand, and this path is Sambhogakaya. They can also synchronize with the universal spiritual power to perform works that comply with the universal laws, the so-called Nirmanakaya path. Besides, they can remain on the earth to help human beings as a Bodhisattva, and this path is Boshivartakya. There are also other paths, but I do not know them very well. From my understanding, the number of people who are liberated is small, but the number of people who remain on the earth to help human beings is even smaller. Currently, all superhuman beings and higher powers are preparing for a new destiny that is the descending from heaven of a future religious authority that is most appropriately called Metteyya Bodhisattva."

Bakhir kept silent for a moment then continued, "Someday, you will understand exactly what I want to say. In fact, these prognostications have been predicted a long time ago and are secretly held at a museum under a subterranean mountain in Tibet. The Dalai Lamas carefully keep these documents."

Professor Mortimer queried, "How can we see those invaluable documents? Tibet still maintains the closed-door policy and refuses to have any relationship with the outsiders, especially the white people."

Bakhir secretly smiled, "My dear friends, I can only say this much, 'Your visit to India is not a coincidence.' You have spent several years searching for the *Truth* but have not found anything. Am I right? That was simply a challenge. Have you noticed that you are able to meet with a number of the wisest and most famous monks in India within a short time and have learned many things that have never been disclosed to any Europeans? If it were not for a message from the true monk and mysterious arrangements, how would you encounter experienced monks that even the most faithful disciples in India could have had a hard time to meet? In a society full of superstition, the notion of the *Truth* seems to be fading. Even the local people have difficulty when they want to have an opportunity with these true monks. Yet you have already received guidance on the invaluable information easily."

Bakhir continued, "Have you ever wondered why it is so? Because of the prejudiced system, a European never wants to sit on a sedge mat together with an Indian. You, however, have eradicated racial discrimination and eliminated national pride to sit next to the monks in rags. This effort is not small. You have dodged through innumerable superstitious people, pretend monks, and dishonest disciples to find persons who are worth meeting and even attentively listen to their teachings. This attempt is not easy to do, perhaps you are not aware of it, but you have overcome extraordinary challenges. Never does Tibet receive a foreign visitor, but an exception has been made for you because you are protected by the true monk. You will be entrusted with a great mission that is to attract the Western world to the East, their spiritual homeland. Their return to the East is not to find a new *Truth*, different religion, or novel knowledge but to understand the *Truth* that is always dormant everywhere. Religions are just different mechanisms that will eventually lead to the same *Truth*."

The entire expedition looked at each other in silence. In fact, they met so many monks and learned numerous invaluable *Truths* within a short time. Hence, their experience was neither luck nor coincidence, but it was rather a pre-arrangement.

Professor Mortimer asked, "You know of the true monk who wants to help us, do you not?"

Bakhir replied, "Exactly, I know about this arrangement; hence, you can meet me today. I know you are craving for knowledge. In fact, some of you had learned religion in the previous life and now return to India as foreigners even though you do not remember what you have previously learned. Once your predestined affinity arrives, you will reinstate your memory. Your destiny has guided you back to Asia to accomplish an important mission . . ."

Everybody was surprised and extremely touched. The longing to meet the mysterious true monk intensified.

Professor Mortimer tried to say a few words, "But when can we meet him?"

Bakhir answered, "It should not be too long. You will know when the time comes. I can only say this much."

The delegation kept silent for a long while before Professor Wentz finally said, "We have been told that you know the art of levitation?"

Bakhir burst out laughing, "This is not strange at all. It is only a simple, negligible means of displacement."

Professor Wentz raised his opinion, "But the art of levitation goes against science. How can we prove it?"

Bakhir smiled and gently knocked on the bamboo stick. Suddenly, he rose into the air in his immobile lotus position as if an invisible string pulled him up. Everyone was astonished. Although the delegation witnessed many miracles, levitation in the air was a strange phenomenon and beyond their imagination. The monk abruptly twisted around, and his body was like a whirlwind that rapidly accelerated him. Within a wink of an eye, he was already tens of meters away from them.

Bakhir reverberated back, "Gentlemen, why do human beings have to crawl on the ground? If human beings have more power than animals, should they fly higher than birds and swim faster than fish? Why can they not do that? Is it the materialism about their nature? Their thoughts only perceive that they can simply walk. Depending on their perception, human beings feel like they are either bound or unbound and perceive as being free or slave. If they know themselves well and develop their abilities properly, they basically can do almost everything."

Bakhir moved swiftly on the serpentine road, and within a few minutes, he disappeared and left a trail of dust behind. Everyone was too moved to say anything. Professor Mortimer held a camera but was not able to take any picture.

CHAPTER NINE

THE INVISIBLE WORLD

Hamoud was a venerable bonze who had a broad knowledge about the invisible world. Unlike all other monks that the expedition had met, he was not an Indian but an Egyptian. He lived alone in a small house built against a mountainside. Hamoud never received visitors, but owing to Dr. Kavir's introduction, he agreed to greet the expedition for a short time. He wore a thin, austere face and carried a fragile body. He dressed in a large gown and wound a turban onto his head in an Egyptian style.

Professor Evans-Wentz started, "We have been informed that you study mysterious phenomena . . ."

Hamoud calmly replied, "Yes, it is true. I specialize in the invisible world."

Professor Evans-Wentz asked, "You then must believe in the existence of ghosts . . ."

Hamoud confirmed with a definite, assertive tone of voice, "That is the *Truth*. It is not only that ghosts and devils exist, but they are also the subject of my study."

Professor Evans-Wentz was curious, "What are the evidences that make you believe they are real?"

Hamoud confirmed, "Everywhere in the world, there are anecdotes about ghosts. Because people are often afraid of what they cannot perceive by ordinary senses, they refuse to accept them. This repudiation results in fear from which they make up dreadful, horrible stories that are not real. If we accept ghosts and devils as we do with elephants and horses, we probably will not be so scared. You demand palpable evidences, do you not?"

Professor Evans-Wentz replied, "Of course, we need an obvious confirmation . . ."

Hamoud said with confidence, "All right, look right here."

The bonze opened a drawer, took out a pair of knitting needles along with a spool of wool, and placed them on the floor at the corner of the room.

Hamoud leisurely said, "We will continue with our conversation, and you will see what happens later."

Everyone was bewildered and did not understand what the bonze wanted to convey.

Professor Mortimer was impatient, "If you study the invisible world, would you please explain the concepts of paradise, hell as well as life after death?"

Hamoud spoke with a serious tone of voice, "That is not a right conception because death is only a transitional stage rather than the end. The universe has many worlds, so this living world is not the only one. The perception of paradise or hell is only a symbol because there is no substantiation of victims being tortured by devils or angels with wings flying around. These symbols are often misunderstood by individual conceptions. I try to present my study sequentially as follows. When we die, we enter the middle stage that includes seven different planes. Fine atoms, the so-called Ether, form each plane, and their vibrations make each astral plane different from one to another. Depending on a person's soul that has sophisticated or coarse vibration, he/she will adapt to a certain astral plane. This is the phenomenon of 'Great minds think alike.'"

Hamoud expanded the conception, "Immediately after death, the elements that constitute the soul are rearranged so that the light layers are inside whereas the heavy ones encase them. This arrangement is similar to dressing for the winter—thinner clothes are closer to the body while thicker clothes are for an overcoat. Since the outer-layer is made up of atoms with slow vibration and heavy composition, it is suitable for the world of the dead where human beings first come. After residing here for a period, the outer layer gradually disintegrates as if a man takes off his coat. The atomic structures of the new outer layer will then determine the next appropriate world for the person. With this protocol and time, when physical materials eventually crumble, the person gradually advances to higher stages. This progression is reminiscent of a gas-filled balloon tied to many sand bags. With the removal of one sandbag at a time, the balloon keeps elevating higher and higher until it is completely free to float through the air."

Hamoud explained, "Among seven planes of the world of the dead, the seventh plane has the slowest atomic vibration and is the heaviest as well as the gloomiest because it is for dishonest souls, criminals, animal slaughterers, societal dregs, and malevolently minded souls with bestiality. Since there is no physical body in the world of the dead, statures of souls often change according to the thought; hence, those with inhuman behavior frequently appear in horrible figures like half-man and half-animal. People who are clearly lacking of knowledge about this world consider the souls with abnormal shapes as devils. This assumption is not too far off from the *Truth* because the majority of these souls have been always deeply resentful, greedy, and revengeful and often search for a way to return to the living world. Depending on these ghosts' desires, they gather around appropriate places, and of course, people in the material world do not see them."

Hamoud gave further details, "The hungry and thirsty ghosts hang around public bars and slaughterhouses where they try to be in tune with the vibrations of the material pleasures. When a person who enjoys good food develops delightful vibrations, the ghosts then try to find a way to take pleasure in the corresponding mindset. These ghosts sometimes attempt to influence and urge people who are weak-minded or inexperienced. Ghosts with sexual indulgences loiter around the houses of pleasure, vibrate with voluptuousness, and try to exert effects on light-minded people. If people drink, a stimulant prevents them from self-control. At this particular moment, these ghosts make an effort to march into them for a second to enjoy lingering pleasures. Because these ghosts are not completely satisfied, their desires gradually diminish and the heavy atoms dissolve accordingly as time goes on. Hence, their souls will have lighter atoms whose faster vibrations are suitable for those in a higher stage, and these souls will ascend to the next corresponding plane. Naturally, a person who has a clean and honest life will not come to this plane. He/she awakens in the appropriate one. Depending on our lifestyle and our way of thinking when we were in the living world, we will come to an appropriate plane after we die. This is the law of 'Great minds think alike.'"

The entire delegation was silent and looked at each other. The Egyptian bonze described the theory clearly by using precise, scientific vocabularies without being lengthy and ambiguous. In any case, this is a very good theory even though it has not been proven yet. May it probably be a hypothesis of nationalities that are highly imaginative like those in Asia?

Hamoud smiled as if he could read everybody's mind, "I wonder whether you are aware of the fact that I am also a Doctor of Philosophy in Physics from Oxford University."

Professor Harding was astonished and yelled aloud, "From Oxford? You had studied abroad in our country?"

Hamoud calmly replied, "Indeed, I graduated in 1864 and was the first Egyptian graduated in this field."

A note from Professor Spalding had cited that the delegation had verified the details. The Oxford University's records have confirmed an Egyptian Doctor of Philosophy [PhD], Hamoud El Sarim, who enrolled in 1856 and graduated in 1864 with a PhD in Physics.

Professor Harding wondered, "But how can you know clearly about this world? Do you read books or rely on evidences from somewhere?"

Hamoud explained, "With many years of religious practice, I have opened special senses of my soul. Even when I was still a graduate student, I was fascinated with metaphysics. I have spent a lot of time to study books about science and noticed that up to a certain level, science has to surrender. Metaphysical research eventually has guided me to mythology, so I have studied this subject thoroughly. Upon my return to Egypt, I was fortunate to meet erudite scholars, so my study advanced much further with time. The study provided me with opportunities to go to India and Tibet where I met a Lama, who specialized in the world of the dead, and learned a great deal from him. Thereafter, I devoted ten years to a secluded practice in religion and managed to open several special senses. Since then, I have freely studied the world of the dead because I can enter this world to study directly. Eventually, I have become very familiar with the world of the dead and made friends with many metaphysical beings who have helped me quite a lot."

Professor Evans-Wentz hesitated, "You mean that you make friends with ghosts?"

Hamoud confirmed, "Of course, because I devote all of my time to activities in the world of the dead, I must have many friends there. The majority of them are souls of deceased people, but a few souls are creatures whose evolutions are different from those of human beings. Some of these creatures are more intelligent than human beings, but others are not even better than animals . . ."

Professor Evans-Wentz asked, "What are the advantages for you to interact with them?"

Hamoud enlightened, "You should know that the world of the dead is strange and convoluted with the natural laws that are completely different from those of the living world. Maintaining a relationship with this world provides me with better knowledge . . ."

Professor Evans-Wentz was curious, "Would it be insidious?"

Hamoud honestly revealed, "Naturally, many creatures or souls are cruel and vicious. A number of sorcerers often maintain connection with these creatures to seek powers as well as privileges, to treat illnesses, to cast spells, or to curse people."

Professor Evans-Wentz was interested, "Can you perform like that?"

Hamoud firmly spoke, "Every single action that deceives nature or goes against the laws of the Creator will result in bad consequences. Searching for personal gain and privilege is strictly forbidden to people who are on the religious path. I do not invest my time in any relationship with those types of souls because they are very dangerous, unfaithful and often kill those who take advantage of them when necessary. Please keep in mind that I am a scientist, neither a low-class magician nor a sorcerer who heals sicknesses."

Professor Evans-Wentz requested, "Would you elaborate more on the world of the dead?"

Hamoud started to explain, "You should know that regardless of which world you are in, everything will not go beyond the scientific laws. For instance, materials exist in three different states, including solid, liquid, and gaseous, and this principle holds true for both worlds. If the natural law reveals that heavy materials sink while lighter ones float in the visible world, the same phenomena are observed in the invisible world. The atoms in the world of the dead vibrate at different speeds comparable to those in the living world. Atoms with faster velocity must be lighter weight than those with slower velocity."

Hamoud concluded, "In summary, depending on the intensity of vibrations, different planes are created. Seven different vibrations generate seven corresponding planes. Atoms with slow vibration must sink because if we bring them to a higher level, the pressure will immediately destroy them. For instance, when we dip a balloon into the water beyond a certain depth, the pressure of water will burst it. This principle also applies to fish. Some types of fish live close to the surface of water while other types live deep down at the bottom of the ocean. If the former group were brought to the bottom, they would not survive because of the water pressure. Vice versa, the latter group would not stay alive near the surface of the water owing to the pressure difference."

Hamoud began with the seventh plane, "The seventh plane is always dark, heavy, and full of souls with horrible shapes, but there are absolutely no devils that torture criminals because being exiled in this plane is already miserable. Let us imagine those souls that are tormented by craving strongly for unsatisfied desires. Being suffered under this condition is hundreds of folds more miserable than being tortured. The souls that yearn for indulgences but can never be satisfied are like those who are starving but cannot eat, or those who are thirsty but cannot drink. Therefore, as time goes on, these souls learn the lessons of endurance and patience until their desires diminish and vanish. They will then be able to go to the sixth plane whose vibrations are similar to those of the living world."

Hamoud continued on to the sixth plane, "In the sixth plane, the souls do not care much for material desires like eating, drinking, and sexual passion, but they are concerned about the little things in life such as self-satisfaction, selfishness, jealousy and anger. The majority of them carry shapes like human beings but appear unclear and glazed. Because their atomic vibrations are closely similar to those of human beings, they often return to the living world. They often embody into sorcerers through requiems and masses to evoke the souls. During these occasions, they mislead the sorcerers and talk vaguely about nonsense things with the intention to please their pride and individual self. Because the majority of these souls are people who were passionately fond of fame, position, and power, they often self-proclaim as this deity or that deity when they embody in the sorcerers. As times goes on, vibrations for desires, self-stubbornness, and reputation eventually vanish, so they elevate to the fifth plane that has lighter and clearer vibrations than those of the living world."

Hamoud gave details about the fifth plane, "Consequently, souls in the fifth plane can rapidly change their shapes and colors. This plane has strange, ostentatious, and alluring sounds and colors. Here the souls have much less greed in personal desires but still long for thoughts and knowledge. The fifth plane is the residence of hypocrites, conservative individuals with prejudices and arrogant intellectuals. This plane is also the world of spirituals, including invisible creatures whose appearances are somewhat like human beings, the so-called Sylphs, Gnomes, and Elves. Some of these spirituals are often persuaded by sorcerers and magicians to perform magic or miracles. This plane also has artificial elements. You should know that when a thought or desire develops, the souls use the essence in the fifth plane to create an appropriate artificial element. The life of these souls depends on the strength of the thoughts. Because the majority of the thoughts of these souls are equivocal, artificial element created only lasts for a short time then disintegrates. A person who deliberately concentrates on thoughts can create an artificial element that can live for several hours or for a few days."

Hamoud elaborated on artificial element, "A high ranked bonze can create artificial elements that can last for a year or for a century. Moreover, these artificial elements stand under his commands. Most sorcerers who practice magic often rely on the principles that can create invisible creatures to take their commands. Not only is an artificial element originated from a soul but also from a group of souls like a nation or a race. When an organization or a nation carries the same thought, it will create a corresponding organizational or national artificial element that will exert an enormous influence on the sentiments, customs, and prejudices of that organization or nation. We can call this organizational or national artificial element as the country's soul or the national character. When a person is born in a country, he/she is somewhat influenced by its national artificial element. Of course, it only influences on the soul that means the sentiment of the nation instead of the spirit of that nation. A person who lives more in the spirit will experience less effect compared to the non-spiritual ones. This explains why one nation has a dreamy mindset like a poet while the other nation carries a realistic way of thinking even though on the geographical aspect, both nations are not too far from each other and more or less share several perceptions about religion, custom, and tradition."

Hamoud started with the fourth plane, "The fourth plane is brighter, and of course, its atoms vibrate very quickly. The majority of the souls in this plane are kind, evolved, and enlightened intellectuals. Intelligentsias who were taciturn but still attached to some kinds of yearning will awaken in this fourth plane after death. Most of them are more or less conscious of the situation, so they immediately start to get rid of their longings and attachments. They also learn from each other and influence one another in this place. They sometimes strike up a relationship and reincarnate together in the same family or nation."

Hamoud continued with the third plane, "The third plane is luminous and has light vibrations. The souls in this plane are kind-hearted but clumsy, for example, monks are devoted but lack of intelligence, and leaders are brilliant but full of prejudices. This third plane is also a habitation for a number of deities [devas] such as Kamadeva [deity of desires], Roupadeva [deity of visible], and Aroupadeva [deity of invisibility]. These deities have a highly developed lifestyle that is more sophisticated than that of human beings."

Hamoud, at last, described the first and the second planes of the middle stage, "The second and first planes are composed of extremely light atoms that vibrate exceptionally fast and are overflowing with luminescence. These planes are for those who are highly advanced, compassionate, and free of yearning as well as greed. The souls remain in the first and second planes to learn from each other, exchange experience, and develop personal virtues before they proceed to higher stages."

Professor Evans-Wentz asked, "Then how long do the dead reside in the middle stage?"

Hamoud firmly explained, "The length of the souls' stay in the first and second planes depends upon the degree of their desires. A few of them only stop by for several hours and then immediately undergo reincarnation. Some of them remain for years while others linger for centuries. To go beyond usual practices, their states of the soul must be disintegrated completely before they can elevate to the highest plane, the so-called Devakhan, or being enlightened. Reminiscent of a flying balloon tied to many sand bags, it can only freely take off through the air when it can strip off all of the sand bags. In summary, terminologies like paradise and hell are merely symbols of the intermediate planes or kamaloka. Depending upon the arrangement of a soul state when a person dies, his/her soul will arrive at an appropriate plane. The issues that devils maltreat and torture victims are only abstract examples when human beings have not had any scientific knowledge about the compositions or vibrations of atoms yet."

Everyone silently looked at each other because what Hamoud explained was entirely logical and scientific and not at all fictitious. However, how could they prove phenomena that experimental science was not able to validate? Whatever it might be, Hamoud was a PhD in physics graduated from the most famous university in Europe instead of an ignorant sorcerer from a desolate region, so he more or less had an objective, unbiased mindset of a scientist. He was neither superstitious nor credulous and did not easily accept disprovable, vague theory. Nevertheless, how could they convince Westerners who are arrogant as well as full of prejudices and absolutely believe in science?

Hamoud smiled and continued, "The comprehension of the invisible world is very important because once we understand what happens after death, we will not be afraid of it anymore. When we die, it is just our physical form, the so-called body, not our life. The physical body ought to die so that its life continues to evolve into another more sophisticated physical form. This progression is a very logical, and science clearly reveals the justice of the universe to us. When alive, human beings have all sorts of desires. Once these desires are satisfied, human beings' gratifications will increase considerably, and at the same time, grotesque materials as well as heavy vibrations will be drawn into the soul state. After death, these desires become more powerful because the spirit is no longer there to control them. Hence, they actually burn us. What else can the devastation caused by desires be other than hell? Just like virtue, good behavior that human beings exhibit during the adolescent period determines the living conditions when they become old. Life in the living world decides life in the world of the dead. This principle is very logical and easy to prove."

Hamoud elaborated further, "For instance, when we are young, we exercise to keep our bodies healthy. Hence, we will rarely be sick when we become old. If we make a great effort in studying at a younger age to assure a stable career, our lives will be guaranteed later in time. Is that right? People who can restrain desire and master demands of their body will not be tortured when they die. The natural laws intend that the body becomes weaker and sick at old age; therefore, human beings are no longer too greedy, and their personal desires diminish accordingly. As a result, their souls can partially filter off heavy, unclean materials so that they will be able to reach higher planes after death. On the contrary, when young people die unexpectedly, their souls are often miserable and stay longer because the greed for desires are still strong when they pass away. Given this knowledge, we need to re-examine our life in the living world, so our soul does not have to stay long in the dark, heavy planes of the world of the dead. Older people must prepare to eradicate attachments, family ties, worries, sorrows, disputes, and angers. They must eliminate all material ties and exterminate all grieves to liberate sooner. The preparation in the living world will shorten the time for the souls to be in the world of the dead and reduce the time for them to reach the upper world."

Professor Evans-Wentz asked, "What happens to ghosts and devils?"

Hamoud seriously explained, "You keep assuming that ghosts and devils are certain entities that are different from human beings. In fact, the majority of them are souls in the seventh and sixth planes. They still attach to the material world and have a passion for desires, so they cannot escape from these planes. Natural laws do not allow these souls to return to the material world, but in some special cases, human beings can briefly see them. Just a minute, let us look over there; my friend has finished his/her job."

Hamoud pointed to the corner of the room where he had previously left a spool of wool and a pair of knitting needles. Everyone stepped closer and saw a handmade woolen jacket, but no one knew since when it was there. The jacket was done clumsily and unskillfully by hand, but Professor Mortimer's name was embroidered on its chest.

Hamoud explained, "This ghost is very mischievous and often loiters around here. I have requested him/her to knit this jacket for you to illustrate. To avoid the fact that you assume I perform magic to exchange another jacket, I also ask the ghost to embroider the name of the person who is most suspicious in the delegation on the jacket. As you are all aware that I have never asked for any names since we have met, who else is this knitted jacket for besides you?"

In fact, the skinny bonze could not fit into the huge jacket that was made particularly for Professor Mortimer. He was a European whose colossal dimension was oversized compared to other Europeans, not mentioning about his unusually large, rare waistline. Furthermore, this jacket could not be a pre-knitted one for sale since the quality was too poor to sell to anyone. In this deserted place, there was no one else besides the bonze and the delegation, so this occurrence was indeed very strange.

Professor Evans-Wentz wondered, "Then does this mean that you can give orders to ghosts?"

Hamoud explained, "I am not a sorcerer who abuses power for personal interest. Simply, I have many invisible friends in the world of the dead. I thoroughly understand the natural laws, including karma, causality, and consequences of worshiping ghosts to seek something in return. I am only a scientist who properly studies the invisible world. The study of metaphysical phenomena is a dignified science instead of superstition. Many people speak scornfully of others who talk about ghosts. Therefore, people who have met ghosts do not dare to disclose because they are afraid of being laughed at or being deranged. If human beings do not believe, they should study and scientifically prove that ghosts and devils are merely imaginary hypotheses. In contrast, if they refuse to provide evidence and dare not prove, they simply find an excuse to conceal their fear. When science cannot yet prove certain propositions, it does not mean that they are not true because some day, science will advance to a level that it can justify them. Common methods like evoking the dead or provoking medium often encounter many mistakes because, as I have presented, the majority of souls that emerge into living bodies have limited knowledge of the plane they stay."

Hamoud explained, "Magicians sometimes cite a few phrases from the Bible, manuscripts, or religious classics to substantiate their words artificially. Technically, they are not different from politicians delivering speeches. The most scientific, accurate method is to come to the world of the dead to study personally. You should realize that our body is not the only medium of our soul, and our senses are not the unique means to study the external world, either. If we accept that the universe has many different planes and each stage of human has a corresponding plane, we instantaneously appreciate the fact that the human body composed of earthly atoms is limited within the living world. Other states of humans also have their own senses; hence, if we can open the senses of our soul state, we can easily observe the invisible world. When we die, our body gradually deteriorates, our senses become impaired accordingly and our soul instantly practices to develop its senses. If we know how to open our soul' senses when we are still alive, we can easily see the world of the dead."

Professor Allen stuttered, "A conception reveals that our soul either ascends to paradise or descends to hell permanently after death. What do you think about it?"

Hamoud shook his head, "This conception is not logical because it conceives that our soul changes completely. This means that after death our soul will lose all of its bad characters, turn out to be perfect, become an angel and rise in paradise. Vice versa, our soul will lose all of its good dispositions, turn into the worst, become some kind of ghost or devil, and tumble down to hell. This is illogical because the evolution must occur gradually; it cannot happen suddenly. In the living world, no one is perfectly kind, and no one is completely cruel. Each one of us has good and bad seeds that accumulate from our karma through many previous lives. Depending on the external environment, those seeds will either germinate and develop or shrink and perish."

Hamoud explained, "A self-improving person is the one who knows himself/herself and nurtures his/her mind to develop good qualities. It is like a gardener who takes care of flowers and pulls out weeds. Realistically, human beings do not change very much from being alive to dead. If they are greedy for food when they are alive, they also remain gluttonous when they die. The only difference is that they cannot feel satisfied anymore because their body has deteriorated and subsequently disintegrated. For instance, upon coming home after death, a person watches his/her children enjoy food extravagantly, but he/she cannot eat anything. His/her voraciousness drastically escalates; hence, he/she feels like his/her internal organs are burning because his/her misery is indescribable."

Professor Allen asked, "As you have said that the hungry ghosts often vibrate with the surroundings, why are they not satisfied?"

Hamoud elaborated, "When the living eats delicious food and has an ecstatic feeling, the hungry ghosts gather around and try to vibrate with the sentiments. They, however, are never satisfied because it is like thinking of good food, feeling pleasurable, and experiencing mouth-watering flavors when they are hungry but none of those satisfies their stomach's needs. Cruel and bloodthirsty ghosts often hang around slaughterhouses to vibrate with fiendish environments; hence, people who kill animals at home have inadvertently invited these ferocious ghosts to come into their house. The presence of these ghosts may cause bad influences, especially for extremely sensitive people."

Professor Allen inquired, "The majority of people assume that ghosts and devils often appear in cemeteries. What is your take on this assumption?"

Hamoud clarified, "The appearance of the cemetery is the manifestation of the etheric body that is deteriorating. There are neither ghosts nor devils nor souls. When a person dies, his/her body disintegrates, and so does his/her etheric body that is the intermediate form between the body and the soul. The etheric body is composed of atoms that are equivalent to those of the living world. However, its composition has more etheric elements that make the etheric body lighter and capable of accumulating the remaining energy from the body in order to prolong life a little longer. Since etheric bodies are deteriorating, they look imperfect. This imperfection explains why people sometimes see headless or legless images that float closely above their tombs. People who are lacking in knowledge call these defective bodies as ghosts. According to my knowledge, cremation is better than burying because the gradual deterioration of the body does not only make the soul miserable but also keeps it in a lethargic, immobile state for a long time. Cremation urges the soul to detach from the body quickly, so the liberation is much faster."

Professor Allen asked, "To what categories in the society do ghosts and devils belong?"

Hamoud elucidated, "They belong to multifarious categories depending upon the kinds of desires that they longed for when they were alive. People who died unexpectedly remain in the world of the dead longer than those who died naturally of old age because the younger people still have more desires and passions in them. Murderers who were executed remain with the impression of imprisonment, feel angry, and still intend to take on revenge. Likewise, a suicidal person who ran away from life continues to be unconscious in the miserable state prior to death for a long time. The laws of the world of the dead confirm that the desires or passions that we yearned for in the living world will determine what plane we will come to and how long we will stay there."

Professor Allen continued, "What is the fate of soldiers who died on the battlefield?"

Hamoud calmly explained, "They still have to follow these rules. Again, it depends upon their personal desires and passions that they had when they were alive. Nevertheless, since they have sacrificed their own lives for an ideal, they have a brighter future because their noble death is a big step toward their evolution. They forget about their own life and live or die for an ideal, so their death is not different from that of martyred saints. Of course, it is not necessarily true that all soldiers live in an ideal. People who kill others because of resentment and hatred or are killed by others for the same reasons are completely different."

Professor Allen continued asking, "As you have said, the dead can always see the living, can they not?"

Hamoud clarified, "It should be said that the dead people cannot continue to rely on the senses of their body, but they can follow everything easily by using the senses of their soul. Moreover, they can read thoughts and recognize sentimental relationships very well even though they can neither hear any sound nor see anything as we do. Since they are able to read our thoughts, they understand what we want to express."

Professor Allen went on, "Are they close to or far away from us?"

Hamoud gave further details, "Immediately after death, they always stay around their loved ones, but as time goes on, they are conscious of their new environment and will detach from family ties to live in their own world."

Professor Allen was curious, "Is there any means for the living to contact their deceased relatives?"

Hamoud explained, "It is not difficult. You just think of them while you are sleeping. In reality, if we understand, we should not disturb them because by doing so, we just create obstacles for their liberation. Death is to walk into a new life. The vital energy that used to radiate outwardly now emits inwardly, and the soul gradually withdraws from his/her body through a secret point on the top of the head. Therefore, both feet slowly become cold before both hands and finally the heart. At this moment, the dead feel very calm, light, and free from material influence. When the soul finally arrives at the brain, it triggers past memories, and the entire lifetime starts to replay like a movie. This phenomenon is known as 'memory projection'. The moment of the replay is extremely important because the 'memory projection' exerts a great effect on the life in the world of the dead. At the same time, the magnetic string that connects the physical body to the etheric body will permanently break. Once this connection has vanished, the dead are completely in a coma and are unconscious so that the soul withdraws from the etheric body. The soul now starts to protect a new life by arranging atomic layers in such a way that the heavy layers enclose the lighter ones. This arrangement determines to which domain the soul will come."

Professor Allen questioned, "How do you travel to the invisible world?"

Hamoud explained, "Your question is not quite accurate since it implies moving from one world to another. All planes are actually in the same place. They are only different from one another by time and space dimension. Going to the invisible world is the transformation of the consciousness and utilization of the soul's senses to recognize the surroundings. This is not a physical relocation. People in the living world cannot see those in the dead world because the atomic composition of the living people is too heavy, and their atomic vibration is too slow to adapt with the rapid vibration of those in the world of the dead. The notion of space is also different because it is the world of thought. Whenever you think of a place, you arrive there immediately. Similarly, when you want to meet a person, you just need to keep the image of that person in mind then you will meet that person right away. Movement in the invisible world is like floating and flying because a soul does not walk with two legs as a physical body does."

Professor Allen inquired, "How do the dead perceive a new life?"

Hamoud explicated, "Except for extremely cruel and terrible persons, the majority of the dead are awakened in the fifth or the sixth plane whose vibrations are not much different from those of the living world. At first, these souls feel strange and puzzled, but they gradually become familiar with it. Depending upon their sentiments and desires in the living world, they act accordingly. For example, I have met a rich merchant's soul who dawdled over his old house for a number of years. He told me that he was very lonely and miserable because he neither had any friends nor needed anyone. He returned to live in his house with old memories but felt very sad because his wife and children paid no attention to him. They believed that he had gone to paradise since they spent a lot of money to organize impressive religious ceremonies, and a monk confirmed that he indeed had gone to paradise. I advised him to disengage from all attachments for liberation, but he refused. Some of his relatives who passed away also came to persuade him, but he did not listen to them, either. He probably will stay there for a long time, or until all of his sentimental attachments fade away."

Hamoud provided some examples, "I have also come across souls that hung around factories they established. They were miserable and angry because they did not have any influence on them. They were very depressed when their successors or their children made wrong decisions that destroyed the business. I have once encountered souls who buried their treasure and throbbingly feared that someone could discover it. They stayed around their hidden places and sometimes tried to reappear and threaten those who came near the area. The jealous souls were even more miserable because they did not want their lovers to share their love with other people. They sometimes became crazy when they witnessed caressing moments between their lovers and others. Of course, they could not do anything, so they felt extremely unhappy. Leaders, kings and authorities who were over-assertive felt very downhearted because they were no longer influential and powerful. They were very miserable."

Hamoud continued, "Sometimes, thoughts of resentment and hatred can create artificial elements that have their own lives and are capable of reacting strongly on the world of the dead. A few years ago, my friend in Calcutta informed me of a beautiful knife with an ivory handle. However, whoever held it always had a desire to kill others. I tried to search for the knife and find an opportunity to hold it. Indeed, I felt strangely aroused. Since I have opened the senses of my soul, I saw a ferocious soul who was very angry with me because I fought against him. Later, my friends in the world of the dead helped me contact this ferocious soul. I learned that his wife committed adultery with his best friend, so he killed both of them with that knife. Thereafter, he used the same knife to kill two siblings-in-law, and then another man who used the same knife killed him. After his death, the hatred within him did not subside, so he prowled around the knife and coerced whoever used it to commit murder. Many people committed homicides. He was very successful until he met me. It took me a long time to persuade him. I finally broke the knife and buried it."

Hamoud shook his head, "In another case, I met a soul who was drunk and killed by a car. He deeply resented this accident, so he waited around the intersection and directed drivers to cause accidents. Many people were killed at this intersection. I spent a lot of time convincing him to leave the place. Of course, these souls will eventually repent, but their actions result in bad consequences that will create a bad karma that he has to pay later. Regardless of whichever world, the universal laws remain unchanged. Another example was about two best friends who loved the same woman. To possess her, one man plotted against his friend who became a victim of a political suspect.   As a result, his friend was arrested and eventually liquidated."

Hamoud continued, "He tried to win the woman over but was unsuccessful.   She later married another man.   He was heartbroken and committed suicide. As a result, the two friends now ended up on the other side of the world, but the assassinated one did not know that his friend victimized him. Since the innocent friend was still fond of his friend, he went to search for him. In contrast, the unfaithful man was not only haunted by his conscience all the times but also constantly tried to hide from his innocent friend. The search lasted for a long time during which the sinful friend constantly felt regretful and miserable. You should be aware that you can avoid people in the living world, but where can you hide in the world of the dead, the so-called world of thought where a soul just needs to think of someone to meet him/her…"

Everyone was silent but deeply felt impressed with what the Egyptian magician described.

Professor Mortimer broke the silence, "Could you please elaborate more on the artificial element?"

Hamoud nodded his head, "When you generate a thought in the middle plane, an artificial element is created accordingly. If your thought is personal, the artificial element flies around you. Of course, when you are alive, you do not realize its existence. However, when you die, you clearly see whether the artificial element generated from your thought is good or bad. Similarly, when you envy or resent deeply at someone, you also generate an artificial element that surrounds the person in the living world. Because the capacity to concentrate on thoughts of human beings is very weak, the artificial elements only vaguely float around and disappear without leaving any trace behind. Nevertheless, when you have a prejudice against a person, you engender an artificial element that cannot only last longer but also enclose that person. The universal law establishes "Great minds think alike" which means that an artificial element can only influence an object that has similar vibrations. A bad person will become worse, but a bad thought cannot harm a good person. Hence, the issues of controlling your thoughts and eradicating prejudices against people are very important because you are responsible for them."

Hamoud illustrated with an example, "I met a very beautiful woman who was very arrogant. She used to seduce young men who thirsted for her beauty and then jilted them. Many men lost all of their fortunes because of her while others were miserable and committed suicide. Thoughts of sulk and resentment from these men had created a vicious artificial element. As soon as she died, this vicious artificial element immediately went after her. The more she ran away from it, the closer it chased after her. Can you imagine that a monster follows you as close as your own shadow?"

Hamoud stopped talking and looked at everyone while the delegation silently looked at each other. They heard about the world of the dead, but no one ever explained it to them as clearly, scientifically and concretely as this Egyptian magician did. Were they supposed to believe in him? How could they verify? The evidence of the woolen jacket made everybody frightened, but the entire invisible world was a too broad yet extensive subject that was far beyond the comprehension of everyone. Was it just a rich, well-thought imagination? Although Hamoud was a Ph.D. graduated from Oxford University, it did not mean that he had an authority to present events that were not provable.

Hamoud smiled as if he could read the delegation's thoughts, "Since I can open special senses of my soul, I can directly see the invisible world without going through any intermediaries. Instead of saying that these books mentioned about this or other documents mentioned about that, I solemnly assert what I present are the experiences that I have been through and studied for many years. Certainly, I do not expect you to accept them, but I hope that you think about them carefully and try to understand them thoroughly. If you have any questions, let us discuss about your problems together. I hope that you examine the matters based upon the scientific spirit and use logic as fundamentals to formulate the issue. The study will be neither simple nor easy but rather difficult and complicated. However, if the nature of the study is so, it will be exciting . . ."

Everyone looked at each other because this magician dared to present an abstract issue like a metaphysical world for discussion.

Professor Allen said, "Up until now, never have Europeans accepted the existence of a world beyond death. They can only acknowledge what you have said as a certain 'belief' instead of a scientific record that is verifiable."

Hamoud smiled, "You can call it a belief if you wish. In reality, religious teachings have taught about the invisible world a long time ago, but it has been mentioned under a symbol or indirect thought. As time goes on, spiritually inexperienced monks cannot understand the concept of the invisible world, so they completely misinterpreted it. Gradually, this conception becomes a superstition under the light of science. It is truly regrettable because science is only a small part of the mythology that has been widely disseminated. If you wish to have a concrete substantiation, I am willing to reveal a key to the world of the dead. What I am about to present is the fundamental of Egyptian geometry that has been lost. In the living world, the knowledge of human beings is limited by a three dimensional space. In fact, there are many more dimensions, but we cannot see them. Our brain can only integrate the length, width and height; hence, the movement and displacement are also restricted in the three dimensional space. If I inform you of the fourth dimension that is perpendicular to the existing three, you cannot imagine it. Nevertheless, when you cannot envisage it, it does not mean that it does not exist."

Hamoud explicated, "To understand the fourth dimension, we must use a comparison. For example, an ant is crawling on a flat piece of paper. If we assume that this ant cannot leave the piece of paper, its world is a surface bound by two dimensions. Even if the ant knew how to deduce, it would not conceive the third dimension that was the height. From our knowledge of the three dimensional system, we can do many ordinary things that appear to be miracles to the ant. For instance, if we place a grain of rice on the piece of paper, the ant will not understand from where the grain came. Because of the limitation of two dimensions of the piece of paper, it thinks that everything must come from the piece of paper and cannot come from anywhere else. If the ant wants to travel from one end of the piece of paper to the other end, it has to crawl along the length of the paper. With our knowledge of the third dimension, we can fold this piece of paper in half so that the two corners along the length touch each other, and the ant only needs to crawl over the edge to reach the other end of the paper's length. The ant cannot understand why the long distance suddenly shortens, and of course, the reason is not strange to us at all. This technique can be used to describe the 'land shortening' of the Tibetan Lamas. Once the fourth dimension is understood, all phenomena in the world of the dead can be easily and scientifically explained."

The delegation looked at each other but exceedingly admired the Egyptian magician who elucidated a convoluted notion by a simple, self-explanatory example.

Professor Allen asked, "What about the fourth dimension?"

Hamoud smiled, "You all know that a straight line is formed by moving a point toward a specific direction. If we move two meters from the original point, we will have a straight line of two-meter in length. If we continue to move for another two meters but perpendicular to the original line until we come back to the starting point, we will have a square. Is it right? Mathematically, a square can be represented as two to the power of two or two square $[2^2]$. This is a straightforward two-dimensional geometry, and nothing is strange about it. If we continue to move vertically and perpendicularly from each corner of the square, we will have a cube that can be represented as two to the power of three $[2^3]$. In summary, we have three figures, namely a straight line, a square, and a cube that are corresponding to 2^1, 2^2, and 2^3. Geometrical space stops here and cannot proceed further because we only know three dimensions. However, mathematics reveals that two can be raised to the powers of four, five, six, and even more. All of these numbers have corresponding figures in geometry."

Hamoud elaborated, "Specifically, two to the power of four or the fourth dimension is the key to enter the world of the dead. Not only does the ancient Egyptian geometry prove the existence of the fourth dimension, but it also has equipments to measure the fourth dimension as well. Returning to the two-dimensional geometry, we use a straight ruler to measure the length. To measure a square, we use another ruler called the square ruler because the straight ruler cannot measure the right angles. Likewise, in space geometry, we cannot use the square ruler to measure a three-dimensional angle because by definition, a square does not have the vertical dimension. If we extend the cube along the fourth dimension, what figure do we have? Of course, we cannot imagine it. Egyptian geometry reveals that it is a figure of four dimensions, the so-called Tesseract, which has sixteen vertices, thirty-two sides, as well as twenty-four faces and is limited by eight cubes. It is worth to note that each cube has six faces, twelve sides, and eight vertices. The day that science can prove this figure is when human beings open the door to enter the four dimensional space. Mathematics discloses that two to the power of four is very easy to prove. This mathematics is applied to build pyramids and to lift rocks of thousands of kilograms to high levels. Although this mathematics has been lost in the past, its vestiges are still engraved with symbols in the Pyramids."

Hamoud was quiet as if his soul wandered to a far distance and continued, "When the veil is opened for the measurement of a fourth dimension, nowadays scientific discoveries are merely insignificant debris. Human beings will be able to travel everywhere in the universe and have powers that are beyond our contemporary knowledge. During the Golden Age, the Egyptians went everywhere in the universe including strange galaxies. Regrettably, their contact with the world of the dead inadvertently exposed them to dangers, but they did not even know about it. Because of this unexpected insidiousness, Egyptian civilization collapsed and disappeared from the earth owing to the lack of spiritual foundation and perspicacious ability to distinguish between true and false. Since the time immemorial, the elders always reminded that the evolution must develop simultaneously with the intellect. Only when the intellect develops, human beings are capable to differentiate between real versus fake and discard irrational ignorance. Unfortunately, Egyptian leaders did not recognize these mutual relationships, so regrettable occurrences happened."

Professor Allen emphasized, "You really mean that the Egyptians have made such enormous progresses?"

Hamoud was confident, "Of course, approximately eight thousand [8,000] years ago, Egyptians lived in societies that were far more advanced than the most developed and civilized society today. As evidence, no one in the world is able to build a pyramid today. There are still many more mysteries that you may understand them some day. My dear friends, what are the purposes that the Egyptians have left behind majestic pyramids and gargantuan knowledge? The majority of Europeans believe that they are the treasures of Pharoah King's preserved corpses. Is that right? There were hundreds of kings under the Pharaoh reign, why did only a few kings build pyramids? Why have people not found any king's corpses in any pyramids? Moreover, why do pyramids not have any secret codes or pictures that describe any kings? Why is it that only the tombs that were buried deeply under the ground contained mummies and paintings? Why do the tombs under the ground contain symbols, secret codes, and pictures while the pyramids are empty? Naturally, people with ordinary conceptions can never understand this observation. If you understand the fourth dimension, you will not look at the pyramids as three dimensional structures."

Professor Evans-Wentz paused for a second and asked, "You mean they have another dimension, do you not?"

Hamoud nodded his head, "You are exactly right, but it is the secret of the pyramids. Therefore, we cannot bring this subject to the table and discuss about it within a limited time. Furthermore, you want to prove the existence of the invisible world, do you not? I hope that my recent mathematical illustrations lend you the key and new fundamental for the progress of your study . . ."

Professor Evans-Wentz timidly queried, "But we still do not have any evidence that says death is not the end."

Hamoud burst out laughing, "For a long time, death has been an ambiguous issue, but it frightens and haunts everybody. Although everyone will eventually die, almost everyone tries not to think about it. Even the old, feeble, bedridden, sick, and miserable people, they are also terrified when they are facing death. The principal reason is that they do not understand death. They neither know how to prepare for it nor can even decide whether they should confront it or accept it. In the life that is impermanent, worthless and ephemeral, death can come at any time, but human beings always try to avoid it as if they postpone paying debts. Understanding about the invisible world helps us accept this obvious *Truth*. Let us ask ourselves a question, 'If death is the end, what is the meaning of this life?' Why are we born to begin with, and why are we on this earth? Why are there differences among individuals although they all have the same consanguinity? Why do they have different living conditions? Why are some of them wise while others are foolish? Why are a number of them extremely intelligent whereas others are ignorant? Refusing to accept death is like denying the *Truth*, so why are we running away from the *Truth*? Is it not better if we endeavor to understand it and to prepare for it?

Professor Evans-Wentz appeared to be worried, "How do we prepare for it? How can we explain to Europeans who are inherently suspicious and reject the fact that there is another life after death?"

Hamoud tranquilly replied, "Those are their problems. It is entirely up to those individuals whether they choose to believe it or reject it. Why are you concerned about explaining it to them? The important issue is that do you believe it? If you believe that death is just like taking off an old shirt, you then remain to be the same person after you die. The issues of angels in paradise or devils in hell are completely illogical because everything will be different otherwise. Scientifically and reasonably speaking, desires and thoughts that a person has in the living world will determine the plane that he/she will come after death. Hence, we clearly see that human beings have a complete control of their destiny whilst they are alive or dead. Is that not a great privilege for human beings?"

Hamoud interpreted, "If we accept that desires and thoughts we create while we are living will fly around our souls and consume its vital energy until exhaustion, we should realize that taking care of our thoughts as well as controlling our lifestyle in the living world is absolutely necessary and important. If these thoughts are purely materials, then of course, our individual situation will be very lamentable since our souls will be unable to satisfy them any longer. Our soul will be miserable, but it will learn valuable lessons on how to refrain from desires for the following life. Of course, once these desires disintegrate, we are able to liberate ourselves. If human beings do not have an intellectual life while they are living, they will be in a very disheartened plane when they die. They will remain inanimate for a long time, or until they are conscientious of the lack of spiritual activity and commit to involve with one in another life. The greatest tragedy of human beings is to die suddenly because they do not accept that they die and endeavor to hold tightly onto their life. Since they do not accept that they are dead, they are adamant to maintain their living conditions, meaning the transitional state in which nothing is clear. Their soul is in the world of the dead while their spiritual thoughts are still with the living world, so they need guidance and advice."

Hamoud elaborated, "For example, let us look at a soul of a drowned man. Since he did not believe that he died, he remained in the state of being suffocated by the water. Because he was in a coma, he did not see the world of the dead and maintained the image of the living world intact, obviously only in his thought. In other words, he lingered on the unconsciousness for many years as if time did not elapse. I tried hard to persuade him, but he did not listen to what I said. I then advised him to return to his home, but he was so deep in oblivion that he could not find the way to his home. With the help of my invisible friends, I found his identity, residence and relatives whom I later contacted and suggested a mass celebration to awaken his soul. Owing to the praying power from the ceremony, I noticed that his soul gradually revived and could listen to prayers. He returned home and witnessed the ceremony offered by his descendants nearly sixty years after he died. Thereafter, he admitted that he was dead and liberated . . ."

Professor Evans-Wentz was surprised, "Do you really think that prayers are influentially powerful that much?"

Hamoud confirmed, "Celebrating a mass for the peace of a soul is very important and useful because it holds an extremely vehement thought. The power and effect of prayers are crucial to the invisible world if a person focuses on prayers with all his heart and mind. Regrettably, common people consider prayers like formalities. They only read prayers from their lips and at the tip of their tongues instead of concentrate on them mindfully; hence, the effect is partially lost. Praying is extremely powerful because it can 'move mountains and fill the rivers'. It is the Tibetan Secret Branch."

Professor Evans-Wentz queried, "As you said, Tibetan religion is very efficacious, is it not?"

Hamoud clarified, "Praying for the dead neither discriminates among religions nor follows any particular ritual or formality. It is essential that the prayer needs to concentrate and pays the utmost attention to praying. According to my knowledge, every religion has its own rites, and all rites are good as long as the prayers are sincere."

Professor Evans-Wentz asked, "Then, is it useful to baptize people before they die?"

Hamoud explained, "A number of people believe that the eternal happiness of human beings depends on the state of mind immediately prior to their death. At that last moment, if they believe that they are saved, they feel as if they received a plane ticket to fly to paradise; otherwise, they will go to hell. This belief has caused unnecessary fears and anxieties. What happens to the people who suddenly die? Are they going to hell? What happens to devoted followers who die on the battlefield where they cannot receive their last rites or viaticum?"

Hamoud expanded further, "The most effective preparation is to have a good and peaceful life. If we have a beautiful and noble life, then our state of mind prior to death is not important. On the contrary, we cannot wish for a bright future in the invisible world even though we receive the best solemn rite and the most sumptuous ceremony. Nevertheless, the last thought we have before we leave this living world is very useful to our life in the world of the dead because it keeps our souls alert to adapt easily to the new environment. A comfortable, peaceful death is always better than a painful, sufferable one. The worst scenario is that the deceased people cannot let go of things. In my opinion, the comprehension about the invisible world and the preparation for death are very important and need to be widely disseminated. Unfortunately, very few people pay attention to these aspects."

Professor Evans-Wentz queried, "Then according to your perspective, what attitude should we take?"

Hamoud graciously suggested, "To Westerners, the philosophy of life from cradle-to-grave needs to change because life in the living world is only a small part of the whole life cycle that is represented by a circle in which life and death are linkages between the states of being alive and dead as well as between the visible and invisible worlds. On the road of evolution, there are innumerable life cycles, and in each of which there are a countless number of lives of every individual. Souls that descend from the upper planes to the lower ones must go through the middle planes, and thereafter return to the upper planes through the middle planes. The living period in the living world is merely a small part of the entire lifetime, but it is important because the circle proceeds deeply into the living world but begins moving upwards. At this moment, the soul is no longer attached to the materials but inclined towards spirituals. Ancient classics outline a worldly life as follows. The first twenty-five years are to study. The next twenty-five years are to take care of a family, but this period is considered as a deep advancement in the living world. The subsequent twenty-five years are to abandon material things for looking after a spiritual life. The last twenty-five years are to eradicate everything for meditating and mulling over jungles as well as mountains."

Hamoud thoughtfully insinuated, "Asians detach from their material life for their spiritual one at the age of fifty, but Westerners are completely different. They are so passionately fond of working that they become scrupulous to a fault. Even in old age, they still strenuously struggle for desires, egos, enjoyments, and survival. Hence, the majority of them lose balance in life and often encounter adversities when they die. In my opinion, the lack of knowledge about the invisible world is the primary reason for people to cause many damages in the visible world. Since people do not place everything in proper perspective, they make mistakes. If they knew the ratio between a living life and the entire life cycle, they would not make a tremendous effort to take care of only one third of their life cycle and neglect other upper worlds. If people were aware of the short life span in the living world relative to their whole lifetime and realized that the life in other planes is even closer to the *Truth*, would they take different actions? Perhaps, because human beings utterly trust their materialistic senses, the majority of them consider this illusive world is real, but other worlds are not."

Professor Evans-Wentz argued, "If you think other worlds are even closer to the *Truth*, why do we drag out our useless life in this living world? Why do we not all go to the other worlds?"

Hamoud smiled, "Although this living world is illusive, it has its own advantages because human beings can only understand who they truly are and improve themselves via superficial vibrations. This living world has many lessons that we cannot find anywhere else. Prior to the final enlightenment, angels and Bodhisattva all have to live through the material life and demonstrate astounding performances as the last challenge. To develop mysterious powers, human beings must be willing to receive lessons from the living world. Thanks to these lessons, they become sensitive to vibrations from the upper worlds."

Professor Evans-Wentz wondered, "How sensitive do you have in mind?"

Hamoud explained, "Since the development of intelligence is like a radio and its vibrations are like waves, people without knowledge resemble a radio that is not tuned to the right wavelength and has the wrong channel. This situation is reminiscent of persons who intellectually remain the same from the first day to the last day of their life. Their learning is nothing, like a radio with inappropriate fine-tuning and cracking noises. Knowledgeable people know how to change themselves in order to tune to the right wavelengths. Certainly, there are many different wavelengths and channels, so they will be overwhelmed with these availabilities until they are able to synchronize sounds, differentiate between good and bad reasons, and select suitable stations. At that moment, they can tune to the right channel to listen to the music they like. The mysterious voice of the Supreme Being is always resounding in the universe for those who want to listen, for those who know how to open their heart to receive and for those who are willing to change their mind to be in-tune with the Supreme Being's fine, noble wavelengths."

Everybody nodded their head to admire the Egyptian magician profoundly because he used concrete examples to elucidate a convoluted subject.

Professor Mortimer wondered, "Besides opening the special senses to study the invisible world, what else have you done?"

Hamoud elaborated, "The study will become meaningless if we just observe like outsiders who just contemplate objectively. Human beings need to learn what happens to them when they die so that they take appropriate changes to accustom to a new life. This learning process does not only benefit them but also their loved ones. The more they know about the world of the dead, the easier they can guide other souls."

Professor Mortimer confirmed, "In other words, you often help souls that just pass away, do you not?"

Hamoud elaborated, "Exactly, that is my job. The majority of the dead people have been often emotional and refuse to accept the fact that they are dead, so they insist on holding onto the living world. As a consequence, they become wandering ghosts. My job is to reassure them and explain to them that if they want to be liberated, they must change completely the way they live in this invisible world. This job is certainly difficult because these souls do not want to listen. Moreover, many souls longingly remember the living world because they still have unfinished businesses which prevent them from being in peace for liberation. Hence, the presence of a living person like me is very useful because I can help them finish their heartfelt desires so that they can be liberated . . ."

Professor Mortimer asked, "Does your work yield any results?"

Hamoud explicated, "These tasks are extremely difficult, so I have to make friends with a number of souls in the world of the dead. If muddle-headed souls adamantly refuse to listen, I have to ask their friends and relatives to persuade and help them. For instance, a man was killed in a fire in London. He was trapped in a three-storied house and not able to escape by any means, so he was asphyxiated by smoke. He did not believe that he was dead; therefore, his conscience still struggled to find a way out of the burned building. I tried to advise him, but he was too afraid of death by burning to believe me. I later asked his mother who passed away many years ago to persuade him. He finally accepted and was liberated."

Professor Mortimer reiterated, "Do you mean that their relatives in the invisible world can help even if they died a long time ago?"

Hamoud confirmed, "Of course, the relationships among people are not accidental but rather established through a predestined affinity for many previous generations. If the love string remains in them, they will continue paying attention to their loved ones even though they are all dead. Even if they have been liberated and ascended to the higher planes, they are willing to descend to the lower ones in the middle domain to help their descendants."

Professor Mortimer was surprised, "So, we can again meet our parents, grandparents and relatives after we die, can we not?"

Hamoud calmly replied, "Of course, as I have been saying, human beings are essentially the same after they die; nothing is changed. If they still love one another, they will find each other. In fact, if we view death as a trip to a new world that is more spacious and bright, we will not feel like we are far apart from our deceased relatives. Realistically, nothing can separate the souls. When we love people with sincere vibrations, we love their souls instead of their bodies. Their bodies may be deteriorating, but their souls are always around us. Although we cannot see them, they can feel our love for them. In addition, they know our sorrows and feelings because they can read our minds. Naturally, if they keep an eye on us, they will receive and even console us when we die. We need to understand this delicate issue thoroughly because we will not only be unafraid of death but also accept it as a natural occurrence once we comprehend it carefully. Regardless of being in the living world or in the world of the dead, the universal laws are always manifest and extremely fair."

Professor Mortimer was curious, "How do we know for certain that we will meet our loved ones when we die?"

Hamoud calmly elucidated, "As I have previously presented, there are seven planes in the Middle Domain, and the awakening in whichever plane completely depends upon people's consciousness whose vibrations are synchronized with those of that plane. The souls in a certain plane can only contact with other souls in the same plane or in the lower ones. The majority of the souls of those who passed away long ago have been purified, so these souls are often in higher planes. Consequently, these souls can contact those in the lower planes if they wish. On the contrary, the souls who awake in the lower planes rarely know those in the higher ones, and the souls who awake in the seventh or sixth plane only want to return to the living world because they are hardly ever conscious of the higher planes. A few souls, after ascending to the higher planes, find their way back to the lower ones. It is not that these souls are passionately fond of the lower planes, but it is an account of the humaneness and love for other souls who are in the same situation as their previous ones or feel lost, lonely and unconscious."

Hamoud remained silent for a while then leisurely said, "Providing help and alleviation to the souls in the world of the dead is absolutely essential because the dead are many and only a few of them are knowledgeable about death."

Professor Mortimer commented, "It is not that everyone is able to perform this task. Must it be the people who have special senses like you do, or you have to wait until you die to help other souls?"

Hamoud shook his head, "It is not true that you can only perform the assistance when you die. When you are alive, you can still help these souls even without having any special senses opened. Everyone who knows how to think will be able to lend a hand. You should be aware that your soul is free to work in the world of the dead while you are sleeping. If you concentrate on the thoughts of supporting services like consoling for the purpose of guidance and alleviating everyone's hardship without any discrimination prior to going to bed, you are able to give a hand."

Professor Mortimer was amazed, "Is that all there is to it? Then who would not be able to do it?"

Hamoud agreed, "Of course, this helping mechanism is not insidious at all because our thought has a special power and extraordinary force in the world of the dead. If we practice on this kind of help while we are living, we will not feel strange or surprised when we die because we are already familiar with it. Besides, we will even be able to meet the souls that have received assistance by our thoughts. Naturally, these souls will welcome us warmly, and we can continue to help other souls . . ."

Professor Mortimer was puzzled, "How can it be that easy?"

Hamoud smiled, "It actually sounds easy, but it requires a serious determination. First, our intention must be non-profit, altruistic and unbiased because the dead world is the world of thought. If we have a conspiracy or bad plan, other souls will know immediately and the consequences are immeasurable. Second, the majority of souls are muddle-headed, obstinate and inconvincible because they still either bind to their destiny or attach to the living world. It may also be that they are too moved to liberate because of their descendants' excessive crying, melancholy or misery. Therefore, this job requires subtleness, cleverness, serenity, tranquillity and self-control. Once we have determined, this mentality becomes a useful instrument that assists us a great deal. In my opinion, a broad knowledge about the world of the dead is the primary foundation."

Professor Allen shook his head, "If you say that I can go to the world of the dead while sleeping, why do I not realize it? Do you not think that you should provide me with obvious evidences?"

Hamoud replied, "Given what you understand about the constitution of human beings, while you are awake, your soul state is the bridge for the environment and conscience. The soul transmits all external interaction, sensibility, and compassion perceived by sympathetic nerves to the conscience before it registers them to the brain. It is substantiated by the fact that we think before we take action, do we not? We sleep because our tired body needs to recuperate, but our soul is different. It continues to be active as evidenced by our realization of our surroundings even when we are sound asleep. Is it true? Our soul always vibrates to adapt to the environment, so it is very sensitive to vibrations of our instinct, desires and passions. Bad temperaments like anger and hatred are only the precipitation of our thoughts. This precipitation becomes a layer to conceal our soul and its influence. Therefore, personality of human beings is merely a habit of their thoughts."

Hamoud interpreted, "As I previously mentioned, whether the thoughts are noble or despicable, they are captured by the souls and directly reflect through the sentiment. For example, a man with a pure soul cannot tolerate the hustle and bustle of cities while the one with a boisterous soul cannot bear with the calm and secluded places. Some people wonder why they cannot sit still at one place and cannot practice meditation. They do not realize that their souls are agitated and fluctuated. They need to know how to manage their feelings and purify their souls. Heavy food such as meat, fish, wine, or stimulus seriously affects our souls. Religious practitioners must absolutely avoid these kinds of food because they instigate excitements against meditations."

Hamoud gave details, "Our body and soul communicate with each other through seven innermost intersections, the so-called Shakras, in which there is a membrane that is composed of earthly atoms to prevent the influence of the world of the dead. Therefore, memories and activities in the invisible world cannot be transmitted to our brain while we are sleeping. Nevertheless, after we wake up, we feel like we see something but cannot remember it. Without consuming stimulated or heavy food, the Shakra is not triggered, so the membrane remains closed. When people devour wine, meat, or other stimulants, this membrane may be destroyed or torn, through which the influences from the world of the dead can transmit to the living world. These influences can make people crazy and derange their nervous system. In some cases, individuals lose their self-control and are possessed by ghosts or evils."

Professor Allen said, "What you have just presented is strange but logical. However, according to our knowledge, science cannot prove these phenomena. Is there any way for us to open our special senses and study the invisible world as you do?"

Hamoud nodded his head, "Opening power points depends upon your heart and mind, so you must train your sentimental consciences before trying to open any other senses. If these consciences have not been purified, none of the special senses can be opened."

Professor Allen said, "Then how do we train our sentimental consciences?"

Hamoud explained, "The spirit is trained by a truthful contemplation. The imagination of human beings is a creative instrument that is very effective. Hence, when we contemplate and imagine, we unintentionally build our spirit. If we only contemplate on good and noble things, we have already trained our spirit. After the spirit is the soul that can only be trained by genuine desires. If we are passionately fond of high-minded yearnings, our soul will develop accordingly."

Professor Allen challenged, "You make it sound very easy. Noble thoughts and genuine desires are too abstract; how can one accomplish them?"

Hamoud clarified, "The majority of people have the same mentality, so they cannot make any progress. Human beings always want to be in power and be liberated, but they would rather wait for a miracle or external force instead of being confident that they have the capability to accomplish it by themselves."

Professor Allen debated, "Even if I want to purify my sentimental consciences, I must have a method, guidance, or technique. Who would not be able to speak abstractly like that?"

Hamoud commented, "From my understanding, all religions teach lofty, beautiful things and apply them to life. Are they not good approaches or purified techniques for sentimental consciences?"

Professor Allen asked, "If it is so, what method do you follow? Let us talk about your own experience first."

Hamoud quietly contemplated and acquiesced, "That is fine. I have learned a specific method at a seminary in Tibet, so I am largely influenced by Buddhism. The first practical approach is to train the body and learn not only how to control and restrain the body completely but also exactly delineate all activities like eating, drinking, or sleeping. Foods are divided into three categories including passive, active and regulatory. The beginner must avoid passive food because it makes the body lose consciousness and become lazy or flaccid. Passive foods are characterized as fermentation, dehydration and alcohols. Active foods include meat and fish that often bestow transient stimulations. All types of meat from dead animals are composed of heavy atoms owing to their bestiality that is not suitable for religious practice or purifying sentimental consciences. Regulatory foods are the only types that have a growing capability and contain vitality like cereals that are about to germinate and sprout. Fruit trees are full of vital energy whereas vegetables absorb solar energy which is necessary for a vigorous, energetic body."

Hamoud continued, "Besides foods and drinks, proper breathing is also very important. Although science proves that human beings are alive because of their breath, it is in fact the vital force, Prana. This vital force permeates everywhere in the body and brings life to all living cells. Prana originates from the sunlight, so it vibrates and intermingles in the air. By breathing deeply and gently, Prana penetrates into the nervous system and circulates everywhere to bring life throughout the entire body. Prana that accumulates in the nervous system creates a flow of human electricity—an essential factor of life. In short, nourishing correctly with regulatory foods and breathing properly are the most important methods to purify the body. As you have seen, these methods are not contradictory to the modern science at all. The actual practice may be different depending upon individuals, for example, some people call it gymnastic while others refer it as meditation. How it is named is not important as long as the primary principle aims at bringing about a healthy and dynamic body."

Hamoud explained, "Persons who train their body need to live in an area that is aerated, spacious and full of sunlight to receive the vital Prana which serves as a supplement to the human electricity. Active food like meat and fish provides the body with brazen vibrations that make this human electric current flow helter-skelter and hard to control. The uncontrollability of the human electricity causes sicknesses or destroys the nervous system. Passive foods such as wines paralyze the nervous system, impede the human electric current and prevent the Prana energy from circulating and delivering vital energy to feed the body. Thus, both active and passive foods present appalling consequences."

Hamoud elaborated on training the soul, "After purifying the body, we continue to train the soul that is the center of our sentiment. Once their feelings are pure, altruistic and charitable, light elements are naturally absorbed through while heavy, bad ones are eliminated through a principle similar to osmosis. Once the souls are pure, their vibrations are on the same frequency with the high-minded thoughts and thus bring the spirits to a higher level. When the vibrations reach a particular cycle, the special senses of the souls start to open, and naturally, human beings begin to have special power. Scientifically speaking, the special senses of the souls are only active in a certain cycle. Only when the souls vibrate in this particular cycle, they are awakened to function. The souls can vibrate in this cycle only when they are composed of very fast, light atoms. All coarse, heavy atoms are eliminated when people actually possess noble sentiment and charitable heart that broadens to cover all creatures. That is the secret to train the souls."

Hamoud went into details of training the spirit, "When the seven senses of the soul are in action, they will open a number of secret points to allow the hot current Kundalini to awake. When Kundalini travels along the vertebral column up to the top of the head, it will stimulate and open the spirit that is eventually developed and unified with true deities. Once the spirit develops and broadens, it will begin to destroy egoism and selfishness of human beings to look toward holy ideals. Very few people can overcome this extremely difficult period. In Buddhist terminology, it is called Buddhahood. In Christian vocabulary, it is referred as self-sacrificing to unify with the

Messiah. In Hinduism language, it is named as 'union with the true self.' Simplistically speaking, this is the moment when the intellect unites thoughts and actions concerning goodwill, humaneness, charity, mercy, intelligence, altruism and forgiveness to crystallize a true self. When the worldly self is destroyed, transitional states are purified. Dissimilarities between others and us and between subject and object do not exist any longer, and all is one. The Spirit is no longer an individual characteristic but becomes the Great Spirit or spirit of prana. Spiritual thought is also no longer an individual thought but develops into the spirit of the Bodhisattva that is completely assimilated with the universal spirit. Both heart and brain widely open to receive the light of *Truth* without any additional learning or debating. In religious practice, this is the stage of enlightenment. People who reach this enlightenment become superhuman beings, founders or saints."

Professor Evans-Wentz questioned, "Based on what fundamental do we know such enlightenment? Should we not have any evidence?"

Hamoud shook his head, "This precious and sacred experience can only be recognized and understood by those who are enlightened. None of the saints will declare that they have reached enlightenment or attained power. Once they arrive at the enlightenment, ranks, titles, fames and positions become meaningless because they do not have the low self like us to distinguish. Only impostors and pretended monks love reputations and positions because their egos are still so big that they need rankings and titles to deceive credulous followers."

Professor Evans-Wentz inquired, "In principle, people behave according to their sense of self, but how about methods and techniques?"

Hamoud shook his head, "There are many methods and techniques, and so are the roads to the *Truth*. Hence, a fixed method or strict technique cannot apply to anyone because everything depends on the origin, the predestined affinity of each individual. Methods and techniques can all be different, but there is one unique principle. Realistically, the *Truth* is always disseminated under one form or another depending on conditions, environments and means. Although the methods are different, the *Truth* is always the same one. Similarly, it is water regardless of whether it comes from a river or spring. Conditions, methods and environments may be dissimilar, but the *Truth* is immutable. Magicians from barbarous tribes or by the founders from religious classics can teach the *Truth*. Although classics or religions may be different in terms of form, they hold common points of view that we must accept."

Professor Evans-Wentz was skeptical, "Is accepting a form of belief?"

Hamoud tried to explain, "A religious path requires faith, but it cannot be an impetuous, blind belief. Faith only comes after the religious followers recognize themselves clearly, understand and prove faith thoroughly. You are all scientists, so you will never believe anything that cannot be obviously proved. Although suspicion is necessary, what would you do if there were occurrences that science cannot or is not able to prove yet? Are you going to reject them? If you refuse to accept them, you lose an opportunity to study them. On the contrary, if you acknowledge them without corroboration, you blindly believe in them. I do not expect that you have to believe in everything that I have just presented, but I surely hope that you will contemplate and study them. If you cannot use experimental scientific instruments to prove these phenomena, you should employ your faculty of reasoning and intuition because studying the invisible world is a field of science rather than an unfounded belief. The knowledge about the invisible world will help many people, so I believe that a number of studies on this subject will be undertaken in the near future."

Professor Evans-Wentz wondered, "Why do you not proclaim your discoveries? Why do you hide yourself in this deserted place? If you want the knowledge of the invisible world to be widely studied, you should take the liberty of initiating the process so that people are aware of it. It may very well be that a number of studies will follow thereafter."

Hamoud smiled, "When human beings have not reached a specific level of understanding, certain things cannot be publicly announced. Former religious founders taught the *Truth* as both 'public heritage' and 'mysterious heritage'. Why did they split the *Truth* into two parts? Why did they specifically teach only a few disciples the mysterious heritage? Was it probably true that they knew only a minority of disciples who could understand the teaching? Scientific study about the invisible world has its own dangers, so it cannot be carelessly disseminated to everybody."

Professor Evans-Wentz requested, "Would you please elaborate further about why it is dangerous?"

Hamoud patiently repeated, "I have just presented to you the method that I have learned how to train body, soul and spirit. Naturally, many other methods lead to similar results, but their final aims are very different. Hundreds of methods develop miraculous power, but religious followers must understand that power is merely an inferior means. It just helps broaden the knowledge and is never the final aim or ultimate objective. Greed for love and admiration will lead people who have the power to heresy. Religious people must clearly realize that they can only be liberated from the illusions of ignorance and truly experience the *Truth* when their sense of self is completely eradicated. The higher the power people have, the more virtuous they should be. They must strictly heighten their vigilance against the illusions of ignorance . . ."

Professor Evans-Wentz insisted, "You talked about ignorance like an abstract subject. Would you give us an example that is easier to understand since we are not familiar with it?"

Hamoud elucidated, "Let us take an example of a person who endures much hardship and ascetic training while practicing religion and begins to develop some rudimentary power like the supernatural vision. Because people with this kind of power are very few on earth, they think that they have made a tremendous progress and become deities. Their arrogance escalates and urges them to believe that they attain the greatest enlightenment, and they are entrusted with noble missions. They self-proclaim with high titles and reputation or sometimes accept a status of sainthood attributed to them by disciples. They believe that they are clear-sighted, superior, and infallible, so nothing can be wrong. They do not realize that mischievous souls in the invisible world often try to mislead novices who just begin to gain some basic power. Naturally, with superficial knowledge, they do not have any criteria which they can rely on to judge and understand phenomena that they witness and test to verify whether such occurrences are compatible with the *Truth* or not. Consequently, they are easily corrupted, and they become subordinates of souls, devils and invisible creatures. As you have seen, magicians, sorcerers, and monks are lacking in clairvoyance, religious hardship, and discipline, so they all fall into the traps of ignorance. They indeed have several kinds of power but use them to serve selfish purposes and harm others rather than to assist human beings."

Professor Evans-Wentz was worried, "But how can they avoid those incidences?" How can a novice know that what he sees are not illusions of ignorance and what he experiences are not groundless lessons from invisible creatures?"

Hamoud somberly declared, "People with a pure life that is characterized by fine thoughts and kind-hearted actions and is not corrupted by selfishness will be protected. Owing to their fine yet noble vibrations, bad influences cannot invade them, and malicious spirits find nothing in them to exploit. On the contrary, people with multifarious ambitions and lack of patience as well as discipline carry in their inner self-unkind vibrations that attract spirits, ghosts and devils. Deep down inside them is full of characters like greed, anger, jealousy, selfishness and dullness that make it easy for the spirits to manipulate them. Regardless of which religion, every religious follower must be disciplined and obey commandments from experienced founders who have been through different paths, are aware of most possible dangers and thus set forth such commandments so that their disciples can avoid."

Professor Evans-Wentz continued, "What are the training methods that use wonder-making powers to cure diseases?"

Hamoud smiled, "It depends on the mind of the trainees, but in my opinion, all training methods without righteousness will unavoidably lead to insidious paths. You should bear in mind that once the trainees have attained a magical power even if it is a low and rudimentary one, they could employ it to perform many things that appear to be extraordinary to normal human beings because the majority of humanity have not had this capacity yet. Because of this abusive mentality, trainees who have already gained some power easily become arrogant. If they are not honest, they will take advantage of their power for evil wills."

Professor Allen shook his head, "You talk about righteousness versus the wickedness as if they are based upon a transparent set of standards. Why do you not think of good and bad like relativity because while Westerners consider a certain matter to be unreasonable, Asians accept it as being sensible?"

Hamoud explained, "You are right. The notions of good versus bad and kind versus evil are more or less influenced by each society. However, as we advance further, we still have the universal laws. According to my knowledge, there are two main roads—the Right Way and the Wrong Way. People who are in the Wrong Way exploit their latent power to gain personal benefit at the expense of others' happiness. This personal benefit or individual development refers to the expansion of special senses, sentiments, or knowledge without any consideration about the damages inflicted upon others. People who take advantage of other's ignorance and weakness to squirrel away money or to satisfy their ambitions belong to the Wrong Way. Let us imagine how dangerous they would be if they had some kinds of mysterious powers. People who are in the Right Way also use mysterious power, but they use it to serve humanity. While serving others, they are willing to sacrifice their comforts and personal ambitions for others' benefits. They also reject sensual pleasures, refuse legitimate respects to which they are entitled and discard worldly self so that they only concentrate on obtaining perfect kindness. People from the Wrong Way use their mysterious power in rituals and ceremonies to create unions or formalities. These formalities may be materials or organizations whose activities are to care neither for a common welfare nor for a noble ideal but are merely the mechanisms through which they can voice their own opinions."

Hamoud continued, "People from the Right Way employ traditional mysterious power of human nature to overcome all limitations of formalities, to liberate their souls from emotional restrictions and transitory imaginations, to avoid temptations as well as dupery of ignorance and finally to serve the sacred, eternal true self. People who study mythology can follow either the Right Way or the Wrong Way. They can find a way to develop their individuality through a strict self-control so that they can develop mysterious powers and acquire knowledge. They can also wish that paradise will be wide open in everyone's heart and in theirs via humanity and altruism. In both cases, the first group of people yearns for knowledge and mysterious power while the second group wants to become the helpful one. The further the two groups advance, the greater the discrepancy is between them. People who use knowledge and mysterious power to serve will become Bodhisattva, and the generous heart of Bodhisattva is the only source of light that can shine and guide human beings to come to the end of the religious path. On the other hand, people who earnestly request knowledge for themselves will meander within individual constraints for a certain time. Owing to the lack of benevolence and intelligence, they may be easily depraved into heterodoxy without even realizing it. Without the guidance of brainpower and intellect, they may effortlessly become victims of ignorance. Their scenario is like that of seafarers who have neither map nor compass. How can they reach a destination by travelling aimlessly?"

Hamoud gave further details, "Reminiscent of a religious path, monks must strictly observe disciplines to improve themselves, and even with that in mind, it is not sufficient. They must establish good intention and determine objectives clearly before they act. Learning a religion goes hand in hand with practicing it; hence, they must contrive their knowledge to serve others. Intelligence must go in parallel with charity. People with a brain and without a heart are like pieces of worthless knowledge or bodies without souls. Conversely, people with a 'heart' and without a 'brain' are not good, either. It is because they can be easily depraved and go astray into heresy. These situations happened in the past, for example, monks without knowledge and intelligence are covered by ignorance, so they venerate the Supreme Being like a deity to worship. They segregate Him from all disciples by announcing that He is too superior to talk to ordinary people. Therefore, all communications with Him must be intermediately done through the clergies. They create all sorts of paraphrases and flowery words into religious teachings so that the followers feel lost in the language and move away from the *Truth*. Gradually, the truly noble philosophies are concealed by various forms of superstition and gobbledygook, which deteriorate the situation. All of these have happened to the Egyptian Religion."

Professor Wentz interrupted, "Would you please elaborate further the collapse of the Egyptian civilization? History still does not yet know why this civilization declined so rapidly."

Hamoud kept silent as if he tried to recollect a certain remote memory and nodded after a moment, "Several hypotheses have been proposed for the decline of the Egyptian civilization. The majority of people imputed the blames to wars, epidemics and natural catastrophes, but very few of them knew the real causes. I do not have any intention to reveal the actual reasons because the objectives of our meeting today are talking and consult about the invisible world. Nevertheless, I am willing to disclose these secrets to you as a special predestined occasion. It is not that I volunteer to divulge, but it is rather a thought message transmitted to me from the true monk. I unveiled these occurrences as a warning to the living world so that human beings do not repeat historical events."

Once again, the existence of the secret true monk was mentioned which really made everybody impressed.

Hamoud looked up at the sky as if he was reviewing the past, "During the golden period, the Egyptian civilization reached its zenith. Monks and sages who taught mythology raised the intellectual standard of humanity to a much higher level than that of today. However, as time went on, many monks did not strictly observe disciplines or did not thoroughly understand the sublime commandments, so they looked for a shorter, easier path that focussed more on technical aspects to attain mysterious power. Magic then became the main objective of learning, not a means anymore. To reach what they were after, they did not hesitate to sacrifice either religious or national interests . . . Owing to the lack of lucidity, these monks entered heretical doctrine and took orders from mischievous motivations. These clergies established gangs and associated with each other to create a powerful influence that even arrogant Pharaoh Kings had to recoil. They abused the names of religions and deities to disseminate hocus-pocuses, conjuring tricks, ominous incantations so that they could attract followers. Given these voodoos, they naturally could do lots of things that ordinary persons would never be able to resist."

Hamoud continued, "Within a short period, people became victims of religious malpractices. The magicians became messengers of the world of the dead. They were devils that camouflaged as humans. They also called the most atrocious ghosts to help them obtain their cruel goals. In temples, sorcery replaced spiritual activity, and genuine monks were quickly eliminated. Consequently, the authentic mythology became lost because no disciples were willing to study. Genuine monks had to run away or left their respectable seminaries. A civilization that was based on mythological knowledge became emaciated when the door to the true mythology was securely shut down. You should keep in mind that in the ancient time, most scientists, physicians, mathematicians, and architects came from the clerical class or learned from religious seminaries because the society did not have any schools or educational system like nowadays. When amulets and witchcraft deceived man's heart, urged people to abandon the Supreme Being and worship ghosts and devils, there was no reason for Astrology, Mathematics and Architecture to exist."

Hamoud unveiled the real facts, "As time passed, the glorious Egyptian civilization miserably declined.   Realistically, fallacious monks with egocentricity and ambition were the origin of the breakdown.   They took advantage of religion, the so-called devilish religion, to make people detach from the Supreme Being and lead Egypt to the road of degeneration.   Instead of trying to liberate themselves from misapprehension, they guided people into paganism.   Instead of obeying religious commandments, they broke their vows and practiced sophism by using flowery words and paraphrases.   Instead of self-criticizing their own conscience and innermost feelings, they established associations and defended each other to cover up their wrong doings.   Although religious rites were no longer sacred, clergies employed superficial appearances to call for an external power to reinforce their authority.   Sincere offerings became obvious bribes.   Monks chose what they wanted most like delicious food and beautiful women to bestow upon deities and then shared them among each other for pleasure afterwards.   The Supreme Being who is charitable and compassionate suddenly became a deity who had full power as well as authority and could reward or punish everybody via clergies as his intermediaries."

Hamoud explained further, "To corrupt people's mind, amulets and hypnoses were practiced to the maximum as if they were necessary mechanisms to satisfy personal ambition.   To prevent the most sacred documents of mythology to fall into unrighteous pagans' hands, true monks used hieroglyphs.   This mysterious type of writing concealed many spiritual meanings that could only be exposed to true monks after they overcame many challenges.   Symbols and parables were utilized fully, and Moses himself later used this communication technique in Jewish books [the Pentateuch].   Since the expansion of paganism was too strong, true monks had to reposition deep into jungles and on high mountains.   Unfortunately, the original mythology was ultimately lost.   At the same time, a number of monks, scientists, mathematicians and architects escaped to Greece to propagate mythology, and a new civilization thus started in this country.   Meanwhile, a religious propagation was established to attract factions and parties, clergies compelled Pharaoh Kings to engage in wars for religious preaching.   These 'holy wars' had created a new social class, the so-called slave."

Professor Mortimer was surprised, "Do you mean there were no slaves prior to that time?"

Hamoud shook his head, "The ancient civilization was fundamentally based on charity and perfection of each individual, so how could there be a slave issue? The slave phenomenon only started when the culture became deteriorated, clergies usurped their power and religious wars broke out. At the beginning, people were war prisoners, but they became slaves thereafter. Shortly later, monks laid out the rules stating that people who did not belong to their religion would be considered as slaves. Since the Jews belonged to a different religion, they were the first victims. This slavery dramatically shaped the Egyptian society because monks did not need to use amulets and hypnoses for personal satisfaction anymore. As a matter of course, slaves had to do whatever their masters wanted."

Hamoud elaborated, "As time went on, the sorcery and amulets were gradually lost because monks did not need them anymore. Once witchcrafts disappeared, the monks' authority also diminished accordingly. Pharaoh Kings then started to restrict monks' powers. When the civilization declined, the splendid *Truths* disappeared. Extravagant life filled with materials, and comforts had made kings and queens become selfish. They only wanted to prolong their lives. Therefore, the custom of tomb construction and mummification became popular because they promised an eternal life. The workmanship processes of gigantic mausoleums had exhausted national treasures and led Egyptian society to retro-gradation . . . Given this situation, Egypt became a very attractive prey to Persia and Greece. History has clearly recorded from this period onward, and I am sure you are well aware of it . . ."

The delegation silently looked at each other because the degradation of Egypt after being dominated by Persia and Greece was not a strange event. However, the fact that Egypt built the majestic pyramids, created innumerable talented people and exerted a tremendous effect on the entire Middle East but rapidly collapsed has remained to be a historical question. Hamoud's explanation provided an invaluable key to the Egyptian history.

Hamoud smiled and looked at everybody, "Human history always changes according to a cycle, so many events that have happened in the past will happen again. Once human beings have gone through the dark and chaotic periods filled with miseries and puzzles, they then long for a magnificent, noble spirit. This yearning will be answered because a saint will be reincarnated into this world. He will open a spiritual door and guide humanity to liberation under formalities and means that are suitable to circumstances, time and space. This reincarnation has happened many times at different places in the world, from China to India and including the Middle East. These saints have preached noble and beautiful *Truths*, but because of ignorance and lack of understanding, human beings marched frantically on the same vestiges shortly after. Once again, noble *Truths* are criticized, altered and falsely preached by monks who are superstitious, fanatic and full of prejudices. Regardless of what happens, the wheel of evolution still turns regularly, and under all circumstances, all eras have individuals who make utmost efforts to liberate themselves from illusions of ignorance and identify the *Truth* . . ."

Hamoud was silent for a moment then leisurely continued, "I want you to remember one thing regardless of whether you consider it as a prophecy or warning. The coming period will be the era of extreme advance in intellectuality but decline in spirituality. All knowledge will concentrate on phenomena instead of cause and nature. Hence, the future science can neither change people's heart nor help them have a clear-sighted view and peaceful mind. The 'phenomenon science' only stimulates senses and external feelings that will make people feel extremely disappointed, anxious, lost and puzzled. In addition, the exhumation of ancient Egyptian tombs will release innumerable devils and extremely cruel forces. As I have just told you, Egyptian monks practiced hocus-pocuses largely during the Egyptian civilization's final episode. The art of mummification is the secret technique that connects the invisible to the visible world; hence, all ancient mausoleums are detentions of invisible forces that guard and maintain evil influences."

Hamoud explained, "Once innumerable devils and cruel forces are released, they will bring voodoos from ancient Egypt back to this century. Naturally, these voodoos will be reformed in a certain way to suit the contemporary. A number of magicians who were emissaries in the invisible world will reincarnate or enter into a body to behave perversely. They will create an utterly dark, depraved society and go against the Supreme Being's evolution. Our world will be the victim of this devilish religion . . . Wars, miseries and instability together with stimulating sensations created by the phenomenon science will thrust human beings into extremely miserable lives.

During this period, the brain and the faculty of reasoning cannot help us with anything. Only comprehension and recognition of silent nature can address our needs. This escaped mechanism is the unique way to liberation."

Professor Allen interrupted, "Is there any evidence of the presence of these invisible forces? How can we warn people about the returning of ancient magicians? Never will the Westerners accept this fictitious and illogical story without obvious substantiations."

Hamoud smiled secretly, "The invisible world is my objective study, so I can illustrate a few data points for you to contemplate as if they are validations. As time goes on, you will witness that what has to happen has been happening. Although the unrighteous ancient magicians cleverly persuade the people with their flowery words and convincingly beautiful doctrines, they still live only like a normal person. No matter what may have happened, they cannot eliminate their past habits. For example, they will work under a religious cover, ask for cooperation from deities, create new commandments to replace noble *Truths* and convince people to deny the Supreme Being. They will utilize terminologies and languages to deceive people. They will die sooner or later, but prior to their death, they will request for their body to be mummified and stored in stony gigantic mausoleums as they had in the past . . ."

Professor Allen burst out laughing, "Then we can easily recognize them. I, however, do not believe that people still want to be mummified and preserved in a large mausoleum nowadays. You should remember that we have been in the twentieth century, not eight thousand [8,000] years ago . . ."

Hamoud smiled, "You will see then. I hope that you carefully record what I have said, and time will answer whether I am right or wrong."

Notes: In the sixteenth edition of this book in 1965, Professor Mortimer commented on Hamoud's prophesy as follows, "Many evidences of mummification of communist leaders bear a resemblance to the ancient Egyptian techniques. Mausoleums built of stones as per the Lenin's will are considerably influenced by the architectures of the ancient tombs that were excavated from the Nile Valley.

CHAPTER TEN

EPILOGUE

"Please stop the research expedition. All financial support is terminated. Please return to London immediately."

The sudden arrival of this telegram had shockingly surprised the delegation. Doctor Kavir informed the delegation about a London newspaper which reported that the delegation of the best scientists from England knelt beside the "naked" Indian monks to listen to their teachings. Owing to an extreme anger, the public demanded Oxford University to terminate the research mission immediately, command the expedition to come back and explain what happened. Without further ado, the expedition took a train to Bombay. Note: at the time, India was still a British colony, and the racial and social discriminations were very dominant.

A part extracted from the diary of Professor Spalding was as follows.

"It was completely unexpected when we received the telegram along with a letter from the Consul General at Bombay together with newspaper clippings that were written about the university professors of the Royal Scientific Society genuflected beside undomesticated Indian magicians to receive lessons. The narrative full of prejudice and malignity of an unwise journalist had destroyed a great effort of research and study that were nicely in progress. How can we explain to the public that besides the complicated customs, confused religions, fabulous mysteries and superstitions, there are hidden noble *Truths* that Westerners need to study? Although India has been sleeping soundly through many centuries, among its material corruptions remains a powerful spirit that is waiting to be awakened. We have learned so much during this research expedition.

Our first lesson was from an English businessman, Mr. Keymakers who taught, 'To study impartially and scientifically, Westerners desperately need to eradicate arrogance and cultural prejudices, always maintain scientific approaches and strict criticism in order to pass through a myriad of superstitious people and search for the *Truth*.' Like a precious stone needing to be polished, the journey to search for the *Truth* was similar. We spent several years arduously seeking and carefully select before we met monks who represented the real spiritual life in India. Owing to accidental chances, we had witnessed noble yet spiritual activities that very few Westerners had the privilege to discover. All of the *Truths* were secretly and charily disseminated in the past were now revealed to us.

As a scientific expedition, we carefully analyzed, vigilantly examined, seriously criticized and sophisticatedly interrogated until everything was clear. Each of us independently recorded what we observed in our diary, and we checked with each other. We then discussed and verified all documented materials until we all agreed on their accuracy before we registered them to the main file. Because of this procedure, we strongly asserted that the registered records were exclusively based on science rather than on personal belief or individual understanding. We hoped that when we publicly disclosed these results, not only would they be a bridge for mutual connection between the two cultures but also urge future research into a deeper and wider level.

The recently sabotaged event had changed everything and destroyed even the humblest wishes. Professor Allen believed that if we returned to London to reveal what we had discovered and clearly explained to the public, people could probably be more sympathetic. I was, however, not that optimistic. Now, it was too early to change the public opinion that was originated from narrow-minded conceptions, prejudices and blind arrogance. Westerners looked down on India like an underdeveloped country and like an ignorant colony full of superstitions as well as illiterates. They would never see fine values and scientific progressions that were carefully concealed under the burning sunlight of the tropical zone.

Professor Mortimer and the American scientists wanted to separate from the expedition and continue with the study because the United States of America was less prejudiced against India somehow. Yale and Harvard Universities were ready to support the study financially, especially since it already had results. As the expedition leader, I did not want the productive study to be interrupted but did not wish to see the American universities taking all the credit, either. In any case, I was a British citizen and proud of English traditions. Since we were trained from Oxford University, we wanted it to be recognized for this pioneering research."

The consul coldly received the expedition in a small room. He showed the article that was written about the research to the delegation because it became the attractive subject that was fully exploited by different media.

The consul raised his voice, "You should be more considerate because in any case, you are not only scientists but also famous university professors and members of the Royal Scientific Society. You are representatives of the most honorable and excellent constituents of England, but you have discredited the prestige of the king. Why did you not stay still in Oxford? What does this oppressively hot country have for you to research?"

Professor Oliver was angry, "It is our own business. What do you know and why do you speak to us in such a tone of voice?"

The consul unsympathetically yet indifferently smiled, "It is no longer your own business because it now involves the honor of the Royal Scientific Society and the reputation of Oxford University. You should know that I am also from Oxford."

Professor Oliver said, "If you graduated from Oxford, you should realize that this study will make our university to be more famous. Someday, people will say that Oxford indeed has pioneered to study mysterious phenomena and yoga."

The consul cynically queried, "Yoga? What is it? Do you mean a certain kind of animal?"

Professor Oliver was so flabbergasted that he could not utter a word. A stupidity as such could only be forgiven if it came from an ordinary, illiterate citizen who had never left his/her house or had never gone any further than the range of the Westminster's church bell. He, however, was a consul who represented the Royal Family, graduated from Oxford University and lived in India more than six years. The consul examined the delegation's passports and informed them that they had to leave India next week.

Another part extracted from the diary of Professor Spalding was along these lines.

"While everybody returned to the hotel and waited for the day to board the boat to go back to London, I had a spiritual feeling that something would happen. I wandered in the crowded city of Bombay with an equivocal mind and did not know what to do. I tried to recollect the events that had happened during the last six months.

Indeed, since the day I had felt disappointed, I wandered in the Benares City and met a big, tall yet extraordinary Indian who conveyed a message from the true monk. From that day, the delegation had always been protected everywhere and was fortunate to meet with people who devoted their lives to search for the *Truth*, conquered nature, mastered invisible forces in the universe and attained mysterious power. Exactly as the true monk said, the study had uncovered issues that the delegation wanted to find, but not everyone still felt satisfied. We longed for meeting with the mysterious true sage whom I feel from my sub-conscience that I had known in the past.

At this moment, I suddenly had a strange feeling. With all the power of my thought, I wished that the mysterious true sage would help us or allow us to meet him. Being completely invaded by this stream of thought, I was suddenly startled. A strange feeling like an electrical current flowing along my backbone made me quickly open my eyes. Beneath a big old tree with luxuriant branches and leaves, an Indian with a radiant face, broad chin, high forehead and brilliant yet attractive eyes appeared. Who else would this be? He was unmistakably the Indian whom I met in the Benares City. He was the person who brought the first message to the delegation. I quickly ran to him and greeted him as if I was meeting an old acquaintance."

The Indian smiled, "How are you? Has your study gone well? I hope that Brahmananda, Sudeih Babu, Mahasaya, Harishinanda, Hamoud El Sarim . . . have not disappointed you."

I was too astonished to say anything. Why did this man seem to know everything?

The Indian smiled, "My dear friend, you asked me whether the true sages were real or not approximately half a year ago. 'If they were real, why did they not reveal themselves and teach human beings?' 'What was good about their seclusion?' At that time, deep down inside, you actually did not believe in the existence of individuals who have advanced far into religious paths. I answered that since we did not know them clearly, the worldly perception could not recognize them properly. Realistically, the all-perfects always appear to help humanity secretly and silently. The majority of people believe that these all-perfect individuals reveal themselves under gorgeous halos and with magic power to change the miserable living world to paradise. This change would never happen."

The Indian continued, "At that time, you did not entirely agree with me. As a Christian, you still believe that 'Christ' has promised to return and save everybody... In fact, 'Christ' has never left us. He is always beside us and helps us. The belief that He will come back under a splendid halo is not correct. We are accustomed to look for the Supreme Being from the external environment as if the Almighty Who is capable of helping satisfy our desires instead of from our innermost where He resides. I hope that the experiences from meetings with the true monks in the recent past will provide you with a strong foundation and vehement self-confidence to continue on with your study."

Again, I was so astonished because not only did this Indian know everything very well but was also able to read other people's mind.

The Indian smiled as if he understood Professor Spalding, "You have been instructed about yoga, nutritious methods, invisible world, mysterious Astrology, universal laws and notions on the worldliness as well as true self. You seem to be very passionate and are interested in them because they are what you have long yearned for; am I right?"

I was utterly surprised and asked, "How . . . How do you know us so well?"

The Indian gently responded, "Because I am instructed to help you, I have personally followed your thoughts since the first day you have set your foot on this land. I am completely sympathized with your disappointment, discontentment and discouragement during the first two years when you visited magnificent temples and interacted with 'famous' monks but did not learn anything new from them. Instead of meeting with sages, you came across swindlers and charlatans who held prestigious social titles and high-ranks but were undisciplined and had negligible religious training. Instead of encountering spiritually experienced teachers, you ran into monks who talked endlessly like running water, but they did not even know about what they were talking. It seems like the sublime *Truths* that they quoted from the classics have nothing to do with their pleasurable, happy life in magnificent temples."

The Indian explained, "All occurrences you experienced and people you met were the challenges of your study. To find a genuine *Truth* that has its real value, you must be able to withstand challenges with time. Likewise, searching for a genuine *Truth* requires a tremendous effort, scientific mentality, and analytical mind to eradicate superstitions and prejudices. Because you deserved to receive the teachings on transcendent *Truths*, I came to meet you at the Benares City and delivered a message from a true master. Thanks to this message, you have met a number of great people who represent the wisdom of Asia. However, as I have said, if you want to go farther to meet true masters, it is a different matter . . ."

I asked, "Do you believe that we can meet the true masters?"

The Indian was optimistic, "Certainly, if you choose this path, your journey will be completely different from your recent one. In this new journey, you cannot be the outsider who just watches, takes notes and studies objectively. This journey must be your personal experience. A knowledge that is neither attained nor experienced by you is merely a shallow, superficial knowledge. A comprehension brought to you by other persons, regardless of any means, is simply their experience. We cannot expect the *Truth* to come to us from the external source because we must know how much is enough to stop and when is the right time to return. To go afar means to come back, and indeed, it is the right path. This journey is not like the previous one that is to go out, to interact with other monk teachers, to record quintessence and to compile documents. It is rather the journey to come back, the so-called *Journey to the East*."

The Indian continued, "You cannot observe and record on behalf of the delegation anymore, but you must be a group of persons who search for the *Truth* and live with the *Truth* that you learn. In this journey, none of the university and the public will accept you. Your reputation may be distorted, and what you learn may be ridiculed and questionable. You will be very lonely, discouraged and desperate. Sometimes, you will be afraid and become suspicious about what occurs. In short, you must think very carefully before you make a decision. If you return to London for a period, you should wait for the public opinion to calm down before you can disclose what you have recorded. However, whether people believe in you or not is a different matter.   If you decide to continue with your study, you must abandon everything and make a trip to the Himalayan Mountains. This is the decisive moment."

I asked, "If we want to continue on with the journey, what should we do?"

The Indian smiled, "Why do you keep asking me what you should do and how you should do it? If you wish to continue, all you have to do is to proceed. It is as simple as that."

The destiny of humanity always undergoes major changes.   Although human beings do not clearly see those changes, they inadvertently approach the predestined destination that has been outlined for them. Less than two weeks later, we were already in the village of Potar that was at the foot of the solemn, majestic Himalayan Mountains. We left everything behind including reputation and position. We utterly broke off from prejudices and eternal self-esteem of the Westerners.

Our journey to the East begins . . .

Introduction to Our New Book

The Four Noble Truths

Vietnamese Author (1965): The Most Venable Thích Thiện Hoa
and Tâm Kiến Chánh (2002)

English Adapters (2012): Sine Nomine, Poven Leace,
Thony Ruthandest, and Hạnh Liễu

CHAPTER TWO

THE TRUTH OF SUFFERING

A. Introduction

I. Life Is a Series of Seas Full of Blood, Toil, Tears, and Sweat.

A large number of us believe that life in this material world is a great long feast, so it is a waste if we do not enjoy it. Hence, we would not let any chance that could potentially bring material pleasures to soar way beyond our reach.

It never occurs to us that those material pleasures are not real. Realistically, we are simply wheedled by ephemeral desires like concupiscence, craving contentment's, physical indulgence, material goods, and immortality. In other words, we are attracted to longings that can never give us genuine satisfactions. Our situation bears a striking resemblance to faint gleams of gratification of thirsty people who drink seawater. The more we drink, the more we thirst. About a minute after we swallow, our throat unpleasantly becomes dry, coarse, and scratchy.

As cited in the *Khế* Sutra, "Tears of human beings are a lot more than seawater in all oceans combined." Indeed, it is true. Life on earth does not fill with happiness's but rather loads with miseries. Even if happiness's exist, they are merely ephemeral in nature. What represents them is just a thin, glossy layer on the outside of everything. Characteristically, the real nature of life is a misery. To be precise, it is a series of seas full of blood, toil, tears, and sweat. In these environments, living beings are bouncing back and forth, tossing up and down, drifting here and there, and throwing from side to side.

The above description is very true, but none of us is capable of recognizing it clearly, understand it thoroughly, and present it truthfully like Sakyamuni Buddha. In part one of his first sermon to the five disciples at Mrgadava—*The Truth of Suffering*, he comprehensively and systematically expounded miseries, one kind after another.

B. Main Contents

I. Definition of *The Truth of Suffering* (Khổ Đế or Dukkha)

Suffering is derived from dukkha. "Du" means difficult. "Kkha" refers to endurance or tolerance. Dukkha means difficult to endure or difficult to tolerate. In Chinese language, Dukkha means suffering, misery, or bitterness.

In a larger sense, it refers to something that makes humans feel highly uncomfortable, distraught, and painful, for example, a deadly sickness, starvation, grief, or horrification. Suffering is the truth that is not only irrefutable and unassailable but also precise and flawless. *The Truth of Suffering* is so unequivocally explicit that no one can deny it or find an excuse to reject it.

Let us now learn about *The Truth of Suffering* that Buddha unambiguously explained, not only methodically and precisely but also meticulously and profoundly.

II. Hierarchical Classifications of Miseries in Life

None of us could ever be able to enumerate miseries that humans suffer in life. Even if we could, we would never be able to finish itemizing them one after another. However, Buddha meticulously categorized them into three general types or eight specific kinds, respectively.

1. Three General Types of Suffering

To describe worldly sufferings unequivocally, Buddha classified them into three general types.

(1) Suffering of suffering (Khổ Khổ)

(2) Suffering of change (Hoại Khổ)

(3) Suffering of action (Hành Khổ)

1.1. Suffering of Suffering (Khổ Khổ)

Suffering of suffering refers to sufferings piling up on each other—layer after layer. Having a body is already an intolerable suffering, but facing many other sufferings imposed by surrounding environments is like living beyond the pale. The existence of these two intertwining strands of sufferings explains why the Buddha called it suffering of suffering. With no doubt, each of us is a victim of numerous miseries, repulsiveness's, and repugnance's.

The body itself is a reeking clump of skin casing flesh, blood, bones, and organs whose distinctive odors are offensively unpleasant. If it does not have a shower or a bath for a few days, it surely releases a revolting smell—probably unbearable.

Moreover, it is not only very non-sturdy and non-lasting but also highly fragile and vulnerable to various forms of attacks. Evidently, being thirsty for three days, suffocating for five minutes, experiencing a broken vein, or being debilitated by a deadly contagious virus can quickly lead the body to death. That is all it takes!

Besides suffering unpredicted causes of death that we have no control over, we also stumble upon many other unavoidable sufferings, for example, long-term sickness's, severe famines, devastating wars, and natural disasters, including floods, tornados, typhoons, hurricanes, hailstorms, earthquakes, windstorms, winter storms, wildfires, heat-waves, droughts, landslides, tsunamis, volcanic eruptions, and etc.

Even just naming a few, these sufferings stack up on top of each other, and indeed, they reflect the notion of *Suffering of Suffering*.

1.2. Suffering of Change (Hoại Khổ)

The *Khẻ* Sutra clearly indicated that the Law of Impermanence affects all living beings that have figures, shapes, and/or dimensions. It simply means that they undergo gradual deteriorations, decomposition, disintegration, and obliterations in due course. Everything in the universe is under the control of this law—nothing can be everlasting.

As hard as iron is, air and heat can rust it. As strong as rock is, wind and water can wear it down to nothing. Even as big as the sun, the earth, and the moon are, they cannot remain the same with time. Hence, as fragile, weak, and small as a human body is, it is much easier to be worn out and much faster to be deteriorating with age. Especially when compared to the sun, the earth, the moon, and rocks, the life span of the human body is as long as that of ephemera.

The ruthless mash destruction of time hammers everything with no mercy and no exception. For every minute and every second we are living, we are also dying. In other words, we are the living dead.

Regardless of how well built, how powerful, how strong-minded, and how wealthy we are, we can never be able to prevent time from destroying us. To time, we are completely powerless. It is miserable, ashamed, and painful to be controlled by *Suffering of Change*, is it not?

1.3. Suffering of Action (Hành Khổ)

From the material perspective, all of us are unintended targets of environmental unpredictability's and of ruthless mass destructions of time. From the spiritual perception, we can be neither independent nor unruffled from the demands because desires that are capable of exciting, urging, and compelling us every second keep torturing our mind.

In addition, the thoughts in our mind ceaselessly transform from one kind to another at the rate that is much faster than we can detect or recognize, so we are not able to follow and control them.

Almost all the times, we fully engage in all sorts of thoughts as if we are restive horses and/or inflatable jumping monkeys that never want to rest. It is exactly as the Buddha said, "Human mind is like a bouncing monkey, and human thought is like a fidgety horse."

This saying simply means that our mind never relaxes. It focuses on one particular thought only for a few seconds then moves on to the next. It is a monkey constantly swinging from branch to branch without pausing in between. Similarly, our thought never dwindles to a trickle. It is bounded among ideas. It is a jittery horse relentlessly chasing after enthralling sceneries with no intention to come to the end.

If we proceed to a deeper level of analysis to see how our mind works, we will realize that besides our conscience, our mind is also under the control of our sub-conscience (sub-conscience mentioned here implies Alaya-Vijnana or Alaya conscience—the eighth conscience).

Although Alaya conscience lies at the deepest level of eight consciences secretly, it exerts the strongest effect and controls everything that is going on inside our mind. It contrives our thoughts, manipulates our actions, and maneuvers our feelings. As evidenced, we are angry; we are happy; we love;

we hate; we are fond of this object; we yearn for that item; we want to accumulate these things; and we must get rid of those possessions; etc. Persistently and incessantly, it commands us what to think, enjoins us how to feel, and instructs us how to behave.

In short, we have no freedom at all. Not only are we always under a tight control of surrounding environments and subjected to obliteration by time, but we are also subservient to the desires and obedient to sub-conscience. Ironically enough, we volunteer to be submissive and are ready to take its orders unconditionally without even realizing it. These layout settings explain why we endure *Sufferings of Action.*

2.   Eight Specific Kinds of Suffering

If we contemplate the abovementioned three sufferings more systematically and scrupulously, we will understand why the Buddha classified them into eight specific kinds in parallel to three general types.

To put it differently, all sufferings mentioned in eight specific kinds are essentially the same as those in three general types. Eight specific kinds of sufferings are as follows.

(1) Birth	(2) Separation from loved ones
(3) Aging	(4) Association with unbeloved ones
(5) Sickness	(6) Non-obtainment of desired goals
(7) Death	(8) Clinging to the five aggregates

2.1.   Suffering of Birth (Sanh Khổ)

Suffering from birth is a kind of back-to-back misery—suffering while being born and while being alive.

2.1.1.   Suffering While Being Born (Khổ Trong Lúc Sanh)

Both the person who gives birth and the person who is born to suffer.

2.1.1.1.   The Mother

When the mother becomes pregnant, her appetite begins to decline owing to the morning sickness like nausea and vomiting, at least during the first six weeks. Sometimes, the mother even experiences hyper-emesis gravid-arum characterized by severe nausea, vomiting, weight loss, and electrolyte disturbance.

Her nighttime sleeping gets shorter for different reasons including, but not limited to, getting uncomfortable in bed, experiencing indigestion or heartburn, feeling restless or insomniac, waking up with leg cramps, and staying awake caused by nausea or worry. Hence, she always feels worn-out and fatigued.

As time goes on, the fetus develops bigger and bigger, so the mother feels heavier and easily becomes exhausted. Standing up and sitting down appear to pose numerous problems. Walking around and doing simple things are no longer common practices or typical routines.

When it is close to the moment of giving birth, the pain experienced by the mother is indescribable. Even if the natural labor delivery has no complication, she still has to go through a labor-intensive process and endures many days of postpartum bleeding. Typically, postpartum bleeding lasts two or three weeks, but for some people, it may prolong up to six weeks.

Besides, she remains to be frail for many months thereafter because she does not only lose a lot of blood, but her five viscera's (heart, liver, spleen, lungs, and kidneys) also become weak. In contrast, if she stumbles upon some kind of complication, she must go through a cesarean section that is not only painful and scary, but it also leaves a long-term scar and some kind of disadvantage for life.

2.1.1.2. The Child

From the time when the fetus is just formed (reincarnation) to the time when the child is born, he/she also suffers, at least, as much as the mother does. Throughout nine months and ten days, he/she is confined within an enclosed space that is not only small and narrow but also dark and gloomy. This living condition is probably much worse than that in jail.

When the mother is hungry or thirsty, the child is floating around in the water sack as if he/she was a partially filled balloon aimlessly drifting afloat in the water. When the mother is full, he/she is squeezed against as if he/she was a sack of rice flour paste securely pressed under a grinding stone.

At the time of being birthed, the child's body manages to jostle along through a narrow pathway to the outside as if he/she was trying to slip through a curved stony wall. Hence, as soon as being out in the air, he/she starts crying as if he/she is trying to convey a message of being miserable.

2.1.2. Suffering While Being Alive (Khổ Trong Đời Sống)

From both the material and the spiritual perspectives, life has a countless number of miseries.

2.1.2.1. From the Material Perspective (Về Vật Chất)

On a daily basis, we need to have a minimum number of demands like food, drink, clothes, housing, and perhaps medicines. In order to have these necessities, we have to work assiduously to earn them. Not only must we work long hours, but we also endure hard labor. In most cases, we trade our own blood, toil, tears, and sweat for what we need.

To many of us, the opportunity to earn a few dollars in exchange for a bowl of rice, a bottle of water, and a few pieces of clothing does not easily come. Regarding housing, the majority of us simultaneously holds a full-time year-round job and a part-time job, but we are still not able to save enough money to buy a decent small house.

It is not that we have to experience starvation and/or become homeless in order to understand a profound meaning of suffering. Irregular eating, being deficient in nutrition, and growing up in poor living conditions are already sufferings.

We do not have to wait until we live in primitive conditions like sleeping on the ground and being protected by the sky roof before we admit that we taste the real meaning of suffering. Insufficiency of clothes to keep us warm in the winter and the inadequacy of housing to shelter us from harsh weather are also considered as sufferings.

Not only do the poor suffer, but the rich also suffer. The sufferings the rich endure are different from those the poor bear. If we want to maintain our wealth, we must work hard by staying up late and waking up early. We must struggle one way or another to keep our high paying job, protect our possessions, and invest our money. From toil, tears, blood, and sweat, we earn our living regardless of whether it is money, property, or labor exchange. Nothing falls from the sky.

So far, we have not even mentioned about unexpected sufferings that none of us can anticipate or can avoid.

2.1.2.2. From the Spiritual Perception (Về Phương Diện Tinh Thần)

As a nature of life, we also endure spiritual sufferings besides those material ones. Intimidation, confrontation, discomfiture, humiliation, degradation, and mortification are inextricable parts. Sometimes, going through these degrading situations is even more painful, tormented, and angst-ridden than suffering from a serious lack of physical materials. There is no need to elaborate on them because we all can endorse for ourselves. Let us look at an example that illustrates many different sufferings we must go through to earn knowledge.

To attain some kind of truth, morals, ethics, common sense, or faculty of reason, we must exert a tremendous effort to learn year after year, not only theoretically but also experimentally. For theories, we can learn from a teacher, a friend, or a book. For experiments, we gain experience by interacting and dealing with various people in life. However, regardless of whether it is a theory or an experiment, we inevitably stumble upon a wide range of difficulties and miseries.

Let us consider a case of learning theories from a teacher in school. The learning process can potentially pose a couple of problems. For example, the subject is difficult, and on the top of it, the teacher delivers lectures at a high level. Then what happens? We become not only disappointed but also up-set and lay the blame on the teacher because we hardly learn anything.

For the same reason, the teacher puts the blame right back on us. He/she claimed that not only we rarely pay attention in class but also have no appropriate prerequisite for the course. As a result, no one is happy with the situation—what a suffering!

What happens when we try to learn the subject from a book by ourselves? What would we do if we came across a difficult excerpt—that wrote about a complex concept or described some convoluted model, and we have no access to related references? Would we be irritated and angry because we were stuck but had no way out? What a suffering!

Experimentally, the only way for us to gain different experiences in life is to interact and deal with various people. Most of the times, we have to pay excruciatingly expensive prices for lessons we learn. Over an extended period, experiences we accumulate are like a plethora of movement patterns that seem to help us figure out how people treat each other, but unfortunately, we can never amass enough.

If it is not this person cheats on us, that person oppresses us. If it is not these people hate us, those folks insult us. If it is not this group of people harm us, that group of people competes against us. The list keeps on growing . . . How many people there are in this world, there are that many personal characters.

Throughout our whole life, we sometimes thought that we endure an infinite number of humiliations, disgraces, condemnations, ignominiousness, sorrows, and miseries, but in reality, experiences we accrue are merely a small trace in the big picture of what life is all about.

In short, irrespective of whether it is material or spiritual, we stumble upon numerous miseries in life. Together, they reflect how birth is suffering.

2.2. Suffering of Aging (Lão Khổ)

There is a saying, "Aging is a scenario of withering, falling off, and ruined—old trees become stunted and deformed whereas elderly people become irrational and foolish." When we are old, not only is our body worn-out, but our mind is also dull-witted. Upon aging with time, we suffer both bodily and spiritually.

2.2.1. Bodily Suffering (Khổ Thể Xác)

The older we get, the worse our vitality becomes. On the inside, not only do five viscera's (heart, liver, spleen, lungs, and kidneys) and six principal internal organs (stomach, bile, gallbladder, urinary bladder, small intestine, and large intestine) get tired easily, but they also deteriorate at a faster rate.

On the outside, organs of sensation including eyes, ears, nose, tongue, body, and limbs enfeeble and render impotent. As evidenced, we experience multiple problems at the same time—blurry vision, deaf ears, snuffly nose, stiff tongue, rhythmic movement disorder, dysfunctional body, shaky hands, and uncontrollable trembling legs.

Given rapid deteriorations at the old age, it is very difficult for us to sit down, stand up, and walk around by ourselves. Even with a cane or a walker, we still need some help from other people because we have neither the strength nor the energy to coordinate the body on our own. Besides, every time when the weather changes, it does not take much for us to get a cold in the winter, get a fever in the summer, and get a chill in the rainy season.

It is sorry to say and sad to admit, but none of the changes due to old age makes us feel good.

2.2.2. Spiritual Suffering (Khổ Tinh Thần)

There is another saying, "The higher the age goes up, the more humiliating it is." Indeed, the older we become, the more embarrassed we feel. Evidently, as we get older, not only does our body become weaker, but our mind also grows duller. We often get confused about where we are going or what we are trying to take. We act as if we have no memory, know nothing, or are foolish somehow.

As time goes on, we eat, drink, and talk as if we have lost our reasons. We do not remember things clearly and orderly. We can neither recall when we eat dinner nor identify whom we talk to last. Sometimes, we scream, scold, and mumble to ourselves . . . Inadvertently, we make ourselves look like a puppet and be a silly clown for the children to have fun. Irrefutably, aging is suffering!

2.3. Suffering of Sickness (Bệnh Khổ)

Nothing can torture the body and make the body suffer more terribly than pain can.

2.3.1. Suffering of Symptoms

Pain—regardless of what kind of pain, from a minor pain like a toothache or headache to a major pain like tuberculosis or cancer—easily makes us groan, feel miserable, and live through unendurable experience. Especially the pain caused by long-term sicknesses, it tortures our body even more.

Often, we are in the mood for neither eating nor drinking because we sense a bitter taste in our mouth and feel as if something is stuck in our lower esophagus. We hope that we could continue staying alive, but we know it would be impossible. On the contrary, we wish that we could die, but we did not have the courage to grant ourselves a death. It is miserable.

2.3.2.   Suffering of Financial Shortage

If sickness continues to get worse with time, our savings gradually disappear as a consequence . . . To some of us, after being sick once, we are completely broke. There is a saying, "If we did not get sick, we could be rich!"

2.3.3.   Suffering of Other Consequences

Besides, our sickness not only makes our loved ones feel worried but also makes them feel sad. Every time, when one member in the family is diagnosed with a deadly illness, trepidation throws the rest of the family into the hustle and bustle of the race course.

Almost all family members are always in a divided unfocused mind. Because they are so apprehensive and angst-ridden, they sometimes do not care much for eating or drinking and have a hard time sleeping at night. The atmosphere in the family gradually but drastically changes as time goes on—not only does everyone want to utter nothing, but all forms of expression that elicit amusement or entertainment also vanish altogether. A few family members do not even feel like going to work. Indeed, sick is suffering!

2.4.   Suffering of Death (Tử Khổ)

Among the four ephemeral phenomena—birth, aging, sickness, and death, death is the one that terrifies nearly all of us the most.

We are so afraid of death to the point that even if we are useful to nothing and are helpful to no one, we still want to live. Logically, we should die to lift burdens off the shoulders of our loved ones. However, when we hear someone talking about death, we do not even dare to think about it.

To a number of less fortunate patients who are diagnosed with cancer or leprosy, although living one more day implies suffering one more day, they still want to stay alive.

How does death have the ultimate power to torture almost all of us?

Why are we so afraid of it?

2.4.1. Bodily Suffering (Về Thân Xác)

If we witness a terminally ill patient who is suffering agonies of impending death, we will understand why death is a terrifying reality. On the brink of death, the patient feels exhausted but is highly anxious because he/she experiences a myriad of physical transformations including suffocation, wide open glaring eyes, deformation at the corner of the mouth extended toward the ear and chin, repetitive muscular contractions followed by twisting and sustained movements, holding arms crossed, fist clenching, knee flexion, and foot inversion.

During the time of impending death, *earth* [representing solids like hair, bones, nails, skin, ligament, tendon, and teeth], *water* [representing liquids like serum, pus, blood, and sweat], *wind* [representing air from breath in and out], and *fire* [representing heat inside the body] gradually fall apart.

For instance, the patient can indistinctly hear sounds but understands nothing, can see things but distinguishes none, can move his/her mouth but releases no noise, can become aware of smells but recognizes no odor, can taste the food but senses no flavor, can touch objects but identify none, and finally can breathe but takes in no air. Shortly after, he/she has absolutely no response and becomes stiff.

If we touch the corpse, we can sense the cold from its core because the whole body is already as hard as a block of wood. Approximately a couple of days later, it starts to deteriorate. Flesh and skin begin to puff up and release malodorous odors. It looks horribly disgusting. After a few more days, the skin becomes cracked, and foul-smelling liquid spews out from the inside. The stench is extremely unpleasant and highly offensive.

2.4.2. Spiritual Suffering (Về Tinh Thần)

Prior to death, the patient is very confused, baffled, and afraid. On the one hand, he/she loves his/her spouse, children, parents, and siblings whom he/she will never have a chance to meet again. On the other hand, he/she worries about himself/herself, not only being alone but also being lost on the other side of the material world. It is true that nothing is more miserable than experiencing this last moment in life.

In short, death makes the body completely disintegrate, and our Alaya conscience or karmic respiratory leads us to reincarnate to where we belong. Truly, death is suffering.

2.5. Separation from Loved Ones (Ái Biệt Ly Khổ)

In the loving relationships between husband and wife, between parents and children, and among siblings, nothing is more distressed and sorrowful than saying goodbye to the loved ones. There are two kinds of separations. The first one is separation caused by imposing obligations, including bilaterally imposed obligation, unilaterally imposed obligation, and self-imposed obligation. The second one is the separation caused by death.

2.5.1. Suffering of Separation by Imposed Obligations (Sanh Ly Khổ)

In a loving family, husband and wife or parents and children live happily together, but for some unexpected reason, they first have to break away from each other. Shortly later, they find out that they must live apart for good because of some kind of duty bound.

Natural disasters as mentioned above are typical leading causes. Human-made catastrophes like chemical contaminations, environmental toxins, and wars are nothing out of the ordinary. Compelled situations like conflicts between mother-in-law and daughter-in-law and extramarital relationships are also very common.

Regardless of whatever the reason is, husband and wife have to live separately, parents and children cannot live together. On one end, the wife anxiously waits for and expects to hear from her husband whereas at the other end, the husband desperately wanders around and searches for his wife.

On this side of the mountain, the parents miss the children while on the other side of the rocky face, the children suffer from being lonely. They are all soaked in tears and drowned in their own broken-hearted situations! There is a saying, "Other than suffering from a death separation, who on earth has the heart to break up a happy family." Sufferings of separation caused by imposing obligations are indescribable.

2.5.2. Suffering of Separation by Death (Tử Biệt Khổ)

Although living separately is suffering beyond description, loved ones, at least, still have a hope to reunite someday. If the suffering of separation by death is the case, the loved ones will never be able to see each other again. Hence, facing separation by death—the forever saying goodbye, who does not feel miserable?

To some of us, when we come across separation by death, we are so afflicted and heartbroken that we do not feel like eating or drinking and have a hard time falling asleep at night. Worse, a few of us are so miserable and despairing that we want to die with our loved one, especially that loved one is our dear life partner. Sometimes, suffering of separation by death can be fatally serious.

2.6. Association with Unbeloved Ones (Oán Tăng Hội Khổ)

While living in happiness, neither of us wants to separate from our loved ones. By the same token, while living in hatred, none of us wants to be with our unbeloved ones.

Paradoxically, they are two sides of the same coin. Nearly nothing in life turns out as we anticipate.

2.6.1. Association with Unbeloved Family Members (Oán Tăng Hội Khổ Với Người Thân)

In life, when we wish to be together, we have to say goodbye to our loved ones or must live apart from them.

In contrast, when we yearn for a splitting up, we have to live together with our unloved ones or must interact with them every day.

The misery that our loved ones and we have to suffer because of obligated separations has the same intensity as the anguish that our unbeloved ones and we have to bear.

There is a saying, "Seeing an enemy is like having a needle poked into the eyes, and living with an enemy is like tasting bitter bile liquid or lying on a bed of nails."

For now, let us hold off on mentioning about interactions with non-relatives like friends, co-workers, colleagues, social collaborates, or business partners.

Awkwardness's can easily happen between our blood-related (parents and children or sisters and brothers) or non-blood-related (husband and wife) family members and us. If our family members and we do not get along for some sort of disagreement or some kind of fighting over something, that is already more than enough for all of us to feel highly uncomfortable with each other.

Although we want to avoid and do not want to talk to each other, we cannot because we live in the same house. We try not to interact with each other, but we are obligated to communicate.

Even though we feel very awkward and embarrassed, we have to bite our lips and face our own shame. We crave to terminate the relationship, but we have no other option.

Because of a financial problem accompanied by a responsibility to our children or because of a respect along with a sense of duty to elders and ancestors, we are obligatory to swallow our own pride and deal with the issue for the sake of keeping the family together. Even within blood-related relationships, anger and resentment drive us not to converse with each other, provoke us not to settle, and prevent us from reconciling or reinstating the relationship. How miserable is it to live a life as such?

2.6.2. Association with Unbeloved Non-relatives (Oán Tắng Hội Khổ Với Người Lạ)

How do people in the society treat each other when they come into conflict or controversy?

Worse, how do people who are neither from the same race nor from the same country react when they deadly hate or bear a deep grudge against each other? If both sides have bitter feelings for one another, it is inevitable that the war is going to happen eventually.

In summary, the abovementioned scenarios are just a few examples of the high prices we must pay for being associated with unloved ones, regardless of whether they are our blood-relatives, non-blood-relatives, or non-relatives.

2.7. Non-obtainment of Desired Goals (Cầu Bất Đắc Khổ)

In a larger sense, non-obtainment of desired goals refers to disappointments at all different levels of consciousnesses. In reality, the more we yearn for things, the more we will become disheartened and disconsolate. The more we expect things to happen in a certain way, the more we will be dissatisfied and embittered.

Who among us does not long for things in life?

Who among us does not expect things to happen the way we want?

The answer is probably none.

Now let us ask ourselves, ". . . So who does not suffer in life?"

Regardless of what type of business we run, what career we pursue, and what part of a professional culture we belong to, the number of us who feel satisfied with our success is, by far, smaller than the number of us who feel discontented with our failures.

Logically, to achieve the best possible outcomes, we must exert a great effort; to be prosperous, we must work diligently; and to be successful, we must be patient and determined. Overall, we must invest lots of energy, time, and money into what we try to accomplish. Unfortunately, neither great effort nor hard work nor patience nor willpower nor energy nor time nor money guarantees any success.

A majority of us neglect our family, skip meals, sacrifice personal hobbies, and even shorten the night sleep so that we can focus on our work, but many times, it still turns out that our dream does not come true . . . Our misery is unutterable and beyond description. Below are a few examples that most of us often stumble upon in real life.

2.7.1. Dissatisfaction Because of Position and Fame (Thất Vọng Vì Công Danh)

In this material world, position and fame are often mesmerizing attractions that almost all of us are dying to go for them at full speed if we have a chance. However, it is not easy at all to fight for those attractions.

Herein, we do not even need to mention about those who want to jump ahead of the game with deception and fraud or to take a short cut because these people usually end up suffering and dying by the faults of their own at last anyway.

We now focus our discussion on situations in which a few of us honestly and sincerely pursue positions and fames with our capability, knowledge, and intelligence. Even with our own genuine talents, we still have to go through numerous discontents, frustrations, and failures before we can reach our goal. This situation is one of the classic examples that Ôn Như Hầu Nguyễn Gia Thiều described in *Ill Feelings of Imperial Maids* or *Grievances of Concubines*.

Specifically, trajectories of our journey searching for positions and fames are always sealcoating and paving with unerasable memories like strenuous struggles against injustices, exhausting fights against exploitations, and sorrowful vestiges of desolation. More to the point, manneristic styles, refined characteristics, distinct qualities, and elegant countenance eventually are transforming away by the dust and the heat of a rough life.

2.7.2. Dissatisfaction Because of Wealth and Honor (Thất Vọng Vì Phú Quý)

The number of us who are disconsolate and disheartened because of positions and fames are many, but the number of us who feel dejected and despondent because of wealth and honor are not less. In fact, it may be even more.

Since we want to be rich as quickly as possible, we connive at a fraud to maintain our high paying job, deprive of others' possessions by violence for our personal gain, or deceive peers and the public. We do everything it takes with the understanding that we would share the spoils among ourselves . . .

However, when our conspiracies concealing crimes like deception, extortion, and corruption are uncovered, our possessions are confiscated, and we become the subject of criminal investigation. While being responsible for illegal charges, not only do we feel mortified, but our family and relatives also feel distressed and humiliated. It is a misery!

2.7.3. Dissatisfaction Because of Romantic Love (Thất Vọng Vì Tình Duyên)

Romantic love is an extremely powerful attachment that seems to plunge most of us into deep misery or profound sadness. More traumatically, it always appears to be a life-changing lesson for whomever encountering it, regardless of whether the experience is positive or negative.

In this world of attachment bond, how many of us actually feel satisfied or become happier in a married life? How many of us go through with no pain? Perhaps, the answer is *no* for the majority of us.

Unquestionably, every day, newspaper headlines shout out details of heart-rending and heartbreaking love stories that lead the lovers to commit suicide. It is very pitiful, but it is outrageous at the same time. In the depths of despair, it is perfectly understandable that many of us intend to take our own life.

Most noticeably, among all non-obtainments of desired goals, dissatisfaction imposed by romantic love is the worst broken-hearted scenario because not only do we think illogically and unreasonably, but we also have the least patience and endurance to suffer through this kind of despair.

As evidenced by the reality through human history, it is rather ironic because most of the times, two typical romantic lovers are not blood related. How could this attachment bond be stronger than those tied by blood relationships could? Logically speaking, it should not be, but in reality, it is.

We have hardly heard that parents, children, siblings, or relatives commit suicide when disappointments arise, but we have learned many heartbroken love stories in which one of the lovers ends up killing or destroy himself/herself by one way or another.

Overall, non-obtainment of desired goals is suffering! Although all three dissatisfactions have their own characteristics, every single one of them is fully capable of turning our life upside down with no problem.

2.8.   Clinging to Five Aggregates (Ngũ Ấm Xí Thạnh Khổ)

As mentioned above, the human body is the combination of five great elements—earth, water, wind, fire, and void, and it exists primarily by *constant exchanges* between the internals and the externals. Although these five elements are interrelated and inseparable, one always attempts to preponderate over the other four.   Strikingly, they simultaneously and constantly change, but their relative proportionation has never been the same twice.   This inequivalent proportionation bears a resemblance to what Heraclitus said, "You could not step twice into the same river."

Let us take a look at human beings from a broader view.   A human, overall, is defined as a combined set of five aggregates[10]—namely, form, feeling, perception, mental formation, and conscience.   Pragmatically, they are the roots of ignorance that keeps all of us from recognizing our very own innate, always-existing Buddha-nature.

Among these five aggregates, form is the only material matter that defines the physical part of the body.   The remaining four—feeling, perception, mental formation, and conscience—are emotional and intellectual factors that constitute the mental and spiritual parts of the human.   Roughly speaking, "form" mentioned here is equivalent to five great elements—earth, water, wind, fire, and void.

Reminiscent of five great elements, five aggregates always compete among themselves, fight against each other, and encroach on one another even though each one of them needs the other four to exist.   Because of their internal competitions, struggles, and conflicts, we have always been suffering a multitude of miseries.

2.8.1.   Being Controlled by the Law of Impermanence (Chi Phối Bởi Luật Vô Thường)

Like the other seven natural laws of the universe, the law of impermanence, in particular, unremittingly controls the human body.   It impinges on every single one of us—from the young to the old, from the healthy to the sick, and from the living to the dead. We always feel anguished and distressed because of its threat.

2.8.2. Being Carried along by Six Passions (Bị Thất Tình Lục Dục Lôi Cuốn)

Because of the five aggregates, we relentlessly attract to six passions—desiring to see the beauty, to listen to melodious sounds, to smell pleasant odors, to taste delicious food, to experience corporal pleasures, and to have mental satisfactions.

Because of the six passions, we become fascinated with six objects of sense—beautiful scenery with vivid colors, pleasing sounds or sweet voices, fragrant odors or delicious smell, tasty foods or succulent dishes, luxurious materials giving rise to better sensations upon contact, and plotted thoughts executed for personal satisfactions.

Because six roots of sensations (eyes, ears, nose, tongue, body, and thoughts) and six knowledge's (the knowledge gained by seeing, hearing, smelling, tasting, touching, and mindful thoughts) go all-out for the six objects of sense, we turn our attention, concentration, and enjoyment into fascination, predilection, and attachment. These interconnections clearly explicate and indicate why it is excruciatingly difficult for us to liberate ourselves from the cycle of life and death.

The six passions are like rabble-rousers that persistently stir up our mind every single second of the day, and almost all of us have no way to keep these passions under control. Realistically and practically, it is a whole lot easier to defeat a powerful, experienced troop than to subside these six passions, especially the last one—a desire to have mental satisfactions.*

Mental satisfactions are often referred to as seven fundamental feelings— *"joy, anger, love, hate, happiness, sadness,* and *penchant"* or *"joy, anger, love, hate, happiness, sadness,* and *fear"*. Regardless of whatever feelings or whichever corresponding combinations we experience, they begin to distort the truth, exhaust our mental capability, deform our sense of purpose, and warp our moral nature.*

For example, joy can effortlessly convert us to an indentured servant or slave for our six passions. Anger not only impedes us from forgiving and being kind but also prevents us from having compassion and being honest to others. Love easily brings us to profoundly deep attachments that not only lead us to being responsible and practical to a fault but also take us to willful blindness. Besides making us be prejudiced, hate also instigates vindictive thoughts to rise in our mind. Not only does sadness throw us into grief and depression, but it also steers us towards carelessness and capitulation. Penchant can easily throw us into a wrong path—a path of being depraved.*

In other words, these seven fundamental feelings are not only different fuel sources to boost up the flame of our resentment fire but are also different kinds of driving forces to intensify the blaze of our desire for more and more . . .*

Thought transformation is our worst enemy because it converts one thought to another at a rate that is excessively fast for the mind to detect. It can quickly swing over to this side but can also easily swerves around to the other side with no break in between. There is a saying that thought is infinitely more talented than the best *Muggers of Magic* because it is fully capable of taking one thing then grasping another thing and transforming both things to something else right in front of millions of people, and strikingly, no one knows how it does it.*

2.8.3. Being Misled by Predetermined Prejudices and Illusions (Bị Vọng Thức Điên Đảo Chấp Trước)

Besides six passions, we also suffer because of vain mirages, opinionated perceptions, and inflexible false impressions. We believe that we can clearly distinguish the differences between both ends of the spectrum, for example, we versus others, win versus lose, gain versus loss, success versus failure, and intelligence versus ignorance, etc. By strongly believing in our vainglorious perceptions, we are always nervous, worried, frightened, and depressed.

III. Why Did Buddha Clearly Present Miseries?

A number of us are perplexed and have been wondering, "Why did Buddha openly describe and lucidly characterize all kinds of misery in this material world?"

If life is a series of seas full of miseries, why did he not cover them up so that we would not feel terrified? The more he concealed those miseries, the less concern and anxieties we have to worry about all the times. Would it be better this way?

Why did he comprehensibly reveal everything in detail to make us feel more frightened and miserable? Would it be more helpful and supportive of us if he showed an optimistic picture of how beautiful, peaceful, and safe life is?

Young children live almost unaffected by the environment they are in, feel unflustered in spite of what happens around them, and enjoy all happiness's that come their way every day because they pay no attention to aggressiveness, competition, resentment. Their way of living indirectly informs them that life has no misery.

Why do we, all the adults, not try to copy the way young children live— attempting to identify no cruelty, no brutality, no ruthlessness, and no heartlessness—so that we can enjoy our life more?

If the Buddha was the greatest being whose unconditional love, compassion, and benevolence are far beyond our imagination, why did he have no mercy on us?

When we first heard about the abovementioned questions, we were inclined to think that they were perfectly logical . . . Indeed, why did Buddha decide to reveal all miseries to us?

Let us take a step back and think. If we carefully and thoroughly contemplate, we will realize that those questions posed are very superficial. Buddha was not merciless when he chronologically and meticulously disclosed all fundamental miseries in life.

On the contrary, he decided to divulge them in detail because he had the unique unconditional love, compassion, and benevolence of all of us. He wanted us to be aware of all miseries for the following reasons.

1. **When We Stumble upon Intricate Situations and Challenging Scenarios, We Are not Terrified (Gặp Cảnh Không Khủng Khiếp).**

All miseries the Buddha presented above are quite fundamental, and none of us can avoid facing them. When we have this body and a life to live, we have no chance to negotiate or no choice to refuse them. After we come to this material world, we are bound to encounter them at one point or another.

- ❖ Who has a life, but he/she was not born to begin with?

- ❖ Who does not get old?

- ❖ Who does not become sick?

- ❖ Who does not die?

- ❖ Who does not say goodbye to loved ones throughout the whole life long?

- ❖ Who has never once lived with or worked with unbeloved ones?

- ❖ Who has attained everything that he/she has ever yearned for?

Hence, even if we wanted to create a beautiful dream or an attractive living example in our mind so that we could live peacefully, our dreaming life would eventually lie in shreds around our throne when ruthless reality came into its own play anyway. By then, regardless of how hard we tried to stay on top of things, we could never stay afloat in the immense ocean of miseries.

To those of us who are accustomed to live vainly in a beautiful dream, we cannot avoid facing traumatic shocks when the real nature of life—ruthlessness, vindictiveness, and brutality—suddenly appears in front of our eyes. Since we have no mental preparation to live a challenging life, we sink right into terrifying depths, irreversible distress, and hopeless desperation at last. In some worst-case scenario, we are so downhearted and despondent that we even take our own life.

The life style of the rich and royal families is a classic example of the above setting. Because we are so comfortable with our own luxurious standard of living—residing in magnificent castles, eating delicious dishes, served by servants, and pleased by expensive entertainments, we do not know how to survive in drastically changed environments. If it happens that we have to encounter terrifying wartime experiences, severe impoverishments, heartless punishments, or cold-blooded slaughters, we immediately become victims of severe emotional attacks and then develop into physically rendered inoperative individuals. Long-lasting dejection and hopelessness, slowly and gradually but definitely, shatter us into tiny pieces, and eventually, we can no longer function.*

In contrast, when we are aware of the fact that life in this material world is full of miseries, we will not be so scared stiff. For example, our mind will not run wild like a restive horse when we stumble upon difficult situations or convoluted problems that appear to be impossible to resolve at the time. With advanced mental preparations, we maintain our composure and remain calm to arrive at the best suitable solution for our problems.

For example, as farmers who live in areas prone to drought or flood, we do not flinch from foreseeing potential consequences of our crops in jeopardy. Since we are well aware of the labor-intensive nature of rice cultivation during the growing season, we keep inventing new lines of attack on the top of maintaining a collection of indigenous strategies every year to minimize the risks posed by extreme climate changes. Hence, harsh weather conditions can hardly make us take an enormous toll.

2. If We Expect Nothing and Yearn for Naught, We Are under the Compulsory Control of Neither Passion Nor External Environment (Không Tham Cầu Nên Khỏi Bị Hoàn Cảnh Chi Phối).

When we realize that life gives us sadder, less happiness, more disappointments, and fewer satisfactions, we should take more control over our six roots of sensation. In addition, we should recognize that the more we long for things, the more we will be frustrated because regardless of how many things we possess, we will never feel we have enough.

By knowing what life offers and how our mind operates, we must learn to bring our desires under control, meaning that nothing is enough. In other words, how much is not enough, and how much is enough? The answer is in our mind.

If we can restrain our desires, we will be neither controlled by environments nor dragged into angry waves of life and nor pulled down into a deep gorge where we end up suffering. This logic bears a resemblance to a clever person who is inadvertently imprisoned for driving violation or for civil disobedience. Unlike all other prisoners, this person thinks about how to use jail time wisely instead of how to fight over jail foods.

3. Diligently Practicing Moral Lessons, Disseminating Compassion, and Cultivating a Lifestyle of Love to Avoid Suffering (Gắng Sức Tu Hành Để Thoát Khổ)

When we know that having this body entails bearing many miseries as a result and are aware that life imposes more sadness than happiness on us, we earnestly wish to escape from this material world. The less desires we want, the easier we can free ourselves from suffering.

The way that we try to rescue ourselves is similar to the way that a whole bunch of children attempts to run for their lives from a burning house. Both the children and we are very fortunate because Buddha warned us in advance. All we have to do are to learn and follow what he taught.

C. Conclusions

I. By Knowing All Miseries in Life, We Must Understand Their Real Causes in Order to Eradicate Them (Biết Khổ Phải Tìm Nguyên Nhân Sanh Ra Khổ Để Diệt Trừ Khổ).

Buddha kindly informed us that three realms—the Realm of Passion (or the material world), the Realm of Beauty, and the Immaterial Realm of Pure Spirit (or the Realm of No Beauty)—are oceans of miseries. The Lotus Sutra (Kinh Pháp Hoa) also reiterates his words, "The three realms are not safe. They are like burning houses."

It is very unfortunate that we are too dull-witted to recognize by ourselves. To be explicit, our ignorance keeps tossing us into the cycle of life and death. We live in misery, but we thought we lived in happiness. The real problem is that *we do not know what we do not know.*

Literally, we are miserable, but we thought that we are happy. We throw ourselves back into the cycle of life and death, but we thought that we are under the control of some kind of higher power.

Now that we are able to recognize the real nature of life—a series of seas full of miseries constantly stirred by massive, violent waves of suffering, we should feel disgusted and determine to get out of it. Most importantly, we must realize that knowing these miseries is a good thing, not a bad thing.

Unlike a number of us who always accept the so-called destiny, we must try hard to unshackle ourselves from bondages of attachments rather than become disappointed, feel depressed, mourn, and finally give up.

Now the question is that how do we eradicate miseries?

To eradicate them, we must know why we become miserable to begin with . . . To be more precise, we must know the real root causes of our miseries.

Likewise, to cure a sickness, an experienced physician has to know the reason that causes the sickness in the beginning. After a thorough diagnosis, the physician then decides what treatment method should be used to cure and which medication should be prescribed to patients.

Similarly, to wipe out a rebellion, a clever leader must know who the person in charge on the other side is, where the rebel base is, and how many people are involved in it. After a careful investigation, the leader then makes a decision on how to encircle and launch a surprise attack to obliterate the uprising.

In short, being conscious of all sufferings does not mean that we will no longer be miserable. To eliminate our sufferings, we must first identify their real root causes and then eradicate them.

In the next chapter, the Buddha explicitly demonstrated different real root causes of every single misery that we all suffer.

NOTE: Now that you know what kinds of miseries sentient beings suffer with no exception. If you are interested in finding out

(1)　The real root causes of your miseries

(2)　How you would feel if you could get rid of them and

(3)　Most importantly, how you can get rid of all of them

Please do yourself a favor by introducing yourself to the book *The Four Noble Truths* written in Vietnamese by The Most Venable Thích Thiện Hoa and translated into English by Poven Leace *et al.*

Made in the USA
Middletown, DE
19 April 2017